Where To Play
GOLF
IN THE BRITISH ISLES

North West England Edition

Where To Play
G⚬LF
IN THE BRITISH ISLES

North West England Edition

**Part of The World Compendium of
Golf Courses series**

ON COURSE PUBLICATIONS LTD.

Produced by On Course Publications Limited,
Freedom House,
32-34 Wood Street, Lytham St. Annes,
Lancashire, England FY8 1QR.

Maps prepared by Freedom Design, Lytham St. Annes.

British Library Cataloguing-in-Publications Data
A catalogue record for this book is available
from the British Library.

ISBN 1 901025 00 4

Printed and bound by St. Ives plc
Typeset by Freedom Design, Lytham St. Annes.
Reprographics by Blackpool Typesetting Services Ltd.

— *Acknowledgements* —

In compiling this North West England edition of Where to Play Golf in the British Isles, the publishers are grateful for the invaluable help given by scores of golf club secretaries and their assistants, professionals and their assistants, senior members, and the compilers of club histories and centenary books. Our thanks go to each and every one.

Because there has not previously been a publication that has given a write-up to every golf club in a given region, no matter what the status of the club, sufficient material was not available in many cases. Indeed, some golf clubs had very little to say about themselves although we will continually endeavour to update and improve the editorial content in future editions.

CREDITS
Original Concept and design of this series of books developed by Mark Sampson and the team at Freedom House Group, (Steven Gill, John Stirzaker, Michealle Kelly, Peter Longworth, Harriot Voss, David Wilson, Barry Band and Stephen Pearson). With a special mention to Paul Houghton of Precision Printing.

EDITORIAL CONTENTS
Barry Band.

RESEARCH AND COMPILATION
Barry Band, David Wilson, Mike Turner, Donald Campbell-Thomson, Warren Smith, Mark Sampson, Andy Ellis.

ARTWORK, ILLUSTRATION & DESIGN
Freedom Design Studio (Steven Gill, John Stirzaker, Gary Lees, Ange Carson, Chris Tominey, Stephen Pearson).

PHOTO CREDITS/GOLF CLUBS
Donald Campbell-Thomson (staff): Bootle, Bowring, Bromborough, Caldy, Castletown, Childwall, Douglas, Formby, Formby Ladies, Grange Fell, Grange-over-Sands, Hesketh, Heswall, Hillside, Hoylake, Morecambe, Peel, Prenton, Ramsey, Royal Birkdale, Royal Liverpool, Rowany, Sherdley Park, Silverdale, Southport and Ainsdale, St. Annes Old Links, Stonyholme, Ulverston.
Warren Smith (staff): Baxenden, Beacon Park, Colne, Dean Wood, Euxton Park, Fairhaven, Fishwick Hall, Garstang, Gathurst, Ghyll, Great Harwood, Green Drive, Green Haworth, Houghwood, Hurlston Hall, Ingol, Leyland, Lobden, Longridge, Mytton Fold, Nelson, Ormskirk, Penwortham, Pleasington, Rishton, Rossendale, Southport Old Links, Stonyhurst, Towneley, Whalley, Wilpshire.
Roger Boyes: (Park House Studio): Royal Lytham and St. Annes.
Dave Clark (Folly Photos): Barrow, Bentham, Brayton Park, Carlisle, Cockermouth, Furness (top pic), Kendal, Keswick, Kirkby Lonsdale, Penrith Golf Club, Seascale, St. Bees, Windermere.
David Wilson (staff): Stanley Park, Fleetwood, Ashton and Lea.
Mike Turner: Miscellaneous contributions.
On the photographic side, the publishers are grateful to club secretaries and members who submitted photographs, some of which have been used but are not individually credited.

PHOTO CREDITS/LEISURE PAGES:
Donald Campbell-Thomson, Cumbria Tourist Board, The Isle of Man Tourist Board, North West Tourist Board, Blackpool Tourism Services.

COVER PHOTO
Royal Lytham and St. Annes, by Roger Boyes.

TITLE PAGE PHOTO
Ulverston Golf Club, by Donald Campbell-Thomson.

With thanks to the Prince of Wales Youth Business Trust for their years of Support.

England's North West

England's North West is not only a wonderland for golfers, it is also a region of contrasting holiday destinations that are being discovered by more and more overseas visitors.

Number one on the tourist trail to the great outdoors is Cumbria's Lake District, the country of William Wordsworth, with its dramatic mountain scenery, rugged fells, picturesque stone villages and sparkling lakes and tarns.

To the south lies Lancashire, the Red Rose County, where the gentle, wooded valleys and silent brooding hills often seem to be Britain's best kept secret. And yet only a few miles away is the excitement and buzz of Blackpool - Europe's largest seaside resort - and historic Lancaster on the River Lune, its castle stating the region's heritage.

South of the River Ribble the coastal plain is fringed by the classic golf links country stretching from Southport to the doorstep of Liverpool, a city with a great maritime history typified by the restored Albert Dock and museums and galleries of national significance.

Improved travel by air and car ferry from North West England to the Isle of Man has added another dimension to leisure pursuits in the region.

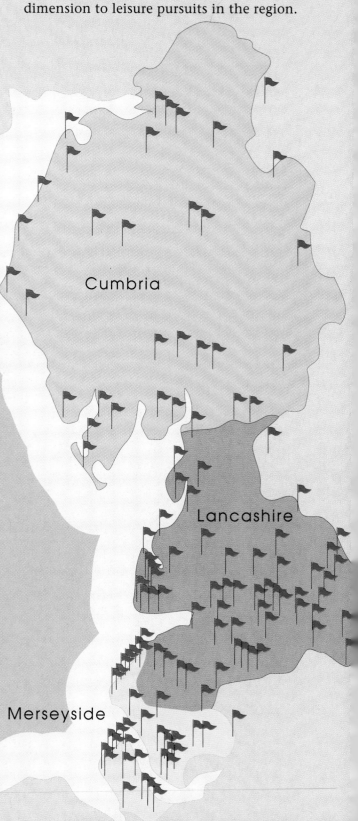

Isle of Man

Cumbria

Lancashire

Merseyside

Foreword

Welcome to the first of 76 volumes that will describe the golf courses of the world. How many golf courses it will involve is not yet known.

One thing certain is that golf is growing in popularity at a remarkable pace. The time is close when the family vacation will include a round of golf as well as a day in a theme park. But first, the global family of golf needs information. That is where The World Compendium of Golf Courses comes to the fore.

Britain alone is thought to have about 3,000 but that's just a short putt when compared with an estimated 12,000 in the United States. And then there are Europe, Africa, Australia, New Zealand, Asia, Japan. And the rest!

After this North West England edition, which establishes the series, there will be books covering Scotland, Ireland and seven more regions of the British Isles, followed speedily by books covering the thousands of golf clubs throughout the five continents, produced to the same format.

We hope you enjoy the variety of courses featured and look forward to placing the worlds beautiful array of golf courses at your fingertips.

Chairman.

On Course Publications

Introduction

There are books about how to play golf, how to play better golf, how not to play golf, how the top pros play golf. But to many golfers, the question of where to play golf away from their home turf can be a mystery.

There is plenty of information available about the premier clubs, who may have a proud history or are the venues of leading tournaments. Trying to play there at short notice, however, is not easy, even supposing you want to pay that kind of fee.

But there are always alternatives - hundreds of alternatives. How to find these clubs and what to expect from them is the purpose of this book. For the first time, they are described in detail and illustrated in full colour, allowing golfers to make an informed choice of 'Where To Play Golf.'

With almost 3,000 golf courses in the British Isles, the travelling golfer has great choice. In the majority of cases, assuming you have a handicap certificate, if you can pay, you can play.

North West England, comprising of Cumbria, Lancashire, Merseyside and the Isle of Man, is the home of great clubs like Royal Lytham and St. Annes, Royal Birkdale, Royal Liverpool, Silloth and Castletown. But the region has scores more places to play - links, parkland, moorland and fell-side courses.

'Where To Play Golf' sets the scene by featuring every golf course in this designated area - and other regions of Britain will be featured in The World Compendium of Golf Courses series.

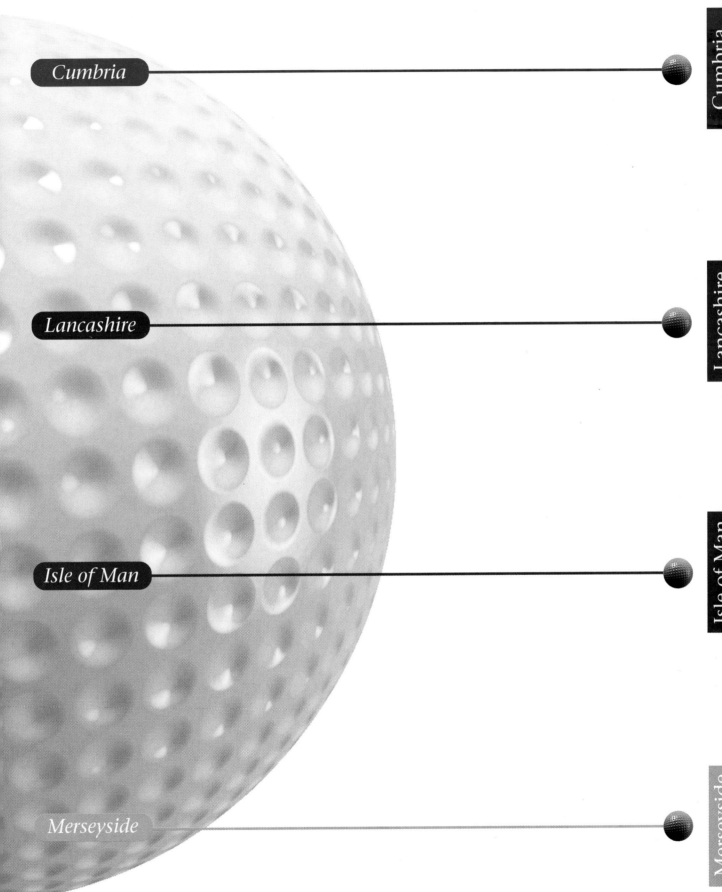

Cumbria

Lancashire

Isle of Man

Merseyside

The plaque marking the location of Bobby Jones' famous shot

Royal Lytham's famous Opens

LYTHAM was mentioned in the Domesday Book and remained unknown outside the Lancashire area for the next 800 years.

The genteel little town then became world famous within a week. All due to golf, of course.

And the town became more and more famous as successive Open Championships were held on the links of Royal Lytham and St. Annes Golf Club because such tremendous headline-making events just seemed to happen there.

The first Open here in 1926 was the 'Bobby Jones Open' when the world's greatest amateur, level with Al Watrous with two to play, landed his tee shot in sandy wasteland, while Watrous hit a perfect drive and then a good second shot onto the 17th green.

Jones, in typically resolute fashion, decided a 175-yard shot was needed to stand any chance of staying in the game. He chose a mashie, a club similar to today's four iron, and hit an 'impossible' shot to a better position than his opponent.

Watrous is supposed to have muttered: "There goes 100,000 bucks." Ashen-faced, he three-putted while Jones got the par four and hoisted the trophy with a four-round total of 291.

The news of what Bobby Jones had done at Lytham St. Annes went around the world and the club later marked his championship-winning shot by placing a plaque at that spot.

The actual club he used is on display in the members' room, underneath a painting of the great man.

Puzzled?

Visiting golfers and fans, incidentally, are still puzzled by the name Lytham St. Annes, which was coined in 1922 when the little seaside resort of St. Annes-on-Sea and the sedate town of Lytham were

The painting of Bobby Jones in the members room and the club with which he made his title-winning shot.

merged into a new borough.

Visitors still get lost, looking for St. Annes in Lytham, and vice versa! For the record, the clubhouse of Royal Lytham and St. Annes is in St. Annes and the course stretches for a couple of miles towards Lytham.

The Open didn't return to Lytham until 1952 when Bobby Locke was at his storming best, making headlines wherever he went. His third open win in four years with a four-round score of 287, put Lytham on the world scene in the press, radio, cinema newsreels and the fledgling television service.

Locke went on to win his fourth Open, at St. Andrews in 1957.

This was also the headline-making achievement of the Australian, Peter Thomson, at Royal Lytham in 1958, winning his fourth open in five years with a score of 278. He added a fifth title, at Royal Birkdale in 1965.

Thomson's great play in the Fifties is worth recalling; for seven years

from 1952, when he came second to Locke, he either won the Open or was runner-up. The Americans, however, were absent for most of that period.

The great Opens at Lytham continued in 1963 when the New Zealander, Bob Charles, became the only left-hander to win the British Open. His score was 277.

It was one of the Open's few play-offs but Charles pasted Phil Rodgers so decisively (winning by eight shots) that the R and A decided future play-offs need not be more that 18 holes.

But probably the most famous Lytham Open victory, and certainly the most significant for British golf, was Tony Jacklin's in 1969, with a four-round tally of 280. He was the first British winner since Max Faulkner in 1951.

Revival

Jacklin's sensational win brought an incalculable amount of publicity for the course and the town, which was further boosted when he won the American Open 11 months later - the first Briton to achieve this since Ted Ray in 1920.

Jacklin's victory inspired a dramatic turnaround in the fortunes of British golf in the next few years.

The Open returned to Royal Lytham in 1974 when the South African, Gary Player, won the title for the third time and put the focus more strongly on Lytham St. Annes when, on the 18th, his ball ran through the green and finished against the clubhouse wall. He had to play a left-handed shot with his putter to get clear.

In more recent times the club was back in the spotlight due to the success of Seve Ballasteros in winning the 1979 and 1988 Opens at Royal Lytham - the second of which necessitated an additional day's play due to the Sunday final being washed out by heavy rain.

ROYAL LYTHAM & ST. ANNES
Golf Club

Links Gate, Lytham St. Annes, Lancashire FY8 3LQ.

Secretary: Lytton Goodwin 01253-724206.
Professional: Eddie Birchenough 01253-720094.

THE most famous golf club in the county of Lancashire, Royal Lytham and St. Annes, is a topic of fascination for golfers everywhere.

Its rich history is woven with the great names of golf and the superb course is often held as the ultimate challenge to a player's accuracy.

Bernard Darwin thought it was "A beast - but a just beast." Peter Alliss once described it as "a rogue."

So many leading players have come to grief on these testing links in nine headline-making Open Championships from 1926 to 1996, that the above descriptions are gentlemanly, to say the least!

For 43 years the great event in Royal Lytham's story was Bobby Jones' recovery from a patch of wasteland at the 17th in the final round of the 1926 Open.

In the 1969 Open at Royal Lytham, the Bobby Jones legend was relegated to second place when Tony Jacklin became the first Briton to win the title since Max Faulkner, in 1951. It inspired a dramatic turn-around in the field of British golf.

These famous stories are recalled in another article in this special Royal Lytham 'Featured Club,' section.

The club's history was written up by Tony Nickson (the centenary year captain) and published in 1986 in a handsome book, titled The Lytham Century.

When the Lytham and St. Annes Golf Club was formed it is likely that only the two instigators, A. H. Doleman and Talbot Fair, had ever played before.

The new club played over nine holes on the inland side of the railway in the centre of the new town of St. Annes-on-Sea. The

Where To Play
GOLF
IN THE BRITISH ISLES

NORTH WEST FEATURED CLUB

FACT FILE

A championship links course of 18 holes, 6685 yards. Par 71. SSS 73. Record 65.

Restrictions: Societies contact the Secretary in advance. Ladies' day Tuesday. No visitors weekends and Bank Holidays. Handicap certificates required.

Fees: £75 per round including lunch.

Dress code: Usual golf attire.

Shop opening: 8am -7.30pm in summer, 9am till dusk in winter.

Facilities:

TO THE CLUB

Half a mile south of the St. Annes shopping centre (not the Lytham end of the town).

'clubhouse' was a room in the old St. Annes Hotel, which was just across the road from the then railway station.

The title of Lytham and St. Annes Golf Club was, perhaps, a wise deference to the old township of Lytham, three miles along the coast. Here dwelled the Squire of Lytham and many other fine citizens, whose membership was sought by the young club.

A year later an open competition attracted members of leading clubs and the winner was John Ball, of Royal Liverpool, who won the first of his record eight Amateur Championships the following year and, in 1890, became the first amateur to win the Open. Ball joined the Lytham and St. Annes club in 1893 and was made a life member in 1908.

In 1890 the club organised the first professional tournament to be held in England. The 10 contestants were all Scots and included four Open winners - including Old Tom Morris, who was 69! The tourney was won by Willie Fernie, the 1883 Open Champion, whose son, Tom, became the Lytham and St. Annes professional in 1926.

In 1893 the club pioneered another event in golf by staging the first Ladies' Championship.

Development values soared in St. Annes and within a few years a new, larger site was acquired half a mile to the south, where the club's professional, George Lowe, who also designed other courses, laid out the new Lytham links in 1897.

Prosperity and success gave the club ambitions to stage the Open Championship and in the early 1920s the course was upgraded by Harry Colt.

The first major event was in 1923, when the North of England Championship attracted the winners of the British and American Opens, Walter Hagen and Gene Sarazen.

Without even a practice round on these daunting links, Sarazen won by two shots from Hagen.

The British Open was duly held in 1926 and the club was honoured with its Royal prefix.

Harry Colt was called in again prior to the Amateur Championship being held at Royal Lytham for the first time, in 1935. He designed a new 15th hole, making it one of the toughest par fours in the world. The top events returned in 1952, with the Open won by Bobby Locke, and the Amateur returned in 1955 and 1986. The Ryder Cup was played at Royal Lytham in 1961.

The British Ladies Amateur

Championship, having first been held here in 1913, returned in 1948 and 1993 and the Curtis Cup was held in 1976.

The Open Championship continues to be played at Royal Lytham - the ninth in 1996 - and for four successive years to 1994, the British

Seniors Open.

The course itself continues to make its heroes. Like all heroes, they have to be straight shooters!

Pictured above is the 10th green. Playing the course is described by professional Eddie Birchenough on the next two pages.

1)   The only par three at the start of a championship course makes it more challenging. Not only do you have to have your right swing with you - you also have to have the right club in your hands. Playing out of trees, you don't really know where the wind is. A very tricky shot.

2)   The secret of this hole is to drive it as close to the out-of-bounds on the right as you possibly can. That leaves a shot straight up the green. If you drive left you will have to play the second shot across the green, which slopes away.

3)   The important thing on this hole is to keep the ball in play. The railway on the right is a threat and there are bunkers on the left. It's a good idea to hit the ball out just short of the drive bunker on the left - perhaps with a three wood - and leave yourself a shot of about 200 yards to the green. It's important not to go through to the back of this green. The hardest bunker on the course is there!

4)   Playing now in the opposite direction to the first three holes, it is usually into the prevailing wind. It's a tough drive and you can't really see the fairway. It's safer to miss the fairway on the left, in which case there is a blind second shot. The ideal tee shot is a long play down the right, which allows you to play the second shot around the mounds. The flat green is difficult to putt. Usually you are looking for more break than exists in the green.

A guide to playing the course, by Royal Lytham's pro Eddie Birchenough

Course Information			
Hole	Yards	Stroke	Par
1	206	13	3
2	420	5	4
3	458	1	4
4	393	9	4
5	188	15	3
6	486	7	5
7	551	3	5
8	406	11	4
9	162	17	3
10	334	10	4
11	485	4	5
12	189	14	3
13	339	18	4
14	445	6	4
15	468	2	4
16	356	16	4
17	413	8	4
18	386	12	4
OUT	3270		35
IN	3415		36
TOTAL	6685		71

5)   Another par three. There is trouble on both sides. You need to

fire a good shot. It plays about 180 yards, usually downwind, so it's the medium-high range. Take the shorter club and allow the ball to roll. The bunkers on the left are particularly deep and difficult to get out of.

6)   A par five that's reachable in two if you can keep the tee shot to the right of the bunker on the corner. If not, it's advisable to lay up short of the four cross-bunkers short of the green and leave a pitch of about 100 yards to a green that is tough to putt, due to the ridge down the middle and some very subtle breaks.

7)   A par five that is usually out of reach of the average golfer. It's important to get the drive into the fairway. There are bunkers on the right and one on the left. A long second shot will usually leave a shot of 120-130 yards over a bridge where only the top of the flag can be seen. You can't see the bunkers left of the green. A small one on the front right catches out many players. The green is big and needs care because it slopes quite severely from the back.

8)   A difficult tee shot from a raised tee to a fairway below. The railway is tight on the right and there's a big bunker in the mound on the left. Again, a three wood will get you far enough to reach the green comfortably in two. The second shot is very deceptive because about 60 yards short of the green is a ridge that looks as if

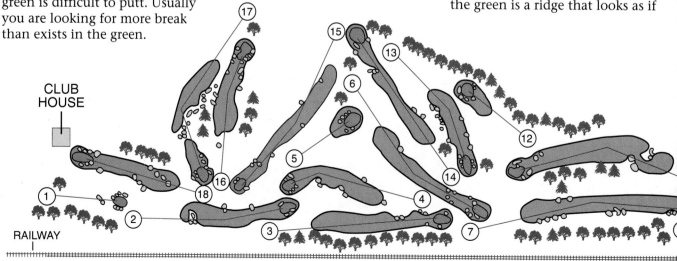

it is right up to the green. There's no reason not to take a bit more club. The flat green on top of a mound is open to the winds we get on this course. In the 1963 Open Championship this hole - although only a short par four - played more over par than any other hole.

9)   A beautiful little short hole surrounded by bunkers. It requires a good solid tee shot into the middle of the green. If you miss the green you are almost certainly in sand and you don't want to over-club here because there's out-of-bounds 10 yards behind the green.

10)   Turning back into the wind again and needing a good tee shot between the mounds onto the fairway. Then it is a pitch to the small green that slopes severely from back to front. If you go past the hole and are putting down the slope and down the wind, it is very difficult.

11)   A par five not often reached in two in the wind. A good tee shot is required, right of the big bunker, and then a second shot with a long iron, making sure you keep the ball in play. Trees to the left will catch anything that's drawn but there is plenty of room right. Usually a long iron leaves you about 100 yards from the green.

12)   This par three was picked by Jack Nicklaus among his 18 most difficult holes in championship golf. It plays at about 190 yards and is just very, very difficult. Playing out of the trees you can't often feel the wind blowing from the left. The green is wider than it

is deep so you can't run the ball. It is ringed by traps and an out-of-bounds on the right.

13)   A short par four. From the tee you can hit anything from a three iron to a driver. The important thing is to miss the bunkers up and down each side of the fairway. If playing your second shot from grass, it's not often more than a seven or eight iron to a green that undulates quite severely in places. Putting needs care on this hole.

14)   This is a tough par four, with prevailing winds off the left. There are bunkers on the right of the fairway to catch any drive that isn't held against the wind. The green is often out of reach with the second shot and it can be a hard slog for the amateur. The green slopes to the back so many shots find their way there.

15)   The toughest on the course into the prevailing wind off the right. Two bunkers on the left need to be avoided - and there's a ridge of cross-bunkers about 90 yards short of the green. So it is often a case of playing a long iron second shot just short of these bunkers and then a pitch of about 110 yards. This is another green with a lot of slope. When the pin is at the back it is difficult to read.

16)   On this short par four an iron is sufficient off the tee if you can hit it far enough to leave a seven or eight iron to the green. Bunkers line the fairway the last 100 yards and the bunker to the left of the green catches many shots that are pitched into the left quarter of the green. Take enough club to carry the bunkers down the right of the green. It is set at a slight angle to the fairway.

17)   This is our signature hole, famous for Bobby Jones' mashie shot from sand on the left onto the green in the 1926 Open. A difficult par four dogleg to the left, it needs a drive down the right because the hole is well bunkered on the left. It's folly to risk going down that side. The second shot from the right hand side is long - a wood or a long iron. Getting in one of the green traps leaves one of those nasty 60-yard shots.

18)   Standing on the 18th tee gives one of the great sights of golf, with the clubhouse and Dormy House behind the green. The first thing to negotiate is the diagonal row of cross bunkers, to gain a long-to-medium iron shot into a green 40 yards long. Pick the right club or you could leave yourself a very long put. A great finishing hole.

FOOTPATH

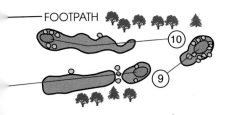

Cumbria

INDEX TO CUMBRIA GOLF CLUBS

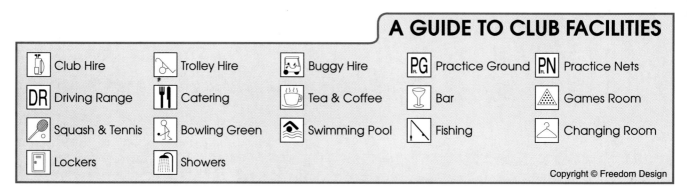

A GUIDE TO CLUB FACILITIES

Club Hire	Trolley Hire	Buggy Hire	PG Practice Ground	PN Practice Nets
DR Driving Range	Catering	Tea & Coffee	Bar	Games Room
Squash & Tennis	Bowling Green	Swimming Pool	Fishing	Changing Room
Lockers	Showers			

Copyright © Freedom Design

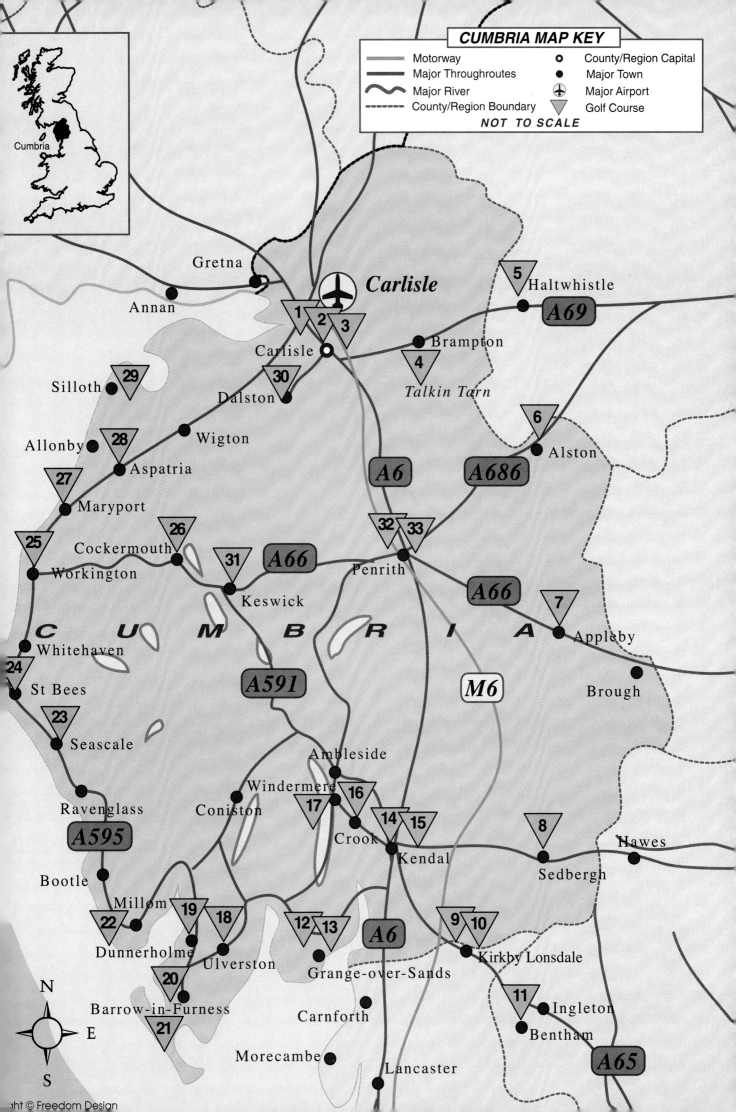

CUMBRIA MAP KEY

Motorway		⊙	County/Region Capital
Major Throughroutes		●	Major Town
Major River		✈	Major Airport
County/Region Boundary		▽	Golf Course

NOT TO SCALE

Gretna

Annan

Carlisle

5 Haltwhistle **A69**

1 2 3

Carlisle

Brampton

4 *Talkin Tarn*

29 Silloth

30 Dalston

6 Alston

28 Wigton **A6** **A686**

Allonby

27 Aspatria

26 Maryport

32 33

25 Cockermouth **A66** Penrith

Workington

31 Keswick **A66**

7 Appleby

C U M B R I A

Whitehaven **A591** **M6** Brough

24

St Bees

23 Seascale

Ambleside

Windermere 16

Ravenglass 17 Coniston 14 15 8

A595 Crook Kendal Hawes

Bootle Sedbergh

Millom 19 18 12 13 **A6**

22 9 10

Dunnerholme Ulverston Grange-over-Sands Kirkby Lonsdale

20 11 Ingleton

Barrow-in-Furness Carnforth Bentham

21

Morecambe Lancaster **A65**

N
W E
S

ıht © Freedom Design

ALSTON MOOR
Golf Club

The Hermitage,
Alston, Cumbria CA9 3DB.

Secretary: Harry Robinson
01434-381354.
Clubhouse: 01434-381675.

THE first club in this directory is testament to a great ethic: There will be golf!

For the Alston Moor course is not only one of the most isolated courses in England, it is also the highest, with part of the course at the 1,500-foot level.

Founded in 1906, the club moved to The Hermitage - a farm believed to date back to 1600 - in 1969.

The present course has 10 holes but planning permission has been granted to develop another eight holes on 65 adjoining acres owned by the club.

When the work starts, the club aims to complete two new holes each year.

Secretary Harry Robinson says that by the turn of the century they hope to have the highest 18-hole course in England.

It is already one of the toughest because of its card-wrecking greens.

Greenkeeper Alan Frater adds "County players come here and can't do a thing with them.

And I once found two Americans lying flat on the ninth, examining the contours. As I got close I heard one say: 'Jeez, I just don't believe this green'. "

With a small membership and a 'miles from anywhere' location, the club offers an unreserved welcome to visitors and societies.

Visitors are surprised to see the lush condition of the greens and the wonderful views. Perhaps the best view is from the seventh, where Cross Fell, the highest point in the Pennines, can be seen framed in trees.

"It's worth the green fee for the view," quips Alan Frater.

Although the course can be played all year - snow permitting - the clubhouse and bar are open only from April 1 to October 31. Simple catering can be arranged for visitors, with more substantial fare available in Alston, where the club has a good rapport with the pubs.

The clubhouse is, in fact, the old farmhouse, to which many alterations have been made over the years and for which the addition of a steward's flat is planned.

It may be remote and little known but to older golfers the name Alston will ring a bell in golfing history for it was in this little Cumbrian village that club heads were made for several leading manufacturers before production went overseas.

The foundry that made club heads for firms like Slazenger, Dunlop and Letters is still in existence although not in the golf business.

In the clubhouse, there is a card on display bearing the signatures of Jack Nicklaus and Greg Norman.

And although local members may wonder what they would make of the notorious ninth hole with its 'hills and hollows' green, the two legends haven't actually been to Alston.

The card was sent in by a Canadian writer, who took it home from Alston a few years ago and later played in a pro-am tournament with Nicklaus and Norman.

Finally, a warning of an unusual distraction at Alston and some other Cumbrian courses - low flying RAF jets, which can appear suddenly with a terrifying roar.

Who knows how many shots they've spoiled?

FACT FILE

A parkland/moorland course of 10 holes, 5518 yards. Par 68. SSS 67. Record 65.

Restrictions: Societies should contact the Secretary in advance.

Fees: Monday to Friday £8 per day (£5 after 5pm). With member £5. Weekend and Bank Holiday £10, £7 with member.

Dress code: Casual and smart.

Facilities:

TO THE CLUB

The course is nearly two miles south east of Alston on the B6277.

Course Information

Hole	Yards	Stroke	Par
1	376	3	4
2	195	14	3
3	340	9	4
4	410	5	4
5	150	11	3
6	476	1	5
7	129	17	3
8	496	7	5
9	189	12	3
10	376	4	4
11	195	15	3
12	340	10	4
13	410	6	4
14	386	2	4
15	129	18	3
16	496	8	5
17	150	16	3
18	275	13	4
OUT	2761		34
IN	2757		34
TOTAL	5518		68

1) Nice and straight for starters - but hook and you're out-of-bounds.

2) A short hole. The green is several feet below the tee.

3) Through a narrow gap in the trees; the fairway slopes right into light rough, out-of-bounds on the left.

4) A long, straight fairway but the ball is attracted like a magnet to the house on the right. Watch for livestock.

5) A very short deceiving hole with some nasty rough on the right.

6) A long uphill par five with danger most of the way on the right. The sloping green is known as cardiac hill.

7) A nice short hole. But go too far right of the green and you will probably not see that ball again.

8) Get behind the stand of trees to the right of the fairway and there is trouble worse than a bunker.

9) Try to keep out of the wood on the left. There's rough on the right and a nasty little bunker, then a green that's undulating but fun!

10-13) Same as the first four holes.

14) Hole six now becomes a par four but is just as dangerous!

15-16) Same as holes seven and eight.

17) A 150 yard carry over a valley. It looks quite easy but don't be fooled. If you drop the ball short the problems are great.

18) Similar to hole nine but it's now a par four with a dogleg to the left. Leave the fairway and you are nearly always out-of-bounds on the left.

Recommended Facilities

APPLEBY
Golf Club

Brackenber Moor,
Appleby-in-Westmorland,
Cumbria CA16 6LP.

Secretary: Basil Rimmer
017683-51432.
Professional: Paul Jenkinson
017683-52922.

COULD this be Cumbria's best-kept secret? Many visitors are amazed when they stumble across the Appleby course with its peaceful setting and fine views of the Lakeland fells and the Pennines.

The course is two miles south-east of the town of Appleby-in-Westmorland, just off the A66 at Coupland Beck and a 30-minute drive from the M6 motorway.

The club was founded in 1894 and moved to its present site at Brackenber Moor in 1903.

The course was laid out by Willie Fernie, of Troon, the Open champion of 1883.

The original clubhouse stood on what is now the 16th tee and was moved to its present site in 1933.

The structure lasted until 1961, when major rebuilding took place and further work was completed in 1991.

Once described by the Manchester Guardian as "the Sunningdale of the north," the club members prefer to regard Sunningdale as the Appleby of the south.

Unlike many courses, Appleby is unique in not having parallel fairways. The circular layout on superb moorland turf enables play in all directions of the compass.

This is as close to links-type golf as it is possible to find inland.

The absence of trees doesn't make this an over-easy course because the excellent greens - which some say are the best in the country - have slopes and steps and with their strategically placed bunkers, make for an enjoyable test of golf.

The Appleby course has stood the test of time and has changed little over the years.

Visitors are impressed by the friendly nature of the members and the warm welcome they receive in the clubhouse.

FACT FILE

A heather and moorland course of 18 holes, 5901 yards. Par 68. SSS 68. Record 63.

Restrictions: Members priority 8 to 9.30am and noon to 1.30pm. Ladies Thursday 1 to 2.15pm.

Fees: £12 to £16.

Dress code: Smart casual.

Shop opening: 8am to 5pm.

Facilities:

TO THE CLUB

Two miles east of Appleby, half a mile off the A66.

Course Information

Hole	Yards	Stroke	Par
1	339	13	4
2	401	5	4
3	341	11	4
4	168	17	3
5	305	9	4
6	404	7	4
7	371	3	4
8	303	15	4
9	414	1	4
10	191	14	3
11	453	2	4
12	258	18	4
13	312	16	4
14	437	4	4
15	179	10	3
16	427	6	4
17	182	12	3
18	416	8	4
OUT	3046		35
IN	2855		33
TOTAL	5901		68

1) An accommodating opening hole with the green best reached from the right.
2) A blind tee shot; the green is guarded by two bunkers and slopes front to back.
3) Drive to the marker post for a good line into the large sloping green.
4) The shortest hole but the trickiest. Don't overdo it on club selection.
5) An intimidating tee shot with room to the left. Best line is just right of the marker post.
6) Superb views from the tee. This longer par four is well guarded by greenside bunkers.
7) Stay short of the road (230 yards) for a better chance on this notorious back-to-front sloping green.
8) Short but not easy. Drive over the marker post for the best line onto a long, narrow green.
9) Tee shot down the right to a large, undulating green. Good putting vital here.
10) A very good par three for its length to a superbly guarded Mackenzie green.
11) Appleby's longest. A good tee shot to the fairway is needed to find the right-to-left sloping green in regulation.
12) A driveable par four for John Daly types. Beware the hidden pot bunker fronting the green.
13) Another short par four with a tricky green protected by bunkers.
14) Probably Appleby's hardest par four. A difficult fairway to hit, needing a good approach shot to the Mackenzie green.
15) With an intimidating river down the right, the green is hidden in a hollow with bunkers front and sides.
16) This long par four becomes tough in the wind. A well struck second can run onto the sloping green.
17) A tough par three with out-of-bounds right, big left-to-right slope and bunkers front and right.
18) Aim for the marker post to give a good line into the long green overlooked by the clubhouse.

Recommended Facilities

BARROW
Golf Club

Rakesmoor Road, Barrow-in-Furness,
Cumbria LA14 4QB.

Secretary: J. Slater
01229-825444.
Professional: N. Hyde
01229-832121.
Clubhouse: 01229-825444.

ALTHOUGH this course can't be considered hilly or exceptionally high, from the front of the clubhouse and from certain points on the course, there are magnificent views of the Lakeland hills to the north and the Pennines and flat-topped Ingleborough to the east.

Blackpool and the Fylde Coast can be seen to the south and to the west is the Isle of Man.

So, like the several courses on the fringe of the Lake District, Barrow has the great boost of scenic splendour but the risk of some lack of concentration!

The course is played on two levels with the round starting at the highest part. At the par-four third hole, play is a dogleg to the green

at the lower level. Players return to the upper level at the 15th, which is a par three.

The club was formed in 1922. Over the years, numerous changes have been made and the course has improved tremendously, thanks to greenkeeper Graeme Munsie, who moved to Barrow from Scotland in 1991.

In October 1993, the club planted 6,500 trees and shrubs to improve the appearance of the course and give shape to the holes.

There is a good test of golf with a variety of holes, but for the player coming in with a good score the last three holes have out-of-bounds that can easily ruin a card.

The club has a busy ladies' section of around 120 members, who have a weekly competition on Fridays.

Changing facilities are available for ladies and gents but it is advisable for visitors to check tee reservations with the professional.

Parties of 12 or more should make advance arrangements with the Secretary.

Daily golf packages can be booked, inclusive of coffee on arrival, a soup and sandwich lunch and an evening meal.

FACT FILE

An undulating meadowland course of 18 holes, 6137 yards. Par 71. SSS 69. Record 66.

Restrictions: Visitors must be members of a recognised golf club and make contact in advance. Handicap certificates advisable.

Green fees: £15 to £25, £10 with member.

Dress code: Usual golf attire.

Shop opening: 8am to 5pm.

Facilities:

TO THE CLUB

From junction 36 of the M6 approach Barrow on the A590. After the Dalton by-pass turn left into Bank Lane and the club is 400 yards on the left.

Course Information

Hole	Yards	Stroke	Par
1	327	13	4
2	168	17	3
3	421	4	4
4	505	7	5
5	407	3	4
6	202	11	3
7	517	2	5
8	299	15	4
9	355	9	4
10	340	5	4
11	327	14	4
12	158	18	3
13	352	10	4
14	487	1	5
15	166	12	3
16	366	8	4
17	308	16	4
18	432	6	4
OUT	3201		36
IN	2936		35
TOTAL	6137		71

1) Relatively easy par four with an approach shot made difficult due to narrow green and exposure to wind.

2) The green is very narrow and not to be missed on the right side.

3) The drive needs to be long to give a flat lie for the approach shot. Distance to the hole for the second shot is quite deceptive.

4) A relatively easy par five - if you hit the ball straight.

5) A long par four needing a good tee shot. Don't miss the green to the left side.

6) A long and difficult par three due to the narrow green being exposed to the wind.

7) A difficult tee shot for the longer hitter, due to out-of-bounds on the right and putting made difficult by the slope on the side of the green.

8) A relatively easy par four but the approach is made difficult due to the bottom of the flag being blind.

9) A challenge for the big hitter to drive to the green - but a watery grave awaits the mishit.

10) A long tee shot is required to carry the bank approach. A difficult shot on a windy day.

11) A relatively easy par four but for the short hitter trouble lies left and right.

12) A long, narrow green, well guarded by bunkers left and right.

14) There's plenty of potential trouble here, due to out-of-bounds running along the left from tee to green.

15) A green exposed to the wind and the course's most difficult for putting - so beware!

16) Out-of-bounds to the left waiting for the hook. The two-tiered green is exposed to the wind.

17) Another challenge to the bigger hitter to drive the green but don't hook.

18) A long and difficult par four due to out-of-bounds along the left. Make sure you leave yourself an uphill putt.

Recommended Facilities

BECKSIDE
Golf Course

Ellerbeck Farm, Crook,
near Kendal, Cumbria.

Proprietors: Mike & Kathleen Jackson
01539-821415.

THIS fascinating and challenging little course owes much of its appeal to its unusual background.

Some ten years ago, Mike Jackson, who farms the land, became fascinated by golf and after a summer of driving balls up his main cow pasture, he had the idea of creating a nine-hole course on some uneven rough grazing land littered with boulders, gorse bushes and bracken.

A large fishing pond had been created some years earlier by damming a stream, and this feature together with the pronounced character of this hilly land, suggested just where each green could be mown.

In turn, this dictated the location of tees and the clearing of the fairways.

Over the past five years, the course has matured with a variety of improvements aimed at lengthening the holes, achieving more sight lines between tee and flag, all against the demanding background of planning restraints in a national park.

Now, most of the greens retain the natural lie of the land, mown and top-dressed from the original field turf but now of a high standard comparing favourably with other golf courses.

The course stands high in its surrounding landscape, giving views of the Lakeland hills and of Morecambe Bay to the south.

Beckside is a good example of farm diversification by its golf-loving owner - but in this tourist area the acid test of a facility is whether it is supported by local people, rather than just by tourists in the peak season. Beckside Golf Course is well used by the local community, who refer to it as 'Royal Crook.' It's certainly good value.

FACT FILE

A pastureland course of 9 holes, 4430 yards. Par 64.

Restrictions: None.

Fees: £5 per 18 holes
(pay and play).

Dress code: Casual.

Shop: Balls and tees available.

Facilities:

TO THE CLUB

On the B5284 road midway between Kendal and Bowness.

Course Information

Hole	Yards	Stroke	Par
1	135	13	3
2	420	15	5
3	320	1	4
4	185	5	3
5	235	11	3
6	185	7	3
7	215	3	3
8	250	17	4
9	270	9	4
10	135	14	3
11	420	16	5
12	320	2	4
13	185	6	3
14	235	12	3
15	185	8	3
16	215	4	3
17	250	18	4
18	270	10	4
OUT	2215		32
IN	2215		32
TOTAL	4430		64

1) A challenging opener requiring an accurate short iron to a small, flat green. Plenty of trouble awaits an aggressive tee shot.

2) Played as a par five, this uphill dogleg to the right demands two long hits to be looking at a birdie. A drive to the left of the guidepin will open up the approach to the green, well protected by natural mounds.

3) Don't be fooled by the yardage; this is a difficult par four. Keep the drive to the right for the easiest approach to the guarded green.

4) A tough hole needing full carry from tee to green. This is the highest part of the course.

5) Enjoy the view from the tee of the Lyth Valley and Morecambe Bay before this downhill hole. The large green will gather balls played right of centre.

6) A four or five iron shot to this downhill, blind hole. Don't expect to two-putt this tricky, contoured green.

7) A par here is well earned. A small green awaits tee shots after a 150-yard carry over a pond. Anything to the right will fall away down a steep bank.

8) Playing from an elevated tee, keep your drive to the left to set up the approach to this blind green. Slicers will find the water.

9) A straightforward hole but beware the open watercourse at about 190 yards.

BENTHAM
Golf Club

Robin Lane, Bentham,
near Lancaster LA2 7AG.

Secretary: Mr. Martin Philipson
015242-62455.
Clubhouse: 015242-61018.

ALTHOUGH the club's postal address is in Lancashire and the club is located in North Yorkshire, they are included in the Cumbria section of the directory because of golf league connections.

The Bentham nine-hole course has been in existence since 1922 and has seen little change in that time.

Although it is in fell country and has a couple of steep climbs, the course is more parkland in nature. It is split by a road, holes one and nine being in the flat area in front of the clubhouse and the other seven being on undulating territory.

These seven offer more of a challenge from trees and ponds but not from bunkers. In fact, the only bunkers are on the second hole.

This is a tight, 500-yarder that offers the full selection of hazards. It has out-of-bounds on the right to catch the super-slice and the tee shot is played over a marker pole and down, but there's a hidden pond on the left. The large green rolls off the fairway and two bunkers stand guard at the front. Walking down the sloping fairway the superb view is of flat-topped Ingleborough. The lack of bunkers may change, however, if the club's hopes of extending the course do not materialise. A feasibility study has been made for 18 holes. The alternative plan is to spend the money on bunkers.

Bentham's second nine holes are played from different tees, giving a few new angles and, on two holes, a distance increase of more than 50 yards.

FACT FILE

A parkland course of 9 holes, 5820 yards. Par 70. SSS 69. Record 69.

Restrictions: Societies confirm booking with the Secretary. Ladies' day Thursday.

Fees: £14 to £20.

Dress code: Usual golf attire.

Facilities:

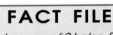

TO THE CLUB

M6 junction 34 to Kirkby Lonsdale. After Caton turn right to Bentham, left into High Bentham. Club on right.

Course Information

Hole	Yards	Stroke	Par
1	371	6	4
2	507	4	5
3	278	17	4
4	369	8	4
5	295	14	4
6	180	16	3
7	310	9	4
8	150	12	3
9	428	2	4
10	433	1	4
11	505	7	5
12	271	18	4
13	328	10	4
14	290	11	4
15	197	13	3
16	365	3	4
17	129	15	3
18	414	5	4
OUT	2888		35
IN	2932		35
TOTAL	5820		70

1) There are trees down both sides on this par four starter. The green is quite large and slightly elevated.

2) A long, tight par five puts golfers to the test. Tee-off over a marker pole and hope to miss the pond on the left. The green is guarded by the only two bunkers on the course.

3) A sharp dogleg to the right is downhill all the way. It is possible to drive to the green.

4) This hole is a slight left dogleg leading to a large green.

5) An uphill hole with out-of-bounds down the right and a ditch on the left.

6) A modest par three slightly downhill to an easy green.

7) A tough par four with streams, out-of-bounds on the right and a sloping green.

8) A short par three going uphill to a large but undulating green.

9) A good finishing hole with out-of-bounds on the right, trees all down the left, and a two-tier green.

BRAMPTON
Golf Club

Talkin Tarn Road, Brampton,
Cumbria CA8 1HN.

**Secretary: Ian Meldrum
01228-23155.
Professional: Stephen Harrison
016977-2000.**

ALTHOUGH the club dates back to 1907 and is played on a course designed by James Braid, the present spectacular course by Talkin Tarn was laid out on land acquired from a local farmer in 1976.

Since then the club has developed and expanded and 1996 saw even more improvements.

When the course opened, the clubhouse was a wooden pavilion. It was replaced by a low ranch-style building in 1986, consisting of a large bar area, dining room, games room and bar, showers and toilets.

The latest additions provide a new dimension in convenience and facilities with a new locker room and changing rooms, an office for the secretary/competition starter, a purpose-built professional's shop and a floodlit car park.

The course has acquired a reputation as a golf challenge, needing solid driving and some long second shots. As the course matured the third and 11th holes became the most feared and now, under winter 1996 improvements, the third has gained 25 yards.

The 11th is perhaps the hardest, for after demanding a long drive, the hole turns sharply to the right onto a sloping green.

The course is very scenic with many fine trees and the wooded shores of Talkin Tarn provide a perfect backdrop. The lake is a popular spot with summer visitors.

The club welcomes visitors and parties are well catered for.

FACT FILE

A rolling fell course of 18 holes, 6407 yards. Par 72. SSS 71.

Restrictions: Visitors and societies apply in writing. Ladies' day Thursday. No visitors Monday, Wednesday and Friday 9 to 10am.

Fees: Enquire by phone.

Dress code: Usual golf attire.

Shop opening: Dawn to dusk.

Facilities:

TO THE CLUB

One and a half miles south east of Brampton on the B6413.

Course Information

Hole	Yards	Stroke	Par
1	173	13	3
2	348	9	4
3	422	1	4
4	556	5	5
5	391	3	4
6	328	7	4
7	277	11	4
8	299	15	4
9	476	17	5
10	336	18	4
11	462	2	4
12	197	8	3
13	401	6	4
14	143	16	3
15	314	14	4
16	315	12	4
17	517	10	5
18	452	4	4
OUT	3270		37
IN	3137		35
TOTAL	6407		72

1) A relaxing par three, normally a five or seven iron. Missing the green on the left is not recommended.

2) Drive left of centre, leaving a short iron to a generous green.

3) A superb hole with a narrow, guarded green that's difficult to read.

4) Two very long shots to reach the green; the second one is tricky with a water hazard down the right.

5) A difficult second shot. Gorse and trees surround the green.

6) A hooker's dream hole - dogleg left off the tee! Unless the second shot is pulled into a huge bunker.

7) A temptation to drive the green but make it dead straight!

8) Lovely view from the tee. Seek position with an iron.

9) After a straightforward drive the hole veers left to a well guarded green. A difficult birdie hole.

10) A lovely driving hole, ideally right of centre, and a short iron to the green.

11) A difficult one as described on the opposite page.

12) The tee shot must carry 100 yards of gorse. Anything from a six iron to a wood, depending on the wind.

13) Drive left of the marker if you want to see the green.

14) A lovely short hole, slightly uphill to a fabulous view.

15) Try to ignore the view from this elevated tee. A short iron second shot to a tricky green.

16) A tight tee shot with out-of-bounds left and a second shot of precise length.

17) A par five that plays longer due to the uphill drive. A birdie chance if the tee shot is good enough.

18) The drive usually leaves a medium to long iron to the green but a sand trap awaits a weak shot. This can be a tricky green to read.

Recommended Facilities

BRAYTON PARK
Golf Club

Lakeside Inn, Brayton,
Aspatria, Cumbria CA5 3TD.

Secretary: Barrie Brown
016973-20588.
Professional: Graham Batey
016973-20840.
Clubhouse: 016973-21059.

OPENED in 1978, the Brayton Park nine hole golf course is set in 50 acres of parkland in the grounds of historic Brayton Hall.

The attractive little course is one of Cumbria's best kept secrets.

But as a pay-and-play course, it is open to everyone and the infrequent player does not have the burden of an annual subscription.

The course was built to cater for a market consisting of beginners, juniors, senior citizens, visitors and golf parties.

For example, societies can book to have coffee on arrival, play 18 holes and then have a two-course dinner - all for £12!

The club's Lakeside Inn offers full bar and restaurant facilities in a beautiful, tranquil setting.

And there is a unique feature forming part of the setting. It is the Brayton carp lake, the oldest wild carp lake in the country.

Brayton Park is easy to reach from the M6 motorway. See the Fact File for details.

FACT FILE

A meadowland course of 9 holes, 5042 yards as 18. Par 64. SSS 64. Record 61.

Restrictions: Visitors and societies phone in advance. No visitors Wednesday pm or Sunday am.

Fees: £4 for nine holes; £6 for 18 holes.

Dress code: Smart and casual.

Facilities:

TO THE CLUB

From south - junction 41 of the M6 onto the B5305 to the A595 and B299 to Aspatria.
From north - junction 44 of the M6, through Carlisle following the A595 to Aspatria.

Course Information

Hole	Yards	Stroke	Par
1	236	7	3
2	286	13	4
3	378	3	4
4	227	5	3
5	197	15	3
6	307	9	4
7	318	11	4
8	402	1	4
9	170	17	3
10	236	8	3
11	286	14	4
12	378	4	4
13	227	6	3
14	197	16	3
15	307	10	4
16	318	12	4
17	402	2	4
18	170	18	3
OUT	2521		32
IN	2521		32
TOTAL	5042		64

1) A very testing long par three. Out-of-bounds down left of the fairway and bunkers each side of the green.

2) A nice view par four hole; second shot to the green well guarded by bunkers.

3) A slight dogleg left from the tee. The pond on the left of the green catches wayward second shots.

4) It's out-of-bounds all down the left of the slightly uphill par three hole.

5) Slightly downhill to a long green with out-of-bounds on the left.

6) A difficult second shot uphill to a long narrow green sloping left to right.

7) There's a risk of over-clubbing the second shot to a penalty ditch behind the shallow green.

8) The hardest hole, driving to a sloping uphill fairway and a narrow green with out-of-bounds all the way.

9) A nice view on this par three hole, slightly downhill with a large pond in front of the green. An intimidating hole.

Recommended Facilities

CARLISLE
Golf Club

Aglionby, Carlisle,
Cumbria CA4 8AG.

Manager: Chris Ward
01228-513029.
Secretary: Mrs Helen Rowell
01228-513303.
Professional: John S. More
01228-513241.

AN exceptionally well kept parkland course designed by Tom Simpson, McKenzie Ross and (later) Frank Pennink.

Carlisle is remembered by visitors for having each hole of a different character and that the four par threes are as good as can be found anywhere. The course was chosen as an Open Championship regional qualifying course in 1996 and has hosted many important events.

It is a mature course with trees that in many places keep the fairways tight. They support a mixture of wildlife including a colony of red squirrels.

Unusually, a tree grows on the fairway at the fifth, forcing the tee shot to be played to the left.

The club professional, John S. More, has been at Carlisle for 40 years.

The present course was established at Aglionby in 1936 after the club was based at Durran Hill Park for almost 30 years. Prior to that, Carlisle golfers had to travel to Silloth, to what was then called the Carlisle and Silloth Golf Club.

With a large and spacious clubhouse - the dining room can seat 100 - and a reputation for having a beautifully maintained course in a very convenient location, the club is an ideal venue for visitors, and welcomes corporate days.

FACT FILE

A parkland course of 18 holes, 6278 yards. Par 71. SSS 70. Record 63.

Restrictions: Societies should phone the Secretary in advance. Ladies' Tuesday. No visitors Saturday.

Fees: £20 to £35.

Dress code: Usual golf attire.

Shop opening: Summer 7.30am to dusk. Winter 8am to dusk.

Facilities:

TO THE CLUB

On the A69 less than a mile east of junction 43 of the M6.

Course Information

Hole	Yards	Stroke	Par
1	388	5	4
2	183	13	3
3	379	7	4
4	149	15	3
5	286	17	4
6	353	11	4
7	415	1	4
8	380	9	4
9	494	3	5
10	385	12	4
11	378	4	4
12	490	8	5
13	147	18	3
14	350	10	4
15	563	6	5
16	441	2	4
17	152	16	3
18	345	14	4
OUT	3027		35
IN	3251		36
TOTAL	6278		71

1) A right to left dogleg. Keep clear of the trees!

2) A difficult par three. Watch those bunkers.

3) An easy driving hole. Hit the second shot left - probably take six.

4) Most difficult on the course. Never over-club and watch the beck on the right.

5) An easy hole. Five wood off the tee, wedge to four feet, birdie three?

6) A good driving hole with a tricky second shot to a long, narrow green.

7) Slight dogleg with a testing second to the low-lying narrow green. Plays a club longer than it looks.

8) A left to right dogleg, difficult to drive the second to a three-tier green. Go left at your peril!

9) An easy par five providing you can keep out of the bunkers and becks.

10) Drive through the narrow gap in the trees. Your club selection for the second is tricky.

11) A blind tee shot then a sharp dogleg. The green slopes severely.

12) Another easy par five if you keep out of the trees.

13) A beautiful par three hole. Must hit the green or risk taking five.

14) A wide fairway - and the second shot must reach the green.

15) The longest hole and yet a relatively easy par five if you steer clear of the large oaks and becks.

16) A good par four needing a good tee shot.

17) Miss the green left and you could end up in the local pub!

18) Another wide fairway to hit - and the most difficult second shot on the course, should you fly it or run it up?

Recommended Facilities

CARUS GREEN
Golf Course

Burneside Road,
Kendal, Cumbria LA9 6EB.

Secretary: F. W. Downham
01539-721097.

Professional: Chris Barrett

THIS 18-hole course opened in the spring of 1995 after a two-year redevelopment of the dairy farm of secretary/proprietor Fred Downham.

It is a pay-and-play course but a club was scheduled to open late in 1996, giving privileges to regulars.

The course, designed by golf architect Will Adamson, is in the process of development and will need time to mature. About 3,000 trees have been planted.

Situated in a level valley on the outskirts of Kendal, it is almost completely ringed by the Rivers Kent and Sprint, which come into play on several holes.

Coupled with the small lake between 11 and 12, they often demand accurate tee shots to avoid fishing expeditions.

There are beautiful views of the Lakeland fells, from Kentmere to the Howgills.

Partners Fred and Eileen Downham, who ran the dairy farm on the site, developed the course after identifying the need for a flat course that could be used by older players who might have trouble on the nearby hilly courses.

At the same time they thought an informal course would be welcomed by players who might be a little shy of trying the established courses.

It is attractively priced to please both categories of clientel, at just £9 per round.

Before it was a farm, the land was a racecourse but no evidence of this was found when laying out the golf course, says Fred Downham.

The clubhouse has been developed from old stables but facilities are limited. There is no bar.

FACT FILE

A parkland course of 18 holes, 5666 yards. Par 70. SSS 68.

Restrictions: None.

Parties: By prior arrangement.

Fees: £9 (pay and play).

Dress code: Smart casual.

Shop: Sales of balls and small items of equipment during course opening hours.

Facilities:

TO THE CLUB

On the Kendal bypass, the A591, turn at the roundabout with the Burneside sign. Turn right at Burneside.

Course Information

Hole	Yards	Stroke	Par
1	149	18	3
2	350	7	4
3	165	14	3
4	339	11	4
5	389	2	4
6	180	9	3
7	479	5	5
8	423	1	4
9	295	16	4
10	351	15	4
11	167	3	3
12	364	4	4
13	476	10	5
14	336	8	4
15	321	12	4
16	237	17	4
17	468	6	5
18	177	13	3
OUT	2769		34
IN	2897		36
TOTAL	5666		70

1) A friendly starting hole with a mid iron to the facing green.

2) A lofted wood or long iron shot to avoid the River Kent at the left.

3) An attractive short hole from an island tee in the river.

4) A straight hole needing a drive and a short iron.

5) A good drive and an accurate second shot are needed on the way to the small green.

6) A mid iron to a large banked green. Beware of the water behind.

7) A long hole with the River Sprint all down the left and a large oak tree guarding the green.

8) A sharp dogleg left. Good positioning on the left of the fairway leaves an easy shot to the Mackenzie green.

9) A straight drive and accurate second shot are needed to avoid the out-of-bounds hedge to the right of the green.

10) A tight drive between hedges leaves a mid iron second shot.

11) A tough uphill par three. Check the pin position.

12) A difficult tee shot between out-of-bounds leaves a mid iron second shot over the ditch to the green - with trouble behind.

13) The right is the best way to the green but watch that pond.

14) Consider the pond and the river but the left of the fairway gives the best view of the green.

15) An easy tee shot and a short iron to the green.

16) Drive and pitch to a small, well guarded green.

17) A well placed tee shot will open a route to the green.

18) A challenging shot for a long iron or wood to carry the river. A bunker to the right of the green catches wayward shots.

Reamended Facilities

Ingmire Hall

Ingmire Hall, a magnificent crenellated and turreted building dates back to the 16th century. Set one mile from the picturesque market town of Sedbergh on the edge of the Yorkshire Dales and yet only half an hour away from Windermere and the Lake District. The Hall has been lovingly restored to provide comfortable accommodation in a peaceful and idyllic location. Rooms are en-suite and have TV, tea and coffee making facilities. There is a residents lounge, a games room with snooker table and a putting green available for the sports minded, or you can relax in the five acres of woodland and gardens. Ingmire is an ideal setting for a peaceful break and is a superb centre for golfing, fishing, touring or a walking holiday. The 'Dales Way' walk and the Howgills virtually on the doorstep, as is picturesque Dentdale and the famous Settle-Carlisle railway.

Ingmire Hall, Sedbergh, Cumbria LA10 5HR. Tel: 01539 621012

CASTERTON
Golf Course

Sedbergh Road, Casterton,
nr. Kirkby Lonsdale, Carnforth,
Lancashire LA6 2LA.

Proprietors: Mr. & Mrs. J. & E.
Makinson 015242-71592.
Professional: Roy Williamson
(teaching capacity only).

CASTERTON may only be a nine-hole course but it is one of the most challenging in Cumbria.

Yes, the course is in Cumbria; the postal address is via Carnforth, Lancashire.

An unusual fact about the course is that it is a private pay-and-play course that depends on visitors.

Years ago visitors went home with tales of a rather tight nine-hole course with interlinking fairways and wire fences to keep sheep off the greens.

In those days the land was rented by the Kirkby Lonsdale Golf Club from the Makinsons, a local farming family.

When the golf club moved down the road to a new course, John and Elizabeth Makinson took over at Casterton and transformed it.

The first step was to despatch the sheep prior to a complete redesign of the fairways and greens.

The course is now built with full advantage into some lovely country and although it still has only nine holes, it has doubled in size.

There are no bunkers but beware the numerous natural obstacles that make it a very tight course.

For instance, the first hole is a 427-yard par four across a steep ridge and down to a dry stone wall that stops balls that have been struck off centre.

The fairway doglegs sharply right to reveal a firm bank to the left of the green. Local players use it to advantage, landing the ball there to get a kick onto the green.

The second fairway is cut out of the rock that lines each side, becoming quite tight after about 150 yards. It's a test of nerve, for sure.

The new Casterton is a young course that is becoming more and more established through the improvements instigated by owner/groundsman John Makinson.

A recent addition is the clubhouse with changing facilities, a shop and a catering unit.

A visit to Casterton is a great day out, with green fees at only £8, it's a bargain, too.

The card on the right hand page is for the white tees. Visitors play off yellow.

FACT FILE

An undulating course with rocky outcrops. 9 holes, 5774 yards. Par 70. SSS 68. Record 64.

Fees: £8 to £10.

Restrictions: Confirm before booking. Group packages available on request.

Dress Code: Smart and casual.

Shop opening: Dawn till dusk.

Facilities:

TO THE CLUB

Off the A683, one mile north of Kirkby Lonsdale.

Course Information

Hole	Yards	Stroke	Par
1	427	3	4
2	316	9	4
3	142	17	3
4	328	7	4
5	168	11	3
6	407	1	4
7	290	15	4
8	332	5	4
9	477	13	5
10	427	4	4
11	316	10	4
12	142	18	3
13	328	8	4
14	168	12	3
15	407	2	4
16	290	16	4
17	332	6	4
18	477	14	5
OUT	2887		35
IN	2887		35
TOTAL	5774		70

1) A superb opening hole needing a big drive but there's no clue what to do next. See the club report opposite.

2) A straight par four down a narrowing gully.

3) A tee shot from up a hill and across rocks to a smallish green.

4) A blind tee shot from another elevated position giving great views.

5) The short hole is hard to par, especially if you slice your longer irons.

6) Another blind shot down a valley with trees, rocks and a wall to impede progress to a large, sloping green.

7) A straight shot over a marker to a three-tier green with a big lip at the front and a slope-off at the back.

8) Lots of natural hazards come into play, with some rough going.

9) A wide open fairway back to the clubhouse.

RIGHT ADVICE EQUIPMENT PRICE · PROFESSIONAL QUALITY · PGA

COCKERMOUTH
Golf Club

Embleton, Cockermouth,
Cumbria CA13 9SG.

Secretary: David Pollard
017687-76941.
Clubhouse: 017687-76223.

THE course is laid out on fell land on the east side of Cockermouth and is easily accessible from the A66 trans-Pennine road.

At 5496 yards it is not regarded as long. Nevertheless, it gives a stern test to the discerning golfer, particularly when the prevailing south west wind blows.

A positive feature of the course is the panorama of fine views from various points.

For example, looking back from the fourth tee the view is of Bassenthwaite Lake, and beyond it, Skiddaw Fell.

Walking down the 10th fairway one can look back over Cockermouth town to the Solway Firth and the coast of Dumfries and Galloway.

From the same fairway on a clear day it is possible to see the Isle of Man.

The testing holes are the 10th and 16th, which were re-arranged by James Braid.

Cockermouth is a historic club celebrating its centenary in 1996 with a busy calendar of events that included a re-creation of an 1897 match against Keswick Golf Club.

The original match was played on the Cockermouth club's first course, a nine-hole layout at South Lodge. In June 1898, the clubhouse burned down.

In 1904 the club moved to the present site at Embleton and a formal opening of the new 18-hole course - described as links, as were all golf courses at that time - attracted the best players in West Cumbria.

In 1924 the club employed James Braid to advise on improving the course and the five-times Open champion was paid 12 guineas for his report.

The club's centenary history assumes the work went ahead in 1925, as members were contributing towards the extension of the course and the clubhouse.

A fascinating slant on the shortages of the post-war years is a reference to members drawing lots for a share of the club's allocation of four dozen golf balls!

Steady progress through the second half of the century, and a VAT windfall, enabled clubhouse extensions and refurbishment to be completed in time for the centenary.

Course Information

Hole	Yards	Stroke	Par
1	252	14	4
2	268	12	4
3	287	8	4
4	182	16	3
5	317	9	4
6	374	5	4
7	392	3	4
8	422	1	4
9	141	18	3
10	298	15	4
11	396	2	4
12	478	7	5
13	374	4	4
14	282	13	4
15	185	11	3
16	339	10	4
17	158	17	3
18	351	6	4
OUT	2635		34
IN	2861		35
TOTAL	5496		69

1) Long-hitters can drive this short par four. But beware the hooked shot and out-of-bounds left.

2) Another shortish par four where wayward drives are penalised.

3) 'Thrombosis Hill' is its name. There's very little run on the fairway and a second shot to a blind hole.

4) A tee shot to a hidden hole. Don't miss the green on the left.

5) A fairway marker post gives the ideal line to the hidden green.

6) A good tee shot is needed here. The important second shot is aimed to come in from the bank on the right of the green.

7) A narrow landing area for the tee shot. The green is guarded by a cross fence, which means a long iron second shot.

8) An uphill par four with another narrow landing area for the tee shot.

9) The shortest hole. Club selection depends on the wind.

10) Long-hitters can eliminate the dogleg to the left.

11) The fairway falls away left on the uphill par four. In dry conditions the ball can run out-of-bounds.

12) A short par five reachable in two by long-hitters.

13) Difficult from the medal tee. A careful second shot is needed as it is out-of-bounds on both sides and behind the hole.

14) The fairway is narrow - and so is the entrance to the green.

15) A difficult par three with a well guarded entrance.

16) The need to drive over two walls makes this an imposing hole.

17) A deceptive par three with potential trouble on the right and out-of-bounds surrounding the green.

18) A dogleg to the left. It's important to hit the fairway from the tee.

Recommended Facilities

DALSTON HALL
Golf Club

Dalston Hall, Dalston,
nr. Carlisle CA5 7JX.

Secretary: Jane Simpson
01228 710165.
Clubhouse: 01228 710165.

OPENED in 1990, Dalston Hall's nine-hole course is situated on the south west outskirts of Carlisle and can quickly be reached from junction 42 of the M6.

Being in the valley of the river Caldew on the fringe of the Lake District National Park, the surroundings are peaceful and wildlife abounds on the course.

Players may well see rabbits, red squirrels, oyster-catchers, herons and even deer during their round of golf.

The clubhouse is small but friendly and catering is provided daily. A caravan park forms part of the complex, making it an ideal venue for those on holiday.

Although most holes at Dalston Hall are relatively short, the strategically placed bunkers, the plantations, a number of internal out-of-bounds, and the prevailing westerly wind will soon catch out the stray shot.

All greens are protected by bunkers and there are a number of fairway bunkers around the course.

Among the spectacular views to be enjoyed is a particularly good one of the Pennines from the second tee. From the fourth tee the Lake District fells provide the backdrop, with Blencathra in good view from the eighth.

Dalston Hall - which is not connected to Dalston Hall Golf Club - provides an historic background to the ninth green.

FACT FILE

A parkland course of 9 holes, 5045 yards. Par 67. SSS 65. Record 65.

Restrictions: Societies make contact in advance. Visitors phone weekends or after 4pm on weekdays.

Fees: £4 to £11.

Dress code: Usual golf attire.

Facilities:

TO THE CLUB

From junction 42 of the M6 follow signs for Dalston on the B5299.

Course Information

Hole	Yards	Stroke	Par
1	282	14	4
2	136	16	3
3	344	12	4
4	476	4	5
5	109	18	3
6	363	2	4
7	330	8	4
8	280	10	4
9	222	6	3
10	276	17	4
11	164	13	3
12	305	15	4
13	398	1	4
14	187	7	3
15	362	3	4
16	335	11	4
17	294	9	4
18	182	5	3
OUT	2542		34
IN	2503		33
TOTAL	5045		67

1) An easy par four to start but beware the out-of-bounds to the left and behind the green.
2) The 30-foot drop to the green provides the main feature.
3) A slight dogleg with out-of-bounds to the right and three large fairway bunkers, each with grass islands.
4) The water hazard about 150 yards from the tee catches the wayward shot. It's a difficult, sloping green.
5) Played from a tee mat out of a small wood to a protected green.
6) An internal out-of-bounds the whole length and tight to the right side spoils many a good card. Beware the ditch behind the green.
7) Tougher than it looks. Out-of-bounds right and a ditch to the left.
8) An easy par four with a deep valley across the fairway. Keep right.
9) A long, difficult par three. The steeply sloping green needs study.
10) A different angle from the first, with a bunker more in play.
11) Much further back than the second. A shot pulled to the left will be in tree country.
12) Similar to the third but less likely to go out-of-bounds.
13) A difficult par four, particularly in the westerly wind. A fairway bunker comes into play.
14) A difficult par three to judge for distance. The green is protected by four bunkers. Local rules apply re overhead wires.
15) As for the sixth but beware the out-of-bounds on the right.
16) The out-of-bounds right is more in play than on the seventh.
17) Similar to the eighth but starting further back.
18) A different tee and green. A good straight shot is needed here.

Recommended Facilities

DALSTON HALL HOTEL

Dalston, Carlisle, Cumbria CA5 7JX.
Tel: 01228 710271 Fax: 01228 711273

Dalston Hall is a Fifteenth Century Mansion, parts of the house and grounds date back even further to the Roman occupation. The Hotel is a unique place in which to escape, relax and soak up the beautiful countryside and colourful history which surrounds this wonderful place.

The Hotel has medieval banquets regularly in the ancient Baronial Hall. Adjacent to the Golf Course. Tee times can be arranged by the Hotel.

Because we want you to feel comfortable when you stay with us, you will find each room in the Hotel has its own warm, relaxed atmosphere - to ensure that you do just that.

Afternoon Tea in the library. Coffee on the Minstrels Gallery. An intimate dinner in the Caldew Restaurant followed by drinks by a roaring fire in the bar. At Dalston Hall each day brings another pleasure.

Elegance and tradition in an age of change

DUNNERHOLME
Golf Club

Duddon Road, Askam-in-Furness,
Cumbria LA16 7AW.

Secretary: Mrs E. M. Tyson
01229-889326.
Clubhouse: 01229-462675.
(Fax: 01229-581400).

DUNNERHOLME is the name of a huge outcrop in the Duddon Estuary and is the focal point of this 10-hole links course.

It is the dramatic location of the sixth green, calling for an accurate drive up to the rock from the 'mainland' part of the course.

This could be reason enough for a visit to this course and when you add the prospect of gorse-lined fairways and the possibility of a wicked wind on your chosen day, the challenge is there.

The club is rightly proud of the rock feature and members delight in telling visitors to take a good look at the sixth green when they are at the fifth tee, for they won't see it again until they get there!

Another point of interest seen from the fifth green is an old Norman farm house up on the hill, from where the area was controlled in medieval times.

The club was formed in 1905 by railway workers and little has changed since but some of the bunkers have grown over, making them no less of a hazard.

There are sheep on the course but they don't cause any problems on the greens. Two groundstaff maintain the course with help and advice from the Sports Turf Research Association.

On the ninth hole, a 349-yard par four, a stream can claim the ball. Local rules apply here. These are, that if your partner witnesses the splashdown, drop a ball with a one shot penalty as there is little chance of finding anything in the deep layer of silt.

A word of warning about another little inconvenience on some holes - the reeds. They make interesting rough as they allow the ball to be found. Then they stop your club as you try to cut through.

The 10 holes are played as 18 by missing the sixth and seventh on the back eight. There are different tee positions on the back section, giving a new perspective to some holes.

The 13th (the third first time round) is extended to a par five with the largest sand bunker in the world to the left as you tee off. It's called Duddon Sands!

The Dunnerholme course is well designed and quite tight. Like many in this area it has the bonus of superb views of Lakeland and the bay.

FACT FILE

A links course of 10 holes with 18 tees, 6154 yards. Par 72. SSS 70.

Restrictions: Handicap certificates required. Societies apply in writing. Ladies' Wednesday pm. Competitions day Sunday.

Fees: £12 to £15, half with member.

Dress code: Usual golf attire.

Facilities:

TO THE CLUB

Turn left over the railway crossing, off the A595 from Dalton at Askam.

Course Information

Hole	Yards	Stroke	Par
1	303	11	4
2	353	10	4
3	456	1	4
4	165	17	3
5	390	4	4
6	129	15	3
7	289	13	4
8	527	7	5
9	349	5	4
10	285	16	4
11	318	9	4
12	364	8	4
13	483	12	5
14	150	18	3
15	413	2	4
16	535	6	5
17	350	3	4
18	295	14	4
OUT	2961		35
IN	3193		37
TOTAL	6154		72

1) The main fairway runs along a ridge with roll-off each side before reaching the large oval green.

2) A stream is invisible from the tee but only big hitters will find it. Reeds to the right pose a bigger threat.

3) Rated the hardest par four in Cumbria because of its length and tightness. Don't risk going for the green with your second shot. There's thick gorse down the left.

4) Aim for the left of the pin on this shortish par three which kicks to the right. The sloping green is bumpy and rimmed by grass bunkers.

5) A large area of gorse in front of the tee will catch anyone playing short and a road is hidden in front of the undulating green. Depending on the pin position, this can leave a hard putt.

6) The best hole for miles with the unseen green atop the Dunnerholme Rock.

7) Teeing off from the rock, this 289-yarder has a wall blocking the green. Play down to the wall and chip over onto a lovely green.

8) A long par five to a fairly open, excellent green. The railway is to the left but it's pretty open to have a lash at it!

9) The stream cuts across the fairway from the right just before the green. So play it short if you are a big hitter. Remember the Local Rules!

10) A great par four up a hill, blind first over a marker post to a little plateau. If you don't make it the second is blind too. A 12-foot high wall poses a problem if you roll away to the left.

Recommended Facilities

EDEN
Golf Club

Crosby-on-Eden, Carlisle,
Cumbria CA6 4RA.

Telephone: 01228-573003 for:
Secretary: Dennis Willey
Professional: Phil Harrison
Clubhouse and Restaurant.
Fax: 01228-818435.

BEAUTIFULLY situated alongside the River Eden, this recently opened club is a golfing enterprise aimed at making the game more accessible to groups and societies.

As such, the club has an extraordinary range of practice facilities. They include a 16-bay floodlit driving range, practice green and bunkers, chipping areas and putting greens. Professional services include tuition, group coaching and a junior development programme.

The club is proud of its professional shop, which stocks a wide range of leisure wear and golfing equipment. Individual attention is given to suit discerning tastes.

The Fairways Restaurant and new clubhouse provide a full range of facilities for members and visitors.

Societies are made very welcome and Corporate packages are available on request.

The management at Eden are always happy to discuss your proposed golf day and will help design a package exactly to your needs. As for the parkland course with gently undulating fairways, it offers a real challenge. The fairways tend to be rather open but there are five lakes and a meandering stream to consider.

Phil Harrison, the ex-European PGA tour professional at the club, points out that most of the greens are raised and protected at the front, causing the player to use a short iron to stay on.

The course is easier to reach than many of the Cumbrian clubs.

FACT FILE

A parkland course of 18 holes, 6368 yards. Par 72. SSS 72.

Restrictions: Groups and societies contact by phone. (£2 per head discount for parties of 10 or more).

Fees: £15 to £20, half with member.

Dress code: Usual golf attire.

Shop opening: Dawn to dusk.

Facilities:

TO THE CLUB

One mile off the A689, five miles east of junction 44 of the M6.

Course Information

Hole	Yards	Stroke	Par
1	365	3	4
2	174	5	3
3	344	13	4
4	433	1	4
5	511	7	5
6	153	15	3
7	371	11	4
8	459	17	5
9	190	9	3
10	353	10	4
11	268	18	4
12	520	2	5
13	160	16	3
14	431	4	4
15	421	6	4
16	329	12	4
17	428	8	4
18	458	14	5
OUT	3000		35
IN	3368		37
TOTAL	6368		72

1) A dogleg with the stream to play 100 yards from the green.

2) A long accurate shot is needed, particularly into the prevailing wind. Out-of-bounds right and behind the green.

3) A dogleg to the left with out-of-bounds right and the river behind the green.

4) A long par four needing two long shots to a well guarded green.

5) With the Eden to the left, a lake to the right and fairway bunkers, accuracy is needed.

6) A lake to the rear and bunkers to the front make this an interesting par three.

7) Out-of-bounds all along the right of the fairway - and a sloping green.

8) A short par five with two good shots earning a birdie chance.

9) An elevated, guarded green needs a good tee shot.

10) A funnelled fairway with out-of-bounds both sides.

11) An eagle chance if you drive the lake; an easier option is to play it as a dogleg.

12) A good par five with a lake to the right and a stream crossing 60 yards before the green.

13) Wind direction decides the choice of club on a sloping par three.

14) A good par four to an elevated, sloping green with bunkers.

15) A sliced tee shot finds a lake, while fairway bunkers lurk to the left.

16) Pin placement affects a birdie chance on this shortish par four.

17) A lateral water hazard lies behind the green.

18) Fairway bunkers and a lake behind the green call for accuracy, making this par five a good finishing hole.

Recommended Facilities

FURNESS
Golf Club

Central Drive, Walney Island,
Barrow-in-Furness,
Cumbria LA14 3LN.

Secretary: W. T. French
01229-471232.
Clubhouse: 01229-471232.

FORMED in 1872 by migrant Scottish workers in the local industries, Furness is the sixth oldest golf club in England.

Originally located on nearby Biggar Bank, the present course was laid out in the early 1900s with the clubhouse being completed in 1916 and opened by the man whose grip is used today by millions of golfers - the great Harry Vardon.

Major alterations to the course and clubhouse have resulted in a fine test of golf and a friendly social ambience.

The course is on Walney Island, bounded by the Irish Sea to the south and west and enjoying lovely views of the Lake District to the north.

The layout gives a good variety of holes to match the prevailing sea breezes, the first six holes straight out towards Earnsie Bay, the second six back along the shore and the final six alternating hole by hole.

The middle six are the most notable, all needing great accuracy and not a little courage. The seventh and eighth, with out-of-bounds to a sandy beach, have been described as having six feet of England to the right and 130 miles to the left.

The par three 10th, resembling the 'postage stamp' at Troon, needs pin-point accuracy, as does the drive on the 11th, which is arguably the best hole on the course.

The ninth and 13th are the most difficult. Long and well directed drives are needed to avoid a blind spot on the former and a gully - fondly named Hades - on the latter.

Although a links course, the fairways do give some relief from that tight lie normally expected from links.

This, coupled with 18 well prepared and varied greens, makes a round at Furness a must for the enthusiast.

After the challenge of the course, the clubhouse and its friendly staff offer the chance to relax over a quiet drink or a game of snooker on the full-sized table.

Catering facilities range from a simple sandwich to a four-course dinner in the well appointed upstairs dining room, which boasts a panoramic view of the course and the Irish Sea.

FACT FILE

A fairly flat links course of 18 holes, 6363 yards. Par 71. SSS 70. Record 65.

Restrictions: Visitors and societies phone the Secretary. Special rates for 10 or more. Handicap certificates required. Ladies' day Wednesday. Competition and members Fridays noon to 2pm.

Fees: £17, £10 with member.

Dress code: Usual golf attire.

Shop opening: 9.30am to 5pm.

Facilities: No catering Mondays.

TO THE CLUB

From junction 36 of the M6 take the A590 to Barrow, following Walney Island signs through the town, over the bridge and straight ahead.

Course Information

Hole	Yards	Stroke	Par
1	537	7	5
2	161	18	3
3	304	9	4
4	323	13	4
5	542	5	5
6	152	16	3
7	432	3	4
8	378	11	4
9	446	1	4
10	174	15	3
11	443	4	4
12	336	10	4
13	410	2	4
14	393	8	4
15	325	14	4
16	271	17	4
17	394	6	4
18	342	12	4
OUT	3275		36
IN	3088		35
TOTAL	6363		71

1) A good loosener needing three strokes to the bunkered sloping green. Big trouble to the right!
2) Depending on wind, a three to a nine iron to a well-bunkered green sloping left to right.
3) A precise drive is needed. Large bunkers to the right and beyond the green.
4) A relatively easy par four. Three bunkers guard a flat green.
5) The longest hole needing a 150 yard drive to the fairway. Bunkers are placed to catch the second shot.
6) In the opposite direction to the second - with similar wind problems.
7) Out-of-bounds all down the right. A long second shot, problematic in wind, to a relatively unguarded green.
8) Out-of-bounds again on the right. Don't be short with the second shot to the green.
9) A difficult hole. Drive well to avoid a blind second shot to a bunkered green. There's gorse to the left and right.
10) A great par three resembling the 'postage stamp' at Royal Troon. Big trouble to the left.
11) Arguably the best hole. Drive long and accurately to avoid out-of-bounds left and right. A long second shot to the sloping, bunkered green.
12) A typical card-wrecker! It looks easy - but misplaced shots to the raised green are costly.
13) A long drive to the uphill fairway, sloping left to right. Remember the Hades gully.
14) Downhill, allowing leeway left and right. A mid-iron second to a blind green.
15) Back up the slope. A reasonable drive leaves an easy mid-iron to the green. Gorse and bunker to the right.
16) Another card-wrecker! Avoid the left side heather and gully known as Titleist Corner. A short iron to a difficult green.
17) A par four with side ditches and a bunkered but flat green.
18) Out-of-bounds to the right. The beautifully shaped green is guarded by four bunkers.

Recommended Facilities

GRANGE FELL
Golf Club

Fell Road, Grange-over-Sands,
Cumbria LA11 6HB.

Secretary: J. B. Asplin
015395-32021.
Clubhouse: 015395-32536.

THIS may be a short course - but what a spectacular short course!

The nine holes are set on a hillside 500 feet above the other Grange club's 18-hole course.

Playing a round at Grange Fell is as much a fell walk as a game of golf.

The holes zig-zag up the fell and because of the tight arrangement and frequent drops in contour, the wayward stroke can be expensive.

The second round is played over the same distances as the first.

The third and the ninth are the killers due to their downhill nature.

There is no respite on the greens. They are small but very undulating. The constant consolation for the little disasters that will befall most players is provided by the terrific views of Morecambe Bay and the Lakeland hills.

In brief, this is a brilliant little course and a great test of skill.

The clubhouse is small but modern and the members are friendly.

FACT FILE

A hillside course of 9 holes, 5278 yards. Par 70. SSS 66. Record 67.

Restrictions: Groups and societies not catered for. Competitions Sundays during season.

Green fees: £15 to £20, half with member.

Dress code: Usual golf attire.

Facilities:

TO THE CLUB

On Fell Road, Grange-over-Sands, the road from Grange to Cartmel.

Course Information

Hole	Yards	Stroke	Par
1	241	9	4
2	274	3	4
3	289	13	4
4	292	11	4
5	161	17	3
6	315	7	4
7	378	1	4
8	479	5	5
9	210	15	3
10	241	10	4
11	274	4	4
12	289	14	4
13	292	12	4
14	161	18	3
15	315	8	4
16	378	2	4
17	479	6	5
18	210	16	3
OUT	2639		35
IN	2639		35
TOTAL	5278		70

1) Beggar's Breeches. A reasonably easy par four with out-of-bounds on the right.

2) Fell End. A par four on a hillside giving difficult lies.

3) Priory Loop. A blind drive with a second shot to a Mackenzie green below. View of Cartmel Priory.

4) High Fell. The difficulty with this par four is a very small green with a bunker.

5) A. B. Davy. Named after the founder of the course, this is a par three with a sloping green.

6) Kestrel Way. Another hillside par four with sloping lies.

7) Lakeland View. A long par four with beautiful views of the mountains.

8) Fell Bent. A good par five, dogleg with out-of-bounds to the left all the way to the green.

9) Bay View. A lovely par three played from an elevated tee to a green 80 feet below.

Recommended Facilities

Graythwaite Manor Hotel

This beautifully furnished country house provides an exclusive, comfortable and tranquil setting in which to relax, enhanced by its peaceful situation in eight acres of private landscaped gardens and woodland on the hillside looking out over Morecambe Bay.

Excellent cuisine, table d'hôte andà la carte, fully licensed.

Fernhill Road, Grange-over-Sands, Cumbria LA11 7JE
Telephone: 015395 32001 Fax: 015395 35549

GRANGE-OVER-SANDS
Golf Club

Meathop Road, Grange-over-Sands,
Cumbria LA11 6QX.

Secretary: J. R. Green
015395-33754 (Fax 33754).
Professional: Steve Sumner-Roberts
015395-35937.
Clubhouse: 015395-33180.

THERE have been many changes since the club was formed and the course laid out in 1919.

But it is still an 18-hole flat parkland course of medium length that plays considerably longer than its length implies.

Well placed plantations, ponds, watercourses and individual trees add to the interest of holes that seem relatively simple, but tee shots straying away from the fairways make a par difficult to get.

The par threes are considered to be one of the features of the course, especially the eighth, a short 134 yards across a stream to an elevated green.

Anyone over-clubbing is in serious trouble and shots falling short require a delicate pitch to be near enough for a par.

Although the course does present certain problems to players who stray from the fairway, they will not be taxed physically. Indeed, it can be a welcome break from coping with hills all around.

Steve and Sue Sumner-Roberts take great interest in the needs and the play of both visitors and members.

The club has a welcoming feel and an excellent bar.

FACT FILE

A parkland course of 18 holes, 5958 yards. Par 70. SSS 69.

Restrictions: Societies write to the Secretary. Handicap certificates required. No visitors Saturdays and Sundays 8.30 to 9.30am and 11.45am to 1.15pm.

Fees: £15 to £25.

Dress code: Usual golf attire.

Shop opening: Summer 8am to 6pm; winter 9am to 4pm.

Facilities:

TO THE CLUB

From junction 36 of the M6, take the A590 and leave at the roundabout signposted Grange. The club is on the left just before entering the town.

Hole	Yards	Stroke	Par
1	326	9	4
2	198	13	3
3	392	3	4
4	318	15	4
5	350	10	4
6	311	11	4
7	337	14	4
8	134	17	3
9	492	5	5
10	410	2	4
11	188	8	3
12	363	7	4
13	291	18	4
14	177	12	3
15	397	1	4
16	402	4	4
17	345	16	4
18	527	6	5
OUT	2858		35
IN	3100		35
TOTAL	5958		70

Course Information

1) There's water only 50 yards from the tee. The undulating green has a bunker to the left.

2) The hazard on this hole is the stream at the back.

3) This dogleg right leads to a green with both a bank and bunkers.

4) A straightforward hole if the trees behind the green are avoided.

5) A fairway bunker and trees are to the right. Bunkers protect the large green.

6) Take good note of the marker on this dogleg right and allow for the stream just 30 yards from the green.

7) Another dogleg right, from an elevated tee, and a pond almost on the green.

8) A short par three that is often over-clubbed. The green is elevated.

9) The second longest hole on the course has water hazards galore.

10) A difficult par four with the only chance being a good tee shot to the marker.

11) Straight but tight, calling for an accurate tee shot.

12) A difficult hole with hidden water hazards.

13) A short par four with bunkers each side of the green to foil wayward drives.

14) Mounds, not bunkers, guard this green and the entrance is narrow,

15) Another straight hole and another unexpected stream.

16) Yellow markers denote a stream, and a bank at the back of the green is helpful.

17) A hard dogleg to the right. Don't go too far left in avoiding the stream.

18) The longest hole with a dogleg, a stream and trees to impede progress to the large green in front of the clubhouse.

Recommended Facilities

Swan Hotel

HOW TO FIND US

Leave the M6 Motorway at junction 36 following the A590 towards Barrow-in-Furness for 16 miles and turn right over Newby Bridge. The Swan is immediately ahead.

GOLF COURSES

Whilst the Lake District is an area of outstanding beauty, there are many Golf Courses within easy reach, 5 miles from both courses in Grange-over-Sands and conveniently situated on the main A590, only 15 minutes from Bowness.

The Swan hotel enjoys a deserved reputation for its charm, comfort and cuisine. Privately owned, the hotel is situated on the banks of the slow flowing River Leven at the Southern end of Lake Windermere, in a setting unrivalled throughout the Lake District.

Your comfort is our first priority and all 36 en-suite bedrooms reflect this. Each one has colour television, radio, direct dial telephone, hairdryer, electric trouser press and full tea and coffee making facilities.

Delicious food, fine wines and excellent service are the hall-marks of the Swans restaurant. Choose the traditional Tithe Barn or the Mailcoach Bar and enjoy imaginative menus, including vegetarian dishes, complemented by a wide and varied selection of wines.

Specifically designed to meet the needs of the smaller conference, the Swan offers a comprehensive range of equipment to facilitate the smooth running of any conference.

Newby Bridge, Cumbria LA12 8NB.
Tel: 015395 31681 Fax: 015395 31917

HALTWHISTLE
Golf Club

Banktop, Gilsland Road,
Greenhead, via Carlisle,
Cumbria CA6 7HL.

Secretary: W. E. Barnes
01434-320337.
Clubhouse: 01697-747367.

THE sound of metal hitting hard objects echoed across the Tyne Valley nearly 19 centuries ago.

It was made by Roman soldiers building a wall to keep out their fierce foes from the north.

Now the sweeter sound of irons connecting with white balls can be heard on these rolling acres on the edge of the Northumbrian National Park.

But Hadrian's Wall is still to be seen here and there, giving the Haltwhistle club a unique distinction of having a world heritage site alongside.

There are truly magnificent views along the valley of the River Tyne.

The course was established in 1966 at the village of Greenhead, which is easily reached from the A69 midway between Carlisle and Hexham. The village is within walking distance of the golf club.

The Roman Vallum actually crosses the course and the famous Pennine Way bisects it at another point. So ramblers are a frequent sight in the area.

The glorious landscape is a big plus with visitors, who are welcome every day except Sunday morning, when the course is fully taken up by members in club competitions.

The clubhouse is admittedly a modest affair but visitors can use the catering facilities and have a drink at the bar. Members reckon they have the reputation of one of the friendliest clubs in the north of England.

Until midsummer 1996 the club was playing only 12 holes but extensions were due to come into play in August.

The new 18th hole calls for a tee shot passing over the Roman Vallum.

It would seem to be a brilliant conversation piece, particularly with American and Japanese visitors!

FACT FILE

A parkland course of 18 holes (from August, 1996) approx. 6000 yards. Previously a 12-hole par 71. SSS 69.

Fees: £10 a day, £30 a week for tourists.

Restrictions: Visitors and societies phone the secretary. No visitors Sunday mornings.

Dress Code: Smart and casual.

Facilities:

TO THE CLUB

On the A69 Carlisle to Newcastle-upon-Tyne road, turn off with the Greenhead sign, about two miles west of Haltwhistle. Follow the Gilsland signs to the club.

Course Information

Hole	Yards	Stroke	Par
1	370	9	4
2	385	3	4
3	262	17	4
4	404	5	4
5	374	1	4
6	288	15	4
7	165	13	3
8	515	11	5
9	295	7	4
10	188	8	3
11	378	10	4
12	395	2	4
13	262	16	4
14	404	4	4
15	349	6	4
16	515	12	5
17	280	14	4
18	139	18	3
OUT	3058		36
IN	2910		35
TOTAL	5968		71

1) A severe dogleg to the left with an open ditch running parallel left of the fairway.

2) Drive straight at the midway marker post. A ditch and two bunkers guard the green approach.

3) Not a long hole but it's out-of-bounds all along the right.

4) Take in the magnificent view before driving downhill with out-of-bounds to the right.

5) Plenty of room for good drives before your uphill shot to a green perched on the course's highest point.

6) Aim over the hawthorn tree centre fairway but note the deep waterway, crossing the course at 250 yards.

7) A short straightforward par three - with the waterway collecting bad tee shots.

8) A downhill drive to a fairway sloping right. Aim left approaching the green to use the slope down to the pin.

9) A hog's back fairway causes terrible trouble all down the right. There are bunkers to the right and left rear of the green.

10) A very hard par three, with a ravine and a bunker on the central fairway.

11) Flat compared with hole 10 but traversing a deep ditch 120 yards from the tee.

12-16) New holes in play from August, 1996.

17) As hole nine but with a different tee.

18) A severe downhill fairway with the tee shot passing over the Roman Vallum, with a deep bunker and plantation waiting behind the green.

Recommended Facilities

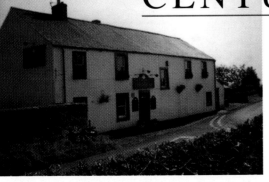

KENDAL
Golf Club

The Heights, Kendal,
Cumbria LA9 4PQ.

Manager: Roy Maunder
01539-733708.
Professional: Dave Turner
01539-723499.
Clubhouse: 01539-274079.

FITNESS is the main requirement on Kendal's course on a hill above the town. It starts with an uphill par three hole and becomes a steady climb until the 14th is reached. Then it plunges down like a miniature commando course.

The result is a variety of back nine holes that are a severe test of golf.

Developments are under way to lengthen the course after the purchase of 30 adjoining acres. Two of the par threes are being taken out and par fives substituted.

The extension will meet criticism that the course is too short although the fell climbing requirement has always made it seem longer than 5515 yards! The purchase of the land has brought to an end the risk of cows getting on the course.

The club also has plans to improve the clubhouse. Among the club's highlights are a spring charity weekend for Kendal Lions and the Northern PGA Pro-Am Tournament.

FACT FILE

A hilly moorland course of 18 holes, 5515 yards. Par 66.

Restrictions: Visitors and societies phone first. Handicap certificates required.

Fees: £16 to £20.

Dress code: Usual golf attire.

Shop opening: Summer 8.30am to 7pm; winter 9am till dusk.

Facilities:

[icons] PG PN

TO THE CLUB

From junction 37 of the M6 to Kendal. Turn left at the lights by the Town Hall with the Underbarrow signs. Turn right at the first crossroads.

Course Information			
Hole	Yards	Stroke	Par
1	232	4	3
2	283	18	4
3	206	8	3
4	381	12	4
5	136	16	3
6	331	6	4
7	221	10	3
8	379	2	4
9	167	14	3
10	401	9	4
11	373	7	4
12	433	5	4
13	397	3	4
14	416	1	4
15	392	11	4
16	319	13	4
17	130	17	3
18	318	15	4
OUT	2336		31
IN	3179		35
TOTAL	5515		66

1) Not an inspiring start, this uphill par three to a squarish green. But a fine view!

2) A narrow fairway with out-of-bounds right and a long green.

3) Another par three of more than 200 yards, uphill to an elevated green.

4) The drive must carry well over the marker to avoid the rough. The green is a real challenge, split by a little ravine.

5) Another difficult green with a steep bank to test your putting.

6) Still going uphill, the tee shot must clear the bank to avoid a big problem.

7) The views improve with height but the tee shot is a downhill line to a large circular green.

8) Climbing back up the hill, avoid the troublesome rough on each side of the fairway.

9) A bank at the back of the squarish green is helpful here.

10) The green is ringed by bunkers and with a trough to the right the approach is the problem.

11) A relatively straightforward hole, still climbing, with a large target.

12) Kendal's longest hole at 433 yards. Fluffed tee shots hit a wall.

13) A spectacular hole from an unusually elevated tee.

14) Stroke index one, earned by the tight fairway and tiny green.

15) The course starts to fall dramatically; big hitters beware the out-of-bounds behind the green.

16) Huge mounds are a barrier to the green which, when seen, is nice and big.

17) Another natural barrier - this time a huge rock - conceals the green and must be carried.

18) A straightforward drive across open territory to the lowest point on the course.

Recommended Facilities

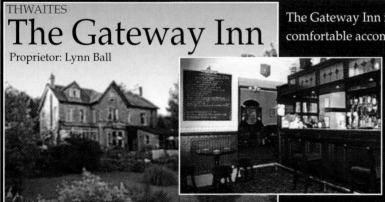

KESWICK
Golf Club

Threlkeld Hall, Threlkeld,
Keswick, Cumbria CA12 4SX.

Secretary: Richard Bell
017687-79324 (Fax 65367).
Professional: Craig Hamilton
017687-79010.

THE story of Keswick's return to the list of clubs is one of the most stirring in the annals of golf in north west England.

From the day in 1941 when the Army moved its bren-gun carriers onto the club's nine-hole course at Spooney Green, and churned it up with high speed training manoeuvres, golf in Keswick ceased to exist.

The club had been founded in 1896 as an amenity of the Keswick Hotel. There was nothing fancy. The clubhouse and locker room was a corrugated iron shed painted green.

After the Second World War the club somehow failed to regain possession and the land was taken over for agriculture.

And so for many years the idea of bringing golf back to this Queenly Lakeland town was just a dream. From time to time there were public meetings and proposals but nothing happened.

In 1964 the Manchester Waterworks Authority offered land, but planning permission was refused. The club appealed at a local inquiry in 1966 and won the day.

Hopes were crushed, however, when the Minister in charge of town and country planning over-

continued overleaf

Recommended Facilities

from previous page

turned his inspectors verdict and a subsequent appeal to the House of Lords was lost.

It was another five years before the club, which had been re-formed in 1965, acquired 200 acres of former farmland at Threlkeld Hall for little more than £10,000.

This time the club gained planning permission and years of fund raising, grant seeking and hard voluntary work by members, resulted in a clubhouse being built in 1976 and a nine-hole course being opened in 1979.

When a further nine holes were laid out in 1983 on a new parcel of land, the Keswick club became one of only two 18-hole courses in the Lake District National Park, the other being the Windermere club.

The official opening of the 18-hole course was performed by Lord Whitelaw in 1985 and to mark the event he was made an honorary vice-president.

FACT FILE

A varied fell and tree-lined 18 hole course, 6225 yards. Par 71. SSS 72. Record 69.

Restrictions: Bookings to the pro shop. Groups and societies must contact the Secretary in advance. Ladies' Thursday 12-2pm

Fees: £15 to £20, half with member.

Dress code: Usual golf attire.

Shop opening: Summer 8am-7pm; winter 9am till dusk.

Facilities:

TO THE CLUB

Four miles east of Keswick opposite Threlkeld village on the A66.

The club has a spare hole, enabling work to be done without reducing the course length.

The clubhouse has recently been enlarged to include changing

Recommended Facilities

Howe Keld

Howe Keld is beautifully situated between the town and the lake with open views of the surrounding fells from all rooms.

En-suite facilities • Dogs welcome • Private car park • Residential lounge bar
Full central heating • Tea & coffee making facilities in all rooms
Open all year round, except Christmas & New Year • Colour TV in bedrooms
B/B from £20 P.P.P.N. • Group discounts available

**5-7 The Heads, Keswick-on-Derwentwater, Cumbria CA12 5ES
Tel: 017687 72417 Props: Reg & Evelyn Tinkler**

rooms, showers, offices and the professional's shop.

Out on the course the visitor must wait until the second hole to appreciate Keswick's joys. It is a 244 yard par three from a raised tee, through a gap in the trees and across a series of streams to a green that is backed by a breath-taking view of Blencathra and its lower fells.

As opposed to other courses in Cumbria, which offer distant views of its famous peaks, Keswick is surrounded by them.

Fortunately the course is built in a river valley and is not that hilly. An exception is the fourth, dubbed 'Cardiac,' which has what seems like a vertical bank to climb in the middle of the fairway.

Watch out for the 11th and 12th holes. They both require a plan of attack before teeing off.

For a relatively new course, Keswick has a lot to offer the visitor. There is a good mix of long holes with wide fairways and shorter holes that are technically difficult.

Recommended Facilities

Derwent Cottage

Derwent Cottage is a large, Lakeland house, part of which dates back to the eighteenth century. It is situated in the quiet village of Portinscale, one mile west of Keswick town centre and just a short walk from Derwentwater. The house is set back from the road within mature grounds of nearly an acre, with terraced lawns and stately conifers.

The accommodation includes five spacious en-suite bedrooms, a dining room, bar and lounge, all of which are fully carpeted, double glazed and centrally heated. Each guest room is large, individually furnished and decorated to a high standard. A four course, candlelit table d'hôte dinner is served each evening at 7pm. Derwent Cottage is a No-Smoking establishment. Children over 12 years of age are welcome but pets are not.

Portinscale, Keswick, Cumbria CA12 5RF
Telephone: Keswick 017687 74838. Resident Proprietors - Mike & Sue Newman

Course Information

Hole	Yards	Stroke	Par
1	385	10	4
2	244	6	3
3	162	18	3
4	370	4	4
5	387	2	4
6	383	12	4
7	499	16	5
8	215	8	3
9	303	14	4
10	373	3	4
11	496	5	5
12	302	17	4
13	421	1	4
14	525	7	5
15	302	15	4
16	173	9	3
17	331	13	4
18	354	11	4
OUT	2948		34
IN	3277		37
TOTAL	6225		71

1) Drive over the help pole into a little dip and green surrounded by trees. The hole slopes the last 150 yards.

2) The hole of the course. A long par three with a big ditch short of the hole and that fantastic view of Blencathra behind the green.

3) A very picturesque green almost surrounded by water but easy to play.

4) Over a pole then sharp left up a steep bank. A very hard par needing a good tee shot to get a second shot at the green.

5) Although the flag is in sight and level with the tee, a big dip catches your drive, leaving a blind second shot.

6) A good drive will set you up for an easy approach. Out-of-bounds to the right from the tee.

7) There's room to open up a little. Straightfoward apart from the 100-foot drop left and back of the green.

8) The tee shot needs to carry all the way to avoid another big dip.

9) Watch for a wall that catches anything fading at about 200 yards.

10) A chance to open up on this tree-lined wide, straight fairway.

11) A daring tee shot slightly right would get past the dogleg and could find a decent position to go at the green for two.

12) Another excellent driving hole with trees all down the left and a pond to the right at about 220 yards.

13) A hard, long hole from the competition tee. Dogleg left with trees all down the left.

14) There's lots of danger to the right and trees to the left on this dogleg left par five.

15) A good drive can clear the dip but still end up in the stream. Otherwise its a short iron to the green.

16) A stream all the way on the left and in front of the green. Watch the barn to the right.

17) Go left or right past the four trees on the fairway. The kidney-shaped green slopes to the right.

18) A stream runs in front of the green on this par four back to the clubhouse.

Recommended Facilities

The *Borrowdale* HOTEL

This stone built Lakeland Hotel is situated at the head of the queen of the Lakes - Derwentwater. Having all the traditional values of a well established family run Hotel.

All 34 very comfortable bedrooms have private facilities, colour TV, radio and baby listening service, direct telephones and tea and coffee making facilities.

All Superior double bedded rooms have Four Poster Beds.

Served in our newly refurbished restaurant is a six course evening dinner offering traditional English and International dishes and complemented by a selection of over 200 wines. There is a well stocked cocktail bar and an added welcome of blazing log fires in the lounge during the winter months. Bar lunches, which are speciality at the Borrowdale are served Monday to Saturday, with a traditional lunch served on Sundays.

Free Golf available Monday to Friday (Keswick)

**Telephone: (017687) 77224
Fax: (017687) 77338**

Borrowdale, Keswick

Recommended Facilities

Skiddaw Grove Hotel

The house was built about 1820 as a Gentlemans residence and has been tastefully modernised to provide ten comfortable bedrooms. There is a bar lounge, a separate residents lounge and spacious dining room, which have superb views over open countryside.

Set admist England's highest mountains and lakes on the fringe of the ancient market town and holiday centre of Keswick and at the heart of Cumbria, Skiddaw Grove Hotel offers peace and tranquility and is within easy travelling distance of most of the country's best Golf Courses

Self Catering

High Meadow is a modern, three bedroomed house, which is situated on a quiet lane, near the Leisure Pool and only five minutes walk from the town centre, available throughout the year. Has a secure garden to the rear and parking for two cars in the front garden. The house is fully equipped, linen is included and there are no meters to feed except for the telephone. Further details are available from the hotel.

- Heated outdoor swimming pool (May-September)
- Bar Lounge
- All bedrooms en-suite facilities, tea/coffee makers, colour TVs, clock radios
- Hotel open throughout the year
- Easy walk to town centre, 10-15 mins via park
- Sheltered sun terrace
- Just 5 miles from Golf Course
- Prices start from £24 p.p.n. B&B
- No smoking - except Bar Lounge

Local Golf Courses

Keswick	5mins	Carlisle	50mins
Cockermouth	15mins	Silloth	50mins
Penrith	25mins	Seascale	55mins
Windermere	35mins		

Skiddaw Grove Hotel
Vicarage Hill
Keswick-on-Derwentwater
Cumbria CA12 5QB
Telephone: 017687 73324

47

KIRKBY LONSDALE
Golf Club

Scaleber Lane, Barbon,
Kirkby Lonsdale, Carnforth,
Lancashire LA6 2LJ.

Secretary: Geoff Hall
015242-76365.
Professional: Chris Barrett
015242-76366.

AFTER several changes of location over the years, Kirkby Lonsdale Golf Club has finally settled on a 163-acre site at Barbon, three miles out of the charming little market town.

Behind that brief summary lies an enterprising story of achievement.

Back in 1991 the club existed on rented land which accommodated nine holes and a wooden hut. The greens were fenced to keep sheep off.

So how did this small club, in the space of five years, leap from that humble existence to their maturing new 18-hole course with a new clubhouse - and do it all for £150,000?

It began when a core group of members began a search for a new site and took a 50-year lease on the Barbon site. Planning permission was granted and the club took over the site in April 1991, with £50,000 in the bank - the proceeds from the old club.

They received a £5,000 grant from the R and A and a £20,000 interest-free loan; a £10,000 grant from the Sports Council and a £10,000

interest-free loan; around £40,000 was raised in membership fees; and £9,000 came from sponsored tees and greens.

But it was only through the physical effort of teams of members that the pasture land was prepared for the course, which was designed by the then secretary, Peter Jackson, saving on a major cost.

All construction work was completed in 1995, with attention turning to an extension of the clubhouse.

The course is a conventional loop circuit of two nines, with the Barbon Brook meandering through the site and coming into play on five holes.

The western edge of the course is alongside the River Lune and the surrounding hills and fells provide a stunning backdrop.

The club had 540 members at the start of 1996 and has some vacancies. It is worth noting that ladies and gents have equal rights and pay the same subscription.

The ladies' section is particularly active and in 1995 they won the

Cecil Leitch Trophy, the prestigious Cumbria County Ladies event named after the international woman golfer from Silloth in pre-1930 days.

The club extends a welcome to visitors, and members are confident they have a course that will quickly gain respect in the region.

FACT FILE

A parkland course of 18 holes, 6472 yards. Par 72. SSS 70. Record 68.

Restrictions: Visitors and societies phone to confirm. Wednesday is ladies' day.

Fees: £16 to £20; £10 with member.

Dress code: Usual golf attire.

Shop opening: Summer 8.30am to 7pm; winter 9am to 4.30pm.

Facilities:

TO THE CLUB

At Barbon, off the A683, about three miles on the Sedbergh side of Kirkby Lonsdale.

Course Information

Hole	Yards	Stroke	Par
1	345	9	4
2	366	11	4
3	168	17	3
4	507	5	5
5	189	15	3
6	396	1	4
7	355	13	4
8	502	7	5
9	374	3	4
10	533	8	5
11	350	14	4
12	388	6	4
13	162	18	3
14	560	2	5
15	356	12	4
16	382	4	4
17	146	16	3
18	393	10	4
OUT	3202		36
IN	3270		36
TOTAL	6472		72

1) A medium length par four down steps to a bunkered green backed by the brook.

2) A straight drive with medium irons to the slightly raised green.

3) This hole plays longer than it looks. Don't miss the green left.

4) Length is important here into the prevailing wind, with a long second shot needed to see the green.

5) A nice view down to the green in the first of the 'Lune loop' holes.

6) The Lune gives the best view on the course. A good tee shot will run down a bank at about 200 yards.

7) Uphill to a plateau green. Too long a drive creates a blind second shot.

8) Fortune favours the brave on this double dogleg card-wrecker.

9) Back to the clubhouse and tee off over the beck to a raised fairway.

10) Dogleg right and out-of-bounds right. A long green allows the longer hitter to hold the green with the second shot.

11) A tricky hole with Barbon Beck twice a threat.

12) A blind tee shot favouring a draw allows a short iron to a receptive green.

13) Could be unlucky for some with a deep bunker and two-tier green that is further away than it looks.

14) A monster of a par five with no short cuts.

15) Climbing out of the woods where the herons live, this par four has a lot in store.

16) The fairway favours a fade; and another receptive green.

17) A little gem that requires thought about the wind and the club to be used. But don't hold back!

18) Don't relax yet! Get between the two large trees to a raised fairway.

Recommended Facilities

MARYPORT
Golf Club

Bank End, Maryport,
Cumbria CA15 6PA.

Secretary: Robert Bell
01900-815326.
Clubhouse: 01900-812605.

A rather unique attraction about the Maryport club is that it offers players nine holes of links golf and nine holes of parkland.

In fact the club has only recently joined the world of 18-holes and the course is in a constant state of development.

A new clubhouse with more parking space would be a boon to members. The present clubhouse dates back to 1905, three years after the club was formed.

The first three holes follow the line of the Solway Firth and give a delightful view of Criffel, on the Scottish side.

After crossing the road that bisects the course, two more links-type holes are played and then the parkland course takes over.

The trees were planted only recently and the dry summer of 1995 has been the death of many. The club has introduced local rules to safeguard those that survived and hopefully they will be saved.

The first hole on the course can be very intimidating as it is a good carry from the tee (even the yellow one) over a stream, more so if the wind is against the direction of play.

The sixth hole can also be a disaster to a card; the stream runs alongside the entire 524 yards and doglegs right, with the out-of-bounds also on the right. And the fairway slopes left to right.

The 14th has also been structured to encourage accuracy of the second shot, the green being on the side of a slope. Any shot other than straight will roll to the bottom, needing a 20 to 30 yard shot back to the green.

The 15th (a links-type) into the prevailing wind has out-of-bounds to the left and the second shot is again one for the straight hitter.

The fairway and the green slope right to left and even a slight hook (or fade by the left hander) goes out.

The continuing saga of the stream dominates two of the remaining links holes. It runs alongside most of the 16th fairway, round the green and doubles back to continue its journey to the sea by crossing the 18th fairway some 200 yards from the tee.

The 16th green is therefore a peninsula.

The 17th is a 219-yard par three with three strategically placed bunkers and out-of-bounds close to the back of the green.

On a good day with light winds, the Maryport course is a reasonable test of golf. On a windy day, no matter what the direction, it is unfriendly. A player would have to hit straight to return a good card.

But the clubhouse is always friendly, with cheerful members, and helpful staff.

FACT FILE

A seaside links and parkland course of 18 holes, 6088 yards. Par 70. SSS 69. Record 70.

Restrictions: Societies must confirm by phone. Ladies' day Thursday, juniors' day Thursday.

Fees: £15-£20, £10 with member.

Dress code: Usual golf attire.

Facilities:

TO THE CLUB ▷

North of Maryport turn left off the A596 onto the B5300 for about two miles.

Course Information

Hole	Yards	Stroke	Par
1	435	4	4
2	440	2	4
3	369	8	4
4	329	12	4
5	164	16	3
6	524	6	5
7	187	10	3
8	337	14	4
9	330	18	4
10	484	9	5
11	175	11	3
12	373	13	4
13	358	7	4
14	379	3	4
15	413	1	4
16	265	17	4
17	219	5	3
18	307	15	4
OUT	3115		35
IN	2973		35
TOTAL	6088		70

1) Out-of-bounds to the right and both a stream and a road cross the fairway.
2) The road crosses at 110 yards, there's gorse and out-of-bounds to the right and the shore on the left.
3) A slight dogleg and long carry to the fairway. More gorse and three green bunkers.
4) Another road crossing and rough over a wall to the right.
5) A stepped green with bunker to the left and two behind. The green slopes right.
6) Keep left and don't be greedy with the tee shot - there's a stream and out-of-bounds the full length. The fairway slopes right. Watch for the hidden green bunker.
7) A tight par three. Plantations left and a stream and out-of bounds right and back of the green.
8) An uphill drive, long carry, and plantations both sides. Blind bunkers each side of the green and a steep drop behind.
9) A straight hole with out-of-bounds left and two fairway bunkers.
10) A dogleg right and easy birdie for long hitters who cut the corner. Out-of-bounds if short.
11) Bunkers left, right and back of the green and plantations each side.
12) The tee shot needs to be accurate on this slight dogleg right. There are trees left and right and a blind approach to the green.
13) A long carry, dogleg right and a hedge masking a steep bank behind the stepped green raised at the right.
14) A difficult drive over a bank and a long second to the green, built on a hillside. Hit short and there's trouble.
15) Out-of-bounds left, rough to the right and a left-sloping fairway and green. Keep the shot left. Difficult in the wind.
16) A straight short par four with a stream running round the green.
17) A long par three, difficult to achieve. Bunkers guard the left-sloping green.
18) The stream is 200 yards from the tee and there's a bank in front of the green. Keep left with the shot to find the way in.

Recommended Facilities

The Old Mill Inn

Pool table, 2 miles from Maryport golf course plus centrally located for Cockermouth, Workington, Braxton Park and Silloth golf courses.
Very attractive rates for all golfers.

The Friendliest Hotel in West Cumbria

We try our best to make your stay as pleasant as possible and do our utmost to meet your requirements.
We guarantee that you will enjoy your time with us and want to return.

Rowbeck, Dearham, Maryport, Cumbria CA15 7JP
Telephone: 01900 813148

51

PENRITH
Golf Centre and Driving Range

Red Hills, Penrith,
Cumbria CA11 0DR.

Phone: 01768-892167 or
Fax: 01768-892268 for
Managers: Tony or Martin Allinson.
Professional: Nigel Burkitt.

THE centre is located on the A66 only two minutes west of junction 40 of the M6.

The complex was opened in 1993 and features a 16-bay floodlit driving range and an extensively stocked shop displaying the majority of golf hardware and fashion brands.

The whole facility is run on a pay-and-play basis, bringing the game of golf to many people who don't have the opportunity to learn or become members of private clubs.

Families are encouraged to visit and use the facilities and there is an abundance of hire sets for those who don't have their own clubs.

The centre is also the venue of one of the new Mizuno Golf Schools, a scheme designed to bring new people into the game through a series of lessons in not only playing the game but also in golf etiquette and the rules of the game.

The schools were established in 1995 by the Mizuno Golf Corporation in association with the Professional Golfers' Association and it has been very successful in bringing new players into the game nationwide.

Being a pay-and-play facility there are not many occasions when there are queues at the first tee, although it is advisable to phone first to check the conditions.

The nine hole course, with spectacular views of the Lakeland fells and the rolling Pennines, was opened in May, 1995.

The development of the course was seen as a logical evolution of the facility and although not long, it has several tricky holes and several more difficult options to the more aggressive-thinking golfer.

Development of the course is on-going, with new tees and bunkers added during the winter of 1995-96.

1) A tight opening hole, out-of-bounds down the left, tree-lined on the right. consider using a putter?

2) Beware you don't go out-of-bounds - right, onto the driving range.

3) Relatively easy, played round the dogleg right. Go for the flag if you're a good golfer.

4) Gently sweeping dogleg right but the prevailing wind may blow your ball out-of-bounds, tight on the right.

5) This hole may look simple but it is easy to hit the ball long into the rough.

6) Gentle uphill dogleg left; a straight tee shot and a short pitch to an elevated green.

7) Straightforward tee shot from an elevated tee. It looks longer than it is!

8) Difficult to stop the ball on the green; it will tend to find the bunker at the rear.

9) An accurate tee shot is needed as the trees on the right encroach slightly.

Course Information			
Hole	Yards	Stroke	Par
1	111	5	3
2	150	4	3
3	229	3	4
4	210	1	4
5	88	7	3
6	204	2	4
7	105	8	3
8	78	9	3
9	110	6	3
TOTAL	1285		30

FACT FILE

The course is nine holes, 1285 yards. Par 30.

Restrictions: None. Pay-and-play.

Fees: £3.95 for nine holes, £5.95 for 18 holes, £2 for club hire.

TO THE CLUB

On the A66 just west of junction 40 of the M6, turn right at the Little Chef and first left.

Penrith Driving Range

- 300yds Driving Range
- Floodlit
- High Quality Simulated 'Turf'
- Mats
- Full Compression Balls
- Club Hire

MIZUNO GOLF SCHOOL

...also at Penrith Driving Range is the **MIZUNO** Golf School which features a course of lessons and a free Mizuno 7-Iron !

PGA PARTNER

PENRITH DRIVING RANGE, REDHILLS, PENRITH, CUMBRIA. CA11 0DR. TEL: 01768 892167

Golf Shop

- On Site Golf Store.
- Major Stockists Of All Leading Brands.
- Full Club Repair Service.
- Full Golf Club Test & Trial Facility

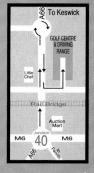

tel: **01768 892167**

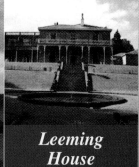

53

PENRITH
Golf Club

Salkeld Road, Penrith,
Cumbria CA11 8SG.

Secretary: D. Noble
01768-891919 (Fax same number).
Professional: G. Key
01768-891919.

PANORAMIC views of the Lakeland fells are enjoyed by players at Penrith Golf Club, situated between the delights of the Eden Valley and the Lake District.

The par 69 course dates back to 1890 and has been developed on land that was formerly a racecourse. There is still evidence of the track on the fairways of the 13th, 15th, 17th and 18th holes.

The parkland course presents a good golfing challenge and visitors are made welcome. Several societies have been regular visitors for 20 years and more.

With easy access from junction 41 of the M6, it is well situated for groups heading for Scotland for golfing holidays.

The course is bisected by a road, which sets the 1st - 4th and 13-18th in the section in front of the clubhouse. This section is relatively flat with some mature trees and fairways lined by heather.

There are several interesting greens, the second in particular. It is almost hidden in trees and can

only be approached at right angles.

The second part of the course, on the other side of the road, is open land sloping in one direction. From this area the views are quite dramatic.

Possibly the most difficult hole is the 12th, which tees off up a hill and over a quarry before doglegging left to the pin.

The Penrith club is committed to a five-year programme of additional tree planting.

The course itself is relatively flat, making 36 holes a pleasure as opposed to a tiring day out.

FACT FILE

A rolling moorland course of 18 holes, 6047 yards. Par 69. SSS 69. Record 64.

Restrictions: Visitors and societies confirm with the Secretary by phone. Parties of eight or more - £5 deposit per person. Ladies' day Tuesday.

Fees: £20 to £25, half with member.

Dress code: Usual golf attire.

Shop opening: 8.30am to 6pm.

Facilities:

TO THE CLUB

From junction 41 of the M6 to Penrith. Turn left immediately on entering the built-up area and the club is one mile on.

Course Information			
Hole	Yards	Stroke	Par
1	363	13	4
2	315	15	4
3	448	3	4
4	174	17	3
5	475	1	4
6	408	5	4
7	374	9	4
8	362	7	4
9	213	11	3
10	105	18	3
11	332	10	4
12	365	2	4
13	385	6	4
14	155	16	3
15	516	8	5
16	183	14	3
17	397	4	4
18	477	12	5
OUT	3132		34
IN	2915		35
TOTAL	6047		69

1) A relatively easy opening hole with an open fairway.

2) A tricky dogleg with a tree close to the long narrow green.

3) Two good hits to the green - but bunkers on all sides.

4) A splendid par three but it demands an accurate tee shot.

5) The longest par four on the course, needing two woods.

6} A testing par four with a copse on the left.

7) A relatively easy four. Trees to the left and right.

8) A slight dogleg with hazards on the right.

9) A par three that would grace any championship course.

10) The shortest of the par threes, the green is well protected by bunkers.

11) A dogleg par four with out-of-bounds on the left.

12) Drive over a quarry; a slight dogleg to an elevated green.

13) A dogleg left with trees on the left and out-of-bounds wall on the right.

14) A mid-iron par three over heather and gorse.

15) A par five reachable with two good woods. There are trees to the right.

16) A tricky par three with bunkers on the left of the green.

17) A perfect drive is required over a slight hill to open up the green.

18) A gamble of a par five over cross-bunkers 30 yards in front of the green.

Recommended Facilities

SEASCALE
Golf Club

The Banks, Seascale,
Cumbria CA20 1QL.

Secretary: Colin Taylor
019467-28202.

WHEN the club was formed in 1893, Seascale was just a dot on the coast of West Cumbria. The population was sparce, even counting the boarding schools and the genteel summer visitors.

A nine-hole course was opened in the April but funds were short and the club used the local railway station until a modest pavilion was finished in July at a cost of £45.

But although Seascale's population peaked at around 1,200 in 1921 and it remained a backwater until the eve of World War Two, the club became a major sporting and social venue of a wider area.

Only five years after opening, the club commissioned George Lowe, the Lytham St. Annes professional, to lay out a second nine holes.

The committee were also adept at publicity and promotion and in the space of three years had the members of 'the great triumvirate' playing on the course. In 1902 they staged a challenge match between Harry Vardon and Sandy Herd, and repeated the ploy three years later with James Braid and J. H. Taylor.

Confidence was high and in 1905 the club spent £2,700 on building and furnishing the present clubhouse.

The building of wartime munitions factories at Drigg and Sellafield set the scene for the golf club's post-war development, when Sellafield was chosen as the centre of Britain's nuclear power development, bringing in hundreds of scientific and technical staff. The golf club lies almost in the shadow of the nuclear site.

The 1980s was a period of financial reorganisation, repair and development and in 1992 the club took another major step by acquiring a 16-acre field for a practice ground.

The story of the club was told by Jack Anderson in a centenary book in 1993.

FACT FILE

A links course of 18 holes, 6416 yards. Par 71. SSS 71. Record 65.

Restrictions: Visitors and societies phone in advance. No visitors before 9.30am.

Fees: £20 to £25 per round; £25 to £30 per day.

Dress code: Usual golf attire.

Shop opening: 8am to 11pm.

Facilities:

TO THE CLUB

On the north west side of Seascale on the B5344.

Course Information

Hole	Yards	Stroke	Par
1	325	9	4
2	339	15	4
3	407	3	4
4	326	11	4
5	187	17	3
6	483	7	5
7	561	1	5
8	199	13	3
9	387	5	4
10	143	18	3
11	470	4	4
12	392	8	4
13	216	12	3
14	499	6	5
15	312	16	4
16	473	2	4
17	344	14	4
18	353	10	4
OUT	3214		36
IN	3202		35
TOTAL	6416		71

1) Drive accurately between the left fairway bunker and the road.

2) A drive to the right of the fairway opens up the green.

3) A choice here of caution or the long drive and an iron.

4) A good drive sets up a mid/short iron into a well guarded green.

5) An accurate tee shot is needed. Conditions dictate club choice.

6) A test of your long game and, with subtle flag positions, putting.

7) An even longer par five - and the green is deceptively flat.

8) A bold tee shot to the green. Balls falling short stay short!

9) A drive left to the plateau gives a panoramic view down to the green. To the right, down the ridge, may give an indifferent lie.

10) Guarded all round by water, sand or rough, this hole needs your best tee shot. The wind can make this a very long par three.

11) The hole for long hitters. Interesting borrows on the green.

12) A straightforward par four if you keep to the middle.

13) Greenside bunkers, out-of-bounds and water make playing short of the putting surface a safe option.

14) More long hitting required along a generous fairway.

15) One of the few par fours where a poor drive can be recovered.

16) Three shots are often needed to the green on this par four.

17) Safety lies in a drive to the left of the fairway marker.

18) A choice of short or long approaches here.

Recommended Facilities

SEDBERGH
Golf Club

Catholes-Abbot Holme,
Sedbergh, Cumbria LA10 5SS.

Secretary: David Lord
015396-20993.
Clubhouse: 015396-21551.

AFTER existing for almost 100 years at the top of a fellside and being described as the worst course in England, and better suited to commando training, Sedbergh Golf Club is now one of the most interesting and beautiful.

It is unusual for a course in this part of the north in that the scenic qualities within the course eclipse the surrounding countryside.

But the club's move to its new course in the Yorkshire Dales National Park, was not without controversy.

Protesters led by singer Mike Harding tried to have the planning permission rescinded and the matter went as far as the National Parks Ombudsman before the scheme went ahead.

The new nine-hole course with 18 tees was built by contractor Terry Redding, of Maxel Golf, on land along the River Dee offered by farming cousins Bruce Wilson and John Handley.

The river and a Roman pack-horse bridge are among the features that make the couse so picturesque.

Only two trees were removed - and 5,000 new ones planted.

All the dry stone walls removed in the laying out of the holes were rebuilt elsewhere on the course.

And the clubhouse is a tasteful conversion of a traditional Dales barn. The log fire is a lovely touch.

The course, although not long, is a great test of ability with an errant shot likely to find water, sand, trees and other hazards. The greens are quite magnificent and all have a distinctive shape.

Compared with the old course, started by seven masters from Sedbergh School in 1896, it's another world.

In their centenary year, the club members can certainly have a laugh at the hardships of not too long ago!

FACT FILE

An undulating grassland course of 9 holes, 5588 yards. Par 70. SSS 67. Record 66.

Restrictions: Visitors and societies contact by phone. Visitors may not play Sunday morning or Bank Holidays.

Fees: £14 - £20 weekdays, £18 - £25 weekends.

Dress code: Usual golf attire.

Shop opening: 7.30am-10.30pm.

Facilities:

TO THE CLUB

One mile out of Sedbergh on the road to Dent.

Cumbria

Course Information

Hole	Yards	Stroke	Par
1	345	13	4
2	109	17	3
3	446	4	5
4	371	7	4
5	156	15	3
6	280	11	4
7	166	8	3
8	476	6	5
9	427	1	4
10	300	14	4
11	109	18	3
12	497	3	5
13	371	10	4
14	156	16	3
15	280	12	4
16	166	9	3
17	506	5	5
18	427	2	4
OUT	2776		35
IN	2812		35
TOTAL	5588		70

1) Out-of-bounds beyond a wall on the left, fairway bunkers and large trees could cause problems.

2) It's short - but a river rushes across your path and the target is narrowed by trees on both sides.

3) This is a long par four with the tee shot facing a narrow gap in the trees. Bunkers dot the fairway at the right.

4) Fairway bunkers are again in evidence and the green is L-shaped with a narrow entrance.

5) Large bunkers guard the large two-tiered green on this shortish par three.

6) A blind drive but a wide fairway.

7) A testing hole played to an elevated green with a steep bank front and sides.

8) Aiming to the right to avoid hazards, the long par five finishes on another elevated green with a great view.

9) The blind downhill tee shot seems to be tight but the hole broadens on the approach to the green.

Recommended Facilities

SILECROFT
Golf Club

Silecroft, Cumbria LA18 4NX.

Secretary: D. L. A. MacLardie
01229-774342.

General Inquiries: 01229-774342.

SWEEPING south west from the central massif of the Cumbrian Mountains, between the valleys of the Rivers Duddon and Esk, the 2,000ft bulk of Black Combe descends to the Irish Sea.

Its silhouette against the northern sky reminded Norman Nicholson, the famous local poet and author, of a lion crouching with its forepaws in the sea.

Sheltered from the worst rigours of the winter north-easterlies, the village of Silecroft rests astride the road that runs for nearly a mile through the coastal plain to the shore, which descends in shingle terraces to one of the finest beaches in northern England.

At low tide, nearly 300 yards of sand stretch to the west, where on fine days the shape of Snaefell, on the Isle of Man, is visible.

Here, where sea and mountains meet, a group of local business and professional men decided to form a golf club.

Seventeen attended the first meeting on November 17, 1902, at the West County Hotel in the nearby town of Millom, whose 8,000 inhabitants depended mainly on the mining and smelting of the local haematite.

The task of the committee that was elected to investigate the means of making a golf links was eased because the proposed site - pasture land along the shore - was owned by three of its members.

The cost of making the links was just £100. How this pasture was transformed into a golf club in a few months, using only manual labour and a horse drawn mower, is difficult to comprehend.

But the fact is that the lease of the course was signed on March 18, 1903, and it opened for play three weeks later.

The site for the 'golf house' was bought for a mere six pence per square yard.

Nearly 90 years later, Silecroft golf course presents a level, well-groomed nine holes with 18 tees, making the second nine holes quite different from the first.

There are nearly 300 members and the course is popular among visitors to the many camping and caravan sites in the area.

The club is located on the coast near the junction of the A595 and A5093, about three miles north of Millom and eight miles west of Broughton-in-Furness.

Practice areas and bar facilities are available to visiting parties. At other times the bar is normally open only on competition days.

FACT FILE

A seaside links course of 9 holes, 5877 yards. Par 68. SSS 68. Record 67.

Restrictions: Societies contact the club in advance. Visitors phone.

Fees: £10 to £15.

Dress code: Usual golf attire.

Facilities:

TO THE CLUB

Near the junction of A595 and A5093, three miles north of Millom.

Course Information

Hole	Yards	Stroke	Par
1	401	5	4
2	435	2	4
3	133	18	3
4	340	12	4
5	324	13	4
6	227	10	3
7	262	16	4
8	424	1	4
9	380	8	4
10	401	6	4
11	407	4	4
12	164	15	3
13	370	7	4
14	401	3	4
15	168	17	3
16	293	14	4
17	367	11	4
18	380	9	4
OUT	2926		34
IN	2951		34
TOTAL	5877		68

1) A straight par four with a fairway bank at 100 yards and out-of-bounds on the right.

2) Out-of-bounds may affect tee shots. Beware gullies on the right.

3) A short par three but the large bunkered green can be tricky.

4) A 100-yard carry to the fairway, a dogleg to the right and out-of-bounds to contend with.

5) A shortish straight hole but an undulating, sloping green is testing.

6) A straight but testing par three. There are bunkers approaching the green and a fairway bank.

7) A straightforward short par four with fairway bunkers to the right.

8) Out-of-bounds on the right - and beware the slope towards a water hazard to the right of the green.

9) The water hazard is in front of the tee, it's out-of-bounds on the right and a bank crosses the fairway at 80 yards.

10) As for hole one with a slightly different tee position.

11) As for hole two with the tee position 30 yards forward.

12) Similar to hole three but the tee is back.

13) A 130-yard carry to the fairway due to the set-back tee position.

14) As for five but the tee is 80 yards back. This can play as a par five in certain wind conditions.

15) The tee is set forward and the bank is now in line with the flag.

16) Similar to seven with the tee 30 yards back.

17) Easier than hole eight because the tee is closer to the green.

18) The same as hole nine.

Recommended Facilities

SILLOTH
Golf Club

The Club House, Silloth-on-Solway, Cumbria CA5 4BL.

Secretary: John G. Proudlock 016973-31304 (Fax: 31782). Professional: Carl Weatherhead 016973-31404.

THE Cumbrian coast is a strange, other world. It's miles from anywhere yet surprisingly industrial.

There are other surprises - the wild, tumbling dunes and rolling tracks of gorse and heather that thrill the lover of links golf when he reaches that remotest of Cumbrian outposts, Silloth-on-Solway, to give the club its full name.

Golf is shared with the oyster-catcher, stonechat and curlew - and the wind of course, which will examine the golfer's technique and resolve to the full.

Dr. Leitch, father of the famous local girl golfer, had a hand in the design of the course, as did Willie Park Jnr.

Alterations were made in 1921 to the plans of Dr. Alister Mackenzie, the noted golf architect.

The name of Silloth has been a part of the vocabulary of British golf for well over a century as a means of expressing the ultimate in natural sea-washed turf.

Yet because of its location in the north west corner of England, it is possibly the best known, least-played course in Britain.

But with the M6 motorway passing within 25 miles, there is no longer a reason not to sample Silloth's delights in person.

The setting has spectacular views over the Solway Firth to the hills and inlets of Dumfries and Galloway. On a clear day the Isle of Man appears on the south west horizon and the Lakeland peaks are to the south.

In such a setting, even a modest golf course would be lifted out of the ordinary but Silloth lives up to the highest expectation its name has come to suggest.

Even the shortest of drive and pitch holes become a test of nerve with the wind the chief problem.

Before the club changed from Carlisle and Silloth to Silloth-on-Solway, its early recognition came with the success of the slim young daughter of a local golfer.

Born in 1891, the year before the club was founded, Charlotte Cecilia Leitch became one of the most successful golfers of her day.

Known universally as Cecil Leitch, she won the British Ladies' Championship four times between 1914 and 1926 and her appearance career as a British international spanned 1910-1928.

In spite of this early connection with the ladies' game, it was not until 1972 that the British Stroke Play Championship was played at Silloth - an event won by Belle Robertson with a four-round total of 296.

The course found favour with the ladies and it was twice the scene of the British Amateur Championship, won in 1976 by Kathy Panton and in 1983 by Jill Thornhill.

The club again hosts the Championship in 1996, and in 1997 is the venue for the British Ladies' Stroke Play Championship.

FACT FILE

Seaside championship links of 18 holes, 6357 yards. Par 72. SSS 71. Record 66.

Restrictions: Visitors and societies contact in advance by phone or Fax. Handicap certificates required.

Fees: £25 to £35, half with member.

Dress code: Usual golf attire.

Shop opening: Dawn till dusk.

Facilities:

TO THE CLUB

South side of Silloth on the B5302.

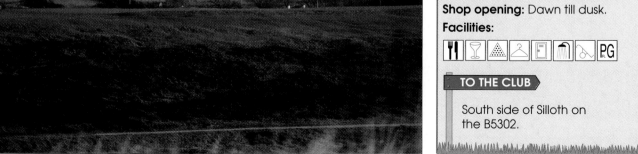

Course Information

Hole	Yards	Stroke	Par
1	380	5	4
2	319	10	4
3	358	3	4
4	372	8	4
5	482	14	5
6	187	12	3
7	403	1	4
8	371	7	4
9	134	15	3
10	308	16	4
11	403	4	4
12	200	11	3
13	468	2	5
14	477	18	5
15	417	6	4
16	182	13	3
17	495	17	5
18	401	9	4
OUT	3006		35
IN	3351		37
TOTAL	6357		72

1) Not a bad opener. Club selection on the second shot is important - as is the hidden green.
2) Long hitters can get near the green; others hit a long iron and wedge shot.
3) A good drive is needed. Play the second shot to the raised green and don't miss it left! The uphill approach may be impossibly long.
4) The course turns its back to the wind. A very accurate approach is needed to a green surrounded by steep slopes and tenacious rough.
5) Into the wind, a straightforward par five. If calm a good birdie chance.
6) A difficult short hole. If windy, play a run-up shot. A difficult putting surface.
7) In the prevailing wind one of the hardest holes. The blind second shot is deceiving.
8) A narrow fairway and well guarded green make this a tough hole. Incredible view from the tee!
9) The shortest hole. When windy anything from a sand iron to a one iron.
10) Two choices here. Long hitters go for the green. Or hit a mid-iron to the corner and then the green.
11) One of the toughest drives in the prevailing wind. If the fairway is found the rewards are there.
12) A long iron par three. Birdie this and you deserve a medal!
13) Not the longest of par fives but if windy there is no harder hole.
14) Another shortish par five. Two good shots and you should get a reward.
15) The undulating fairway makes for a tough second shot with a medium-long iron.
16) A good tip here is to hit your shot short of the green and allow the ball to run up the slope.
17) The drive is important as there is a carry of more than 100 yards.
18) Keep the drive down the left; there are bunkers right.

Recommended Facilities

The Golf Hotel

Criffel Street, Silloth-on-Solway. Tel: (016973) 31438

The Golf Hotel is a well appointed, licensed hotel, conveniently situated in Silloth-on-Solway, overlooking the Solway Firth, located in close proximity to the Lake District, Silloth is only a short drive away from the Roman Wall and also the picturesque Galloway region of South West Scotland, visible on the opposite shore of the Solway Firth.

Snooker room, flexible bar hours for residents, 150 yds from golf course.

ST. BEES SCHOOL
Golf Club

St. Bees, Cumbria CA27 0DS.
Clubhouse: 01946-824300.

ST. BEES School built its own golf course in 1929, according to this extract from the school magazine in that year: "Early this term a new golf course was planned and laid out on the rough ground on the Lesser Heads" (cliffs).

"Under the direction of Mr J. S. Boulter (housemaster) and the golf committee, an energetic band of volunteers from the school cut out the teeing grounds and greens."

The first school golf club in 1929 had 80 school members and in 1931 several local residents applied for membership.

Today, in addition to pupils who have free access to the course at various times, there is a thriving village club on the course with more than 375 members.

In the early days, boys and a local farmer would maintain the course. One of those boys, Eddie Park, who was a pupil at St. Bees School from 1941-1943, later became one of the country's leading experts on greenkeeping and course maintenance.

He had many articles published in 'Golf Monthly' and 'Greenkeeper' magazines in the 1970s and 1980s, culminating in a series titled: 'The Management of British Golf Courses,' written in collaboration with his son, Nicholas Park, which was later printed as a booklet and distributed widely to British golf clubs.

The original nine-hole course was over 2,000 yards with five par fours and four par threes. Recently, extra tees have been constructed so that the second nine holes have different lengths and different angles of approach.

Being of a hilly nature on the cliffs by the sea, it is a difficult course on which to score well - accuracy being more important than length. The standard scratch score of 65 matches the par over a total length of 5122 yards. There is only one par five.

From the course there are magnificent views of St. Bees Head and out across the Irish Sea to the Isle of Man, with Scotland in the distance across the Solway Firth.

The school has produced many fine golfers of county standard, including an Oxford Blue, E. S. Browne, and more recently the captain of the English Universities golf team in 1993, David Sim.

Two of the village club's most recent county players, who played most of their early golf at St. Bees and still play locally, are Ken Richardson and Eric Gullikson. The latter holds the record for the most appearances for Cumbria.

Recently the village club has built a new clubhouse on the course with help from the school and a healthy spirit of cooperation exists between the two main users.

FACT FILE

A clifftop course of 9 holes, 5122 yards. Par 65. SSS 65.

Restrictions: Visitors are welcome but are advised to avoid competition times at weekends.

Clubhouse opening: Wednesday 5-9pm, Weekends noon-6pm.

Fees: £10 and £12.

Dress code: Usual golf attire.

Facilities:

TO THE CLUB

The course is on the B5345 road, four miles south of Whitehaven.

Course Information

Hole	Yards	Stroke	Par
1	312	8	4
2	288	17	4
3	360	5	4
4	194	14	3
5	147	11	3
6	397	4	4
7	215	9	3
8	450	1	4
9	163	16	3
10	330	6	4
11	286	18	4
12	365	3	4
13	201	12	3
14	143	13	3
15	406	2	4
16	215	7	3
17	470	15	5
18	180	10	3
OUT	2526		32
IN	2596		33
TOTAL	5122		65

1) An uphill dogleg left with a valley 120 yards short of the green.

2) A straightforward hole but avoid the cross bunker at 220 yards.

3) A good drive is essential to enable a precise second shot to a high plateau green which falls away on all sides.

4) A long downhill par three. It is difficult to hold the green.

5) A short par three, well bunkered on the right, falling away left.

6) A good drive over a mound, with a steep drop-off to the left, is essential on this hole. The second shot to the green is downhill.

7) Uphill all the way on this 215-yard par three. Into the wind it is impossible to drive the green.

8) An uphill drive over a marker post often makes it impossible to reach the green in two - unless you hit two perfect shots.

9) A downhill par three requires a precise shot to hold the green - or do you try and run it on?

Recommended Facilities

STONYHOLME
Golf Course

St. Aidan's Road, Carlisle,
Cumbria CA1 1LS.

Manager: John Hodgson
01228-27555 (Fax 514547).
Professional: Stephen Ling
01228-34856 (Fax 34856).

SET near the centre of Carlisle, Stonyholme is an award-winning 18-hole municipal course bordered by the Rivers Eden and Petril with water coming into play on no fewer than seven holes.

Although the course is not long, it has been designed to be demanding by strategically placing the bunkers to affect the average golfer. The fairways are tree-lined and the greens are excellent.

The course is a real tester, anyone playing to their handicap would be doing well.

BBC Golf Magazine voted Stonyholme one of the best municipals in the UK. The course management asks golfers to come along and see why.

Stonyholme is situated next to Carlisle United football ground and is used by several soccer players.

The course was built in 1974 as 9 holes and was extended to eighteen in 1984.

The extension coincided with the formation of the Stonyholme Golf Club, whose clubhouse was recently refurbished and a pro shop opened.

The Stonyholme course has two measured putting greens marked with yardage and bunkers for chipping practice.

A short drive from Stonyholme is Swifts, a par three pitch and putt course ideal for beginners. It is used to supplement the practice area at Stonyholme.

Swifts also has a 16-bay driving range with practice and teaching facilities.

An application has been made to the R and A for Swifts to be measured with a view to it becoming a recognised golf course.

FACT FILE

A parkland course of 18 holes, 5787 yards. Par 69. SSS 68. Record 64.

Restrictions: Societies phone in advance.

Fees: £6.75 to £8.50 (municipal course).

Dress code: Smart and casual.

Shop opening: Dawn till dusk.

Facilities:

Off Warwick Road (A69) on the east side of junction 43 of the M6.

Course Information

Hole	Yards	Stroke	Par
1	387	6	4
2	342	10	4
3	327	12	4
4	160	18	3
5	370	4	4
6	172	16	3
7	361	2	4
8	330	8	4
9	193	14	3
10	377	5	4
11	366	11	4
12	402	3	4
13	482	1	5
14	308	15	4
15	348	7	4
16	319	13	4
17	169	17	3
18	374	9	4
OUT	2642		33
IN	3145		36
TOTAL	5787		69

1) A right to left dogleg with water down the left. Cut the corner if you dare!

2) A straight par four to a two-tiered green. Out-of-bounds left.

3) Straightforward apart from bunkers at driving distance.

4) Uphill to a blind three-tiered green.

5) A tight tee shot. Catch the downslope for extra distance.

6) A lovely enclosed par three with a green ringed by trees.

7) Water, water everywhere! Rivers cross and border this hole.

8) Stay left of the tree for the best approach shot.

9) A long, straightforward par three.

10) Beware the practice ground down the right. It's out-of-bounds.

11) A demanding, tight tee shot through an avenue of trees.

12) More of the same - but the second shot is harder!

13) Keep it straight for a good birdie chance.

14) Watch out for the pond. An easy hole if you get your drive away.

15) It's amazing how many land in the river! So take care.

16) Don't leave the second shot short or overhit the first.

17) This 169-yard par three is longer than it looks.

18) A tough par four to finish.

Recommended Facilities

ULVERSTON
Golf Club

The Clubhouse, Bardsea Park,
Ulverston, Cumbria LA12 9QJ.

Secretary: P. Wedgwood
01229-582824.
Professional: M. R. Smith
01229-582806.

THE Ulverston club, which celebrated its centenary in 1995, stands on a hill with superb views of Morecambe Bay and the Lakeland mountains.

And to match the scenery there is some excellent testing golf, on a course that will be a tremendous discovery for visiting golfers.

The present course dates from 1910 and was designed by H. S. Colt in an old deer park in wooded country in the Furness foothills.

It is a quality downland course on a lime sub-soil that recovers quickly from even the heaviest rain.

The hilly course has some fascinating holes, moulded by the contours like ridges, banks and ground that falls away steeply, giving a constant challenge.

Combined with the sand traps and well planned fairways, the result is a course that must be treated with respect.

If concentration fails, then consolation comes in the exceptional views, particularly the sunset seen from the final few holes. The last two holes are so often the deciders and merit descriptions in detail.

The 17th, agreed by most players to be the best, is a real thriller, for right in front of the tee is the face of an old limestone quarry. Even a good drive, if the trajectory is too low, will fail to carry the face.

Once on the plateau, a narrow fairway between rocks has a bunker some way short of an open green.

The 18th is a dogleg to the right, round the trees that form the boundary of the course.

If the tee shot does not take off too much of the corner there is a straightforward second shot downhill, over a couple of cross-bunkers to a green built out of a falling slope.

FACT FILE

A parkland course of 18 holes, 6201 yards. Par 71. SSS 70. Record 65.

Restrictions: Societies apply in writing. Other visitors phone. Handicap certificates required. No visitors on competition days.

Fees: £20 to £30, half with member.

Dress Code: Usual golf attire.

Shop opening: Tuesday to Thursday 9am-2pm and 4-6pm. Weekends 9am-2pm. Closed Monday & Friday.

Facilities:

TO THE CLUB

From junction 36 of the M6, the A590 into Ulverston and left onto the A5087 to Bardsea, then right after Conishead Priory.

Course Information

Hole	Yards	Stroke	Par
1	341	9	4
2	319	14	4
3	418	3	4
4	509	5	5
5	157	16	3
6	397	7	4
7	368	1	4
8	161	18	3
9	348	11	4
10	142	17	3
11	484	6	5
12	341	13	4
13	488	8	5
14	191	15	3
15	395	2	4
16	324	12	4
17	382	4	4
18	436	10	4
OUT	3018		35
IN	3183		36
TOTAL	6201		71

1) A blind tee shot over a bank brings the elevated green into view.
2) A good drive gives the chance of a par four on this 319-yarder.
3) Trees down both sides make this a tight hole. A huge bunker blocks the right front of the green.
4) Out-of-bounds right but a wide fairway on the longest hole.
5) A good short hole needing a tee shot up to the green. Just don't veer to the right!
6) A dogleg left from an elevated tee. The green is superb.
7) A good tee shot is rewarded with a bounce forward from a dip 200 yards from the tee.
8) Sand traps abound on this 161 yard par three.
9) The great views from previous holes continue on this relatively easy uphill par four.
10) A two tier green makes this short par three a bit tricky.
11) The green is reachable in two but watch for the big grass bunker on the right.
12) Fairway bunkers are the hazard on this straightfoward par four.
13) A good drive between two bunkers gives a position to gamble on a well struck second shot to a guarded green.
14) A longish par three with trees along the right.
15) A blind tee shot over a marker starts this difficult hole.
16) Sand traps at the back of the green are the main problem here.
17) The views are fantastic on this great hole, described on the opposite page.
18) Another great hole, described on the opposite page.

Recommended Facilities

Grasmere
Red Lion Hotel

Red Lion Square, Grasmere
Telephone: 015394 35456

Offering newly refurbished, 4 crown, 3 star accommodation, situated in one of the most beautiful areas of the country. We have our own solarium, sauna, steam room, jacuzzi and mini gym with power shower and guests enjoy free membership of a nearby luxury leisure club.

Enjoy a warm welcome with friendly staff and good food. Excellent base for golfing, walking, fishing and touring. Ideally situated for both Keswick and Windermere Golf Courses.

Ambleside
Salutation Hotel

Lake Road, Ambleside
Telephone: 015394 32244

Recommended Facilities

QUARRY GARTH

This gracious and mellow Edwardian Country House is set in eight acres of peaceful Lakeland gardens and woodland near Lake Windermere.

Residents are captivated by excellent cuisine, antique furniture, original paintings, collectors items, open fires, candlelight and a relaxed family style welcome that is without a trace of pretension. Access to fellside walks direct from the hotel car park.

Jim and Margaret Wilkinson
Quarry Garth Country House Hotel
Windermere, The Lake District LA23 1LF
Telephone: 015394 88282
Fax: 015394 46584

AA Rosettes

WINDERMERE
Golf Club

Cleabarrow, Windermere,
Cumbria LA23 3NB.

Secretary: Ken Moffat.
Professional: Steve Rook
015394-43550.
Clubhouse: 015394-43123.

WINDERMERE is the premier club in Cumbria and the course is held in awe by golfers as the ultimate challenge.

There is nothing easy or usual here. For a start, it's a short but very tight course without bunkers. Just rocks and heather and a lot of bumps and card-spoiling quirks.

It's because the course is threaded through the natural features of this little patch of Lakeland that it is often referred to as a miniature Gleneagles.

Famous names who have 'run the rule' over Windermere include the noted golf course architect Robert Trent Jones and the American golf guru Paul Runcorn.

Jones thought it one of the best examples he had ever seen of the use of natural features in the design.

Runcorn thought every golfer should play Windermere at least once.

Windermere's great attribute is that every hole is so individual but the constant factor is the unpredictable effect of the natural hazards.

In this respect it calls for a good deal of luck for there are several blind shots and the landing areas are invariably littered with rocks and bumps.

continued overleaf

Recommended Facilities

When not playing blind the need is for accuracy and judgment, which favours the experienced eye.

Windermere is a go-ahead club with its own residential accommo-dation and tuition courses.

Founded in 1891, it is one of only two 18-hole golf courses in the Lake District National Park (the other is Keswick) and has the most glorious views of the Lakeland mountains.

These can be of small consolation to the golfer who embarks on this challenge - and finishes a round looking decidedly pale!

FACT FILE

A hilly heathland course of 18 holes, 5006 yards. Par 67. SSS 65. Record 58.

Restrictions: Visitors and societies phone in advance. Must have handicap certificates.

Fees: £23 to £28.

Dress code: Usual golf attire.

Shop opening: Summer 8.30am to 6pm, winter 9am to 4.30pm.

Facilities:

TO THE CLUB

One and a quarter miles before Bowness on the B5284.

Recommended Facilities

Course Information			
Hole	Yards	Stroke	Par
1	315	11	4
2	232	5	3
3	252	17	4
4	365	1	4
5	291	9	4
6	354	7	4
7	371	3	4
8	130	15	3
9	269	13	4
10	199	4	3
11	259	14	4
12	291	18	4
13	306	8	4
14	146	16	3
15	187	6	3
16	480	12	5
17	356	2	4
18	203	10	3
OUT	2579		34
IN	2427		33
TOTAL	5006		67

1) Get used to the stunning views first! The first green tucked between rocks needs a cautious approach.

2) Pitch over a pole and hope for a useful lie. The green is small.

3) Out-of-bounds left and thick heather to the right leave little margin for error. And, again, it's a small green.

4) More heather and bracken! The distance is deceptive and the green is just beyond the marker.

5) Beware the hidden pond at the left. And rocks can deflect the ball.

6) There's a lot of rough to carry and a pond close to the green.

7) Down a steep gully and then up to the green. The fairway is roomier and the green larger but it's rimmed by rocks and heather.

8) The task is to drive over a ravine to a green with no back room.

9) For the first time there's room to open up. The green in one?

10) Not visible from the tee, a stream crosses just short of the green.

11) The clubhouse has been hit on occasions by golfers aiming to clear both the dip and the bumpy landing ground.

12) Luck is needed with a blind tee shot to bumpy, rocky ground.

13) Not too bad if you can keep out of the bracken.

14) Trees and heather are all that stand in the way of a par three!

15) Out-of-bounds left and a stream to the right call for accuracy.

16) The course's only par five, with a tree-lined fairway and big green.

17) A comparatively open par four to a huge green by the clubhouse.

18) A long uphill par three with a last chance of finding a rock or a clump of heather!

Recommended Facilities

WORKINGTON
Golf Club

Branthwaite Road, Workington,
Cumbria CA14 4SS.

Secretary: M. W. Addison
01900-603460.
Professional: Adrian Drabble
01900-67828.

THE club's course was designed by James Braid and was opened in 1907.

It is only a couple of miles from the centre of Workington but is built into such scenic countryside that it is easy to feel 'away from it all.'

There are marvellous views to the north across the Solway Firth to Scotland; the Lakeland mountains form the dramatic backdrop to the south east; and the Isle of Man is visible in the south west.

The Workington course is well-wooded with a minor river running through in a gully that is steep in places and comes into play on six holes. Members regard the 10th as the keynote hole.

This is a course where good putting is called for because several greens are on two tiers or are undulating.

A road splits the course into two sections but this is of little account.

The Workington club was in existence before James Braid's course was laid out. It was founded in 1893 and started on a different site with a nine hole course arranged by Mungo Park the 1874 Open champion and later the greenkeeper at Silloth. Only a year later it was extended to 18 holes.

The man behind that first Workington course was Dr. Andrew Highet, a Scot who was appointed as the local medical officer. He was an experienced golfer with connections at the Royal Troon Golf Club.

He proposed the formation of a golf club at a public meeting in Workington's Green Dragon Hotel in 1893.

The club welcomes visitors and societies.

FACT FILE

An undulating meadowland course of 18 holes, 6250 yards. Par 72. SSS 70. Record 65.

Restrictions: Societies phone the pro in advance. Handicap certificates required.
No visitors before 9.30am or from noon to 1.30pm.

Fees: £12-£25.

Dress code: Usual golf attire.

Shop opening: Summer 8am to dusk; winter 9am to 5pm.

Facilities:

TO THE CLUB

On Branthwaite Road, Workington, off the A595, two miles south east of the town centre.

Course Information

Hole	Yards	Stroke	Par
1	394	5	4
2	311	15	4
3	589	1	5
4	517	7	5
5	338	9	4
6	152	17	3
7	208	11	3
8	315	13	4
9	389	3	4
10	178	8	3
11	492	14	5
12	124	16	3
13	472	2	5
14	500	12	5
15	223	4	3
16	359	10	4
17	301	18	4
18	388	6	4
OUT	3213		36
IN	3037		36
TOTAL	6250		72

1) Care is needed with the shot to the green. The out-of-bounds is to the right and back.

2) The tee shot needs to be left of the fairway. The green is well bunkered.

3) A good par five hole. Keep to the left of the fairway.

4) The right side of the fairway will give you a flat lie.

5) The left side of the fairway is favoured.

6) Expect plenty of trouble if you top your tee shot.

7) The green is well bunkered. Don't be short on here.

8) Hit the tee shot left of the marker for an easy approach.

9) A blind tee shot, usually a blind second shot - and trouble left and right of the green.

10) An accurate tee shot is required. A stream crosses in front of the green.

11) Favour the left side of the fairway, a blind second shot, an easy par five?

12) The shortest hole on the course but not that easy. The green is small and well bunkered.

13) Beware the second shot running into the stream.

14) A straightforward par five. The clubhouse roof is your line in here.

15) It's difficult to stop the ball on this green!

16) Keep the tee shot up the left side of the fairway.

17) This one shouldn't present any difficulties.

18) The left of the fairway gives the best line onto the green.

Recommended Facilities

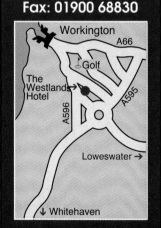

THE KESWICK COUNTRY HOUSE HOTEL
KESWICK
★★★★

PRINCIPAL HOTELS

Station Road,

Keswick-on-Derwentwater,

Cumbria, CA12 4NQ

tel: 017687 72020

fax: 017687 71300

Welcome to The Keswick Country House Hotel, the principal hotel in Keswick.

We are part of Principal Hotels, one of Europe's most progressive hotel groups renowned for individual, distinctive hotels, with an uncompromising commitment to good taste, high standards, and above all, excellent service to you, our guest.

Built in 1863, The Keswick Country House Hotel reflects the romance of the Lake District and the tranquillity of one of the United Kingdom's most delightful regions.

The 66 en-suite rooms enjoy superb views of the inspiring lakeland mountains. Each bedroom has colour television, direct dial telephone, hairdryer, trouser press and welcome refreshments tray.

There are boundless opportunities for leisure - golf, sailing, windsurfing, pony trekking, tennis, water skiing and squash, in addition, of course, to the excellent walking. The Keswick Spa Leisure Centre is conveniently placed at the end of the hotel's drive, not to mention the added bonus of free Golf for residents on Keswick Golf Course Monday to Friday.

The Keswick Country House Hotel is easily accessible, 20 minutes from the M6 via the A66 and less than two hours from Manchester, Leeds, Glasgow and Edinburgh. There is ample parking for guests at the front of the hotel.

A LAND MADE FOR POETS!

"THE loveliest spot that Man hath ever found," said William Wordsworth of his beloved Lake District.

Few would disagree. The heart of the Lake District National Park has a grandeur all of its own in its crags and peaks, its fells and green valleys and its sparkling lakes, tarns and rivers.

Such spectacular scenery provides a paradise for outdoor activities the whole year round; walking, climbing, riding, cycling, sailing and golf.

Picturesque villages and sturdy, stone-built towns do much to create the Lakeland spell. Bustling Bowness-on-Windermere and Ambleside dominate the largest lake, linked by steamers and cruisers as well as by road.

Keswick, at the head of Derwentwater, in the north, combines interesting shops, museums and an indoor leisure pool with the appeal of a market town.

Even more photogenic are Grasmere, where Wordsworth lived, Hawkshead with its squares and cobbled alleys, and Sawrey, the 'birthplace' of Beatrix Potter's characters.

Furness and Cartmel

THE vast sands of Morecambe Bay guard a grim secret.

Many a stagecoach lost its race with the tide on the dash from Morecambe to Grange - still accessible 'over sands' by guided walks from the Area of Outstanding Natural Beauty at Arnside.

Now a sheltered resort with a long seafront promenade, Grange-over-Sands is the centrepiece of Cumbria's Riviera, backed up by the 12th Century Cartmel Priory Church and stately Holker Hall and Gardens, home of the Lakeland Motor Museum.

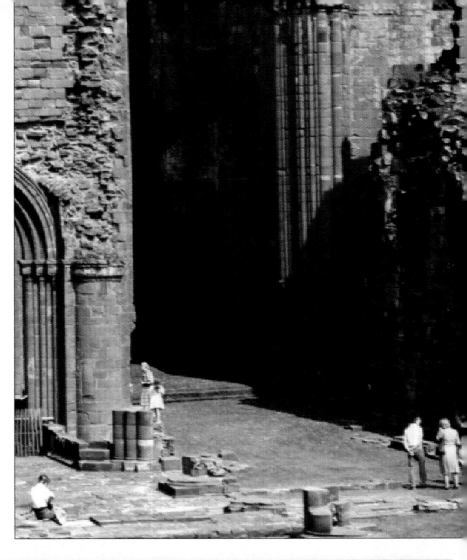

Nearby Flookburgh also begs a visit for its plaice-like flukes, netted around the Levens Estuary, which divides the peninsulas of Furness and Cartmel.

Furness adds attractions of its own: Ulverston, complete with market and Town Crier, the Laurel and Hardy Museum and Cumbria Crystal; the soaring

ruins of the imposing Furness Abbey, Dock Museum, South Lakes Wild Animal Park, Classic Bikes Motorcycle Museum, Heron Glass, or Piel Island's Norman castle, reached only by boat.

Today the castle stands watch over seabirds nesting on Walney Island, whose sandy beaches mark the westernmost point of the bay.

The popular rail trip from Haverthwaite provides a link with Lakeside, on Windermere.

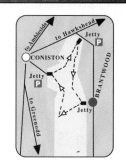

Calder House Hotel
(PRIVATE)

THE BANKS, SEASCALE, CUMBRIA CA20 1QP
Tel and Fax: 019467 28538

A GOLF WEEKEND BY THE SEA
ALL-IN-PRICE of £130 per HEAD

Arrive Friday, possibly play golf in the afternoon and then play a further two games on Saturday, followed by a game on Sunday.

Included in the price are two days Bed and Breakfast and Dinner plus three days green fees at the well known Seascale Golf Club, Championship Links Course...
...only 150 yards from the Hotel.
Other attractions in the area include the MUNCASTER CASTLE & GARDENS, BIRD SANCTUARIES, THE ESKDALE MINIATURE RAILWAY AND THE SELLAFIELD VISITORS CENTRE.

Your Tee-Off times will be arranged at the time of your initial booking.

Then we will send you a booking form for you to choose your room for the weekend. The booking form must be returned with a non-refundable £10 per head booking fee.

Calder House is a family run licensed hotel. Many rooms have all facilities including colour TV and many have sea views.

We have a very comfortable well stocked Bar-Lounge and during the weekends the Bar is open almost continually.

We also have an extensive Menu for Bar Meals and snacks, this is a basis for a complete menu in the Restaurant.

We can cater for small parties of up to 45, for wedding receptions - set menu or buffet arrangement.
All parties and set menus must be booked in advance so that arrangements can be made as to the cost and type of arrangement.

...So try our Golfing Weekend by the sea, You will enjoy it!
Ring Bill Neal for a friendly response to your requirements.

Carlisle and the Borderlands

HISTORIC Carlisle offers a unique experience for visitors, blending its rich heritage with modern shopping centres in a traffic-free environment.

This great border city is steeped in myth and romantic legend; a legacy bequeathed by the Emperor Hadrian, William Wallace, Rob Roy, Robert the Bruce, Bonnie Prince Charlie and the notorious Border Reivers.

Venture out into the Borderlands to see the market town of Brampton, the 11th century Lanercost Priory and Longtown - strongly linked with Arthurian legend - and the dramatic

Birdoswald Roman Fort on Hadrian's Wall, a superb introduction to Britain's greatest Roman monument.

And in complete contrast see how cloth is woven for top designers Chanel and Jean Muir at the Linton Tweeds Centre.

Eden and the Pennines

THE Eden Valley is a surprise to first-time visitors. Rich green pastures and arable lands, a river stocked with salmon and trout, and prosperous villages and market towns give the area the idyllic feel echoed in its name.

It's a valley where all roads meet at Penrith, a leisurely country town of unexpected squares and outstanding gardens.

To the north lie the wooded hillsides of Armathwaite and Kirkoswald, both built of blush coloured local stone, and the smart villages running into Carlisle.

East lies Appleby, a market town of some interest with a broad, tree-lined main street, a castle - and the River Eden at its mellowest. To the south, near Kirkby Stephen and Brough, the landscape assumes the sterner feel of the nearby Yorkshire Dales while to the west Ullswater is just a 20-minute drive.

Western Lakes and Coast

WINDING past the mountain eyrie of a ruined Roman fort, the spectacular Hardknott Pass (with a gradient of 1-in-3) descends through picturesque Eskdale to Cumbria's sandy coast.

Here, the Ravenglass and Eskdale Railway, a miniature public line affectionately known as 'La'al Ratty,' starts its scenic journey from Ravenglass to Eskdale. Dating back to the 16th century, Eskdale Mill, in one of the loveliest valleys in the Western Lakes has an exhibition on local life.

There's Wastwater, where the forbidding rock screes rise straight from the deep, dark waters at the base of towering Scafell; gentler Ennerdale Water, Loweswater, Crummock Water and Buttermere, all ringed with mountains, Bassenthwaite Lake and Derwentwater, right on the doorstep of Keswick.

The old, unflurried town of Cockermouth - where Wordsworth's birthplace is open to the public - provides another gateway to the coast, to St. Bees with its priory church, extensive beaches and cliffhead bird reserve, and on to Georgian Whitehaven, Workington and Maryport, with its harbour and maritime attractions.

The road then hugs the shingle shore to Silloth, famous for its fine golf links, stunning sunsets and views across the Solway Firth to Scotland's mountains.

Tourist Information *i*

The Tourist Information Centres in the Western Lakes and Coast area have a wide range of services to offer, including an Accommodation Booking Service, a comprehensive range of free literature and holiday guides, as well as saleable books, maps, souvenirs, stamps, etc.

Whether visiting the area on holiday or business, the friendly staff will be pleased to give you advice that will help make your visit to Western lakeland much more enjoyable.

Western Lakes & Coast - A Little Further, A Lot to Enjoy

Cockermouth
The Town Hall, Market Street
Tel: 01900 822634

Egremont
Lowes Court Gallery, Main Street
Tel: 01946 820693

Keswick
Moot Hall, Market Square
Tel: 017687 72645

Maryport
Maritime Museum, 1 Senhouse Street
Tel: 01900 813738

Sellafield
Sellafield Visitors Centre, Seascale
Tel: 019467 76510

Silloth
The Green, Tel: 016973 31944

Whitehaven
Market Hall, Tel: 01946 695678

Workington
Central Car Park, Washington Street
Tel: 01900 602923

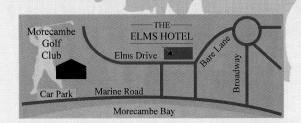

Lancashire

1. ST. ANNES OLD LINKS
2. ROYAL LYTHAM & ST. ANNES
3. FAIRHAVEN *(Lytham St. Annes)*
4. GREEN DRIVE *(Lytham)*
5. BLACKPOOL NORTH SHORE
6. BLACKPOOL STANLEY PARK
7. HERONS REACH *(Blackpool)*
8. POULTON-LE-FYLDE
9. FLEETWOOD
10. KNOTT END *(Preesall)*
11. HEYSHAM
12. LANCASTER
13. MORECAMBE
14. LANSIL *(Lancaster)*
15. SILVERDALE *(Lancaster)*
16. GARSTANG
17. ASHTON & LEA *(Preston)*
18. INGOL *(Preston)*
19. PRESTON
20. PENWORTHAM *(Preston)*
21. FISHWICK HALL *(Preston)*
22. LEYLAND
23. SHAW HILL *(Chorley)*
24. CHARNOCK RICHARD
25. DUXBURY PARK *(Chorley)*
26. EUXTON PARK *(Chorley)*
27. CHORLEY
28. HURLSTON HALL *(Ormskirk)*

29. ORMSKIRK
30. DEAN WOOD *(Up Holland)*
31. BEACON PARK *(Up Holland)*
32. GATHURST *(Wigan)*
33. HOUGHWOOD *(St. Helens)*
34. LOBDEN *(Rochdale)*
35. BACUP
36. ROSSENDALE *(Haslingden)*
37. DARWEN
38. PLEASINGTON *(Preston)*
39. ACCRINGTON
40. BAXENDEN
41. GREEN HAWORTH *(Accrington)*
42. TOWNELEY *(Burnley)*
43. BURNLEY
44. MARSDEN PARK *(Burnley)*
45. NELSON
46. COLNE
47. GHYLL *(Barnoldswick)*
48. CLITHEROE
49. WHALLEY
50. GREAT HARWOOD
51. STONYHURST PARK *(Hurst Green)*
52. LONGRIDGE
53. BLACKBURN
54. WILPSHIRE *(Blackburn)*
55. MYTTON FOLD *(Blackburn)*
56. RISHTON

A GUIDE TO CLUB FACILITIES

Club Hire	Trolley Hire	Buggy Hire	PG Practice Ground	PN Practice Nets
DR Driving Range	Catering	Tea & Coffee	Bar	Games Room
Squash & Tennis	Bowling Green	Swimming Pool	Fishing	Changing Room
Lockers	Showers			

Copyright © Freedom Design

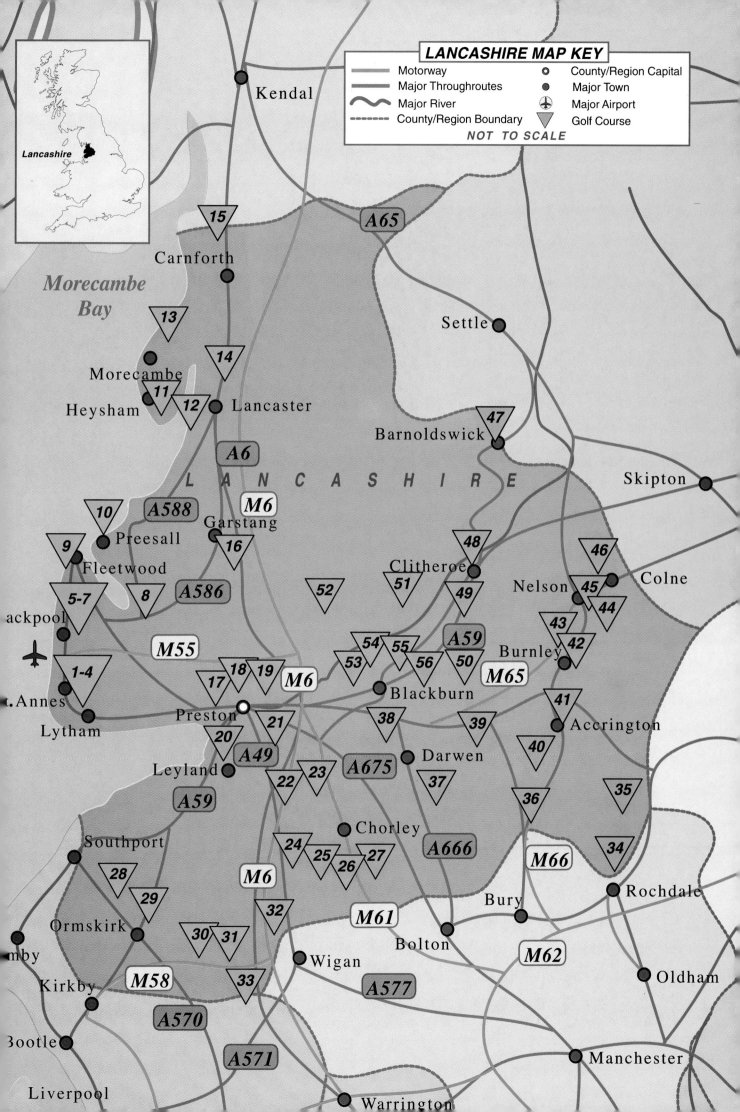

Motorway
Major Throughroutes
Major River
County/Region Boundary

County/Region Capital
Major Town
Major Airport
Golf Course

NOT TO SCALE

Lancashire

Kendal

Morecambe Bay

Carnforth

15

13

A65

Settle

Morecambe

14

11

12

Lancaster

Barnoldswick

47

Heysham

A6

L A N C A S H I R E

Skipton

10

A588

Garstang

M6

48

Clitheroe

46

9

Preesall

16

51

Nelson

45

Colne

Fleetwood

8

A586

52

49

44

5-7

ackpool

53 54 55

A59

43

42

Burnley

1-4

M55

17 18 19

M6

53

56

50

M65

t.Annes

Preston

21

38

Blackburn

41

Accrington

Lytham

20

A49

39

Leyland

22 23

A675

Darwen

40

A59

37

36

35

Southport

24 25 27

Chorley

A666

34

28

26

M6

M66

29

32

Bury

Rochdale

Ormskirk

30 31

M61

mby

33

Bolton

M62

Kirkby

M58

Wigan

Oldham

A570

A577

3ootle

A571

Liverpool

Manchester

Warrington

ACCRINGTON
Golf Club

Devon Avenue, Oswaldtwistle, Accrington, Lancashire BB5 4LS.

Secretary: J. E. Pilkington
01254-232734.
Professional: Bill Harling
01254-381614.
Clubhouse: 01254-232734.

OVERLOOKING the towns of Accrington and Church, the course is situated in pretty countryside with views dominated by Pendle Hill and the Ribble Valley.

The Accrington and District club, to give its proper name, moved to the site in 1908 after the owners of the original nine-hole course donated the land to the local council.

Before moving, the club sought advice from Alex Herd, who thought they had a splendid piece of golfing ground which should produce a very fine nine-hole course.

The club went ahead and rented the 60-acre site for an annual fee of £75!

Nearly 20 years later a second nine holes were opened, designed by James Braid, who was impressed by the texture of the turf.

The present clubhouse was built in 1914 and has been extended three times.

After the third extension in the 1980s, attention turned to the course, with major investment in machinery and treatments.

In 1991 an automatic watering system was installed with financial support from the members.

The finishing touches to the club's appearance was the resurfacing of the car park in time for the 1993 centenary.

The Accrington course has a good reputation as a golfing challenge. The club has produced several Lancashire county players.

The head greenkeeper, Trevor Foster, is a two-time Lancashire champion and current team member.

The course is 'next door' to the Rishton Golf Club.

FACT FILE

A moorland course of 18 holes, 6044 yards. Par 70. SSS 69. Record 64.

Restrictions: Groups and societies on application.

Fees: £15 to £18.

Shop opening: Summer 8.45am to 8pm. Winter 9am to dusk.

Facilities:

TO THE CLUB

Two miles from Blackburn on the A679.

Course Information

Hole	Yards	Stroke	Par
1	191	7	3
2	352	11	4
3	414	9	4
4	149	17	3
5	534	3	5
6	410	1	4
7	301	13	4
8	335	15	4
9	328	5	4
10	347	14	4
11	350	10	4
12	154	18	3
13	406	2	4
14	163	8	3
15	382	12	4
16	533	6	5
17	363	4	4
18	332	16	4
OUT	3014		35
IN	3030		35
TOTAL	6044		70

1) A testing first hole with out-of-bounds left and right.

2) Drive to the left of the fairway to allow for the slope. Rather tight.

3) A blind tee shot over a steep incline. If playing the second shot short, play to the left side of the green.

4) There's a canal to the right and the green is ringed by bunkers.

5) Long hitters should allow for the stream across the fairway.

6) The incline all the way from the green makes this hole play long.

7) It's difficult to see the green from the tee. The line is just inside the left of the trees.

8) Drive and second shot should be left of target to allow for the slope.

9) It's out-of-bounds right and a dogleg to a protected green.

10) There's a water hazard on the right and the green is well protected.

11) The second shot needs to be short and left to allow for a steep slope down to the green.

12) A testing hole with a bunker and a water hazard.

13) A good par four needing a tee shot left and a long second shot. There's water down the right and the green has four big bunkers.

14) Large bunkers in front of the forward-sloping raised green suggest problems here.

15) A straightforward hole and one of the easiest.

16) This calls for a well-hit second shot to clear large cross bunkers.

17) Water to the right, trees to the left - but no bunkers.

18) Sloping down to the bunkered green, a good line is just left of the pro's shop.

Recommended Facilities

ASHTON & LEA
Golf Club

Tudor Avenue, Blackpool Road,
Preston, Lancashire PR4 0XA.

Secretary: M. G. Gibbs
01772-735282 (Fax 735762).
Professional: Mike Greenough
01772-720374.
Clubhouse: 01772-726480.

DISPLAYED on a wall in the lounge in Ashton and Lea's smart new clubhouse is a gold record album awarded to band leader James Last.

The German maestro in turn awarded it to the golf club in appreciation of the hospitality shown to him on several visits when he was touring Britain and visiting Preston Guild Hall in the 1970s and 1980s. Apart from that gift, gold objects were in short supply for most of the club's history.

As the commemorative booklet pointed out on the occasion of the club's 75th anniversary, in 1988: "Unlike many golf clubs, Ashton and Lea was never greatly endowed with wealthy patrons who could pick up the bill for large items of expenditure. All income, and much of the physical work, came from members who would, after each setback, roll up their sleeves and get on with the rebuilding of the course and the clubhouse."

An early disaster was the fire that destroyed the clubhouse in 1927. Twenty years later the Government requisitioned the clubhouse and part of the course in order to build homes for workers at the nearby Springfields atomic energy works.

That particular clubhouse is still standing as the headquarters of the works sports and social club!

Ashton and Lea's story has many references to special meetings called to approve levies on their long-suffering members.

After the war the club struggled to restore and extend the course to 18 holes - but couldn't afford the upkeep and reverted to playing nine holes for a while.

After avoiding liquidation in 1967, the situation was turned around and three years later the club tried to buy the course from the de Hoghton estate. Other attempts failed and a new 35 year lease was negotiated in 1984.

The club's strength was always in long service from several stalwarts, notably Herbert Calvert, the first captain and president from 1917 to 1953, and Alan Alston, twice captain, chairman of the post-war reconstruction committee and president from 1965 to 1985.

The course has been transformed to a high standard in recent years. An irrigation system was installed in 1990 and the clubhouse was rebuilt in 1995.

The club is commercially-minded and caters for conferences, seminars, social functions and fitness training, as well as a selection of golf packages.

FACT FILE

A parkland course of 18 holes, 6346 yards. Par 71. SSS 70. Record 65.

Restrictions: Visitors and societies make contact in advance.
No visitors before 9.15am or 12.15 to 1.45pm.

Fees: £20 to £23.

Dress code: Usual golf attire.

Shop opening: 8am to 7pm.

Facilities:

TO THE CLUB

Off the A5058 (Blackpool Road) at Lea. Turn off opposite the Pig and Whistle.

Course Information

Hole	Yards	Stroke	Par
1	374	9	4
2	172	16	3
3	435	1	4
4	420	3	4
5	358	8	4
6	165	12	3
7	396	2	4
8	311	13	4
9	481	17	5
10	422	5	4
11	141	14	3
12	336	11	4
13	317	18	4
14	360	10	4
15	388	6	4
16	477	15	5
17	395	7	4
18	398	4	4
OUT	3112		35
IN	3234		36
TOTAL	6346		71

1) A gentle start from a sheltered tee. Beware the wind from the left.

2) Don't miss right and end up in the 'bomb hole'

3) A monster hole so early in the round! Par will feel like a birdie.

4) A deceptive carry for the second shot. It may fall short.

5) It may look easy but there is trouble left and right. Take the four!

6) The green is long. Front edge it and three-putt for a nice four!

7) The green is so small you may wonder if it's there. Hit it in two shots and call yourself a golfer.

8) Have a go at the green. The locals don't. Short and left leaves a great shot over the trees.

9) The right of the fairway leaves the best angle. Depending on the wind it can be a second shot with a driver or a wedge.

10) There's a pond on the right from the tee, and a partially blind second shot. Don't miss left.

11) Please allow following players through after five shots!

12) As easy as it looks.

13) The big eagle chance if you can miss the trees, ditch, bunkers etc!

14) Lay up unless down wind. The carry is further than it looks.

15) Lay up a long way. It's very fast ground to the pits.

16) A long carry over water and bunkers to a huge green.

17) The hardest green to read. You must be to the right off the tee.

18) Again, it may look easy but good golfers have taken nine here. More than once.

Recommended Facilities

Preston Marriott

Formerly the old farm house for the Broughton Park Estate, and now sympathetically refurbished over 1995 with a spend of £2.5 million.

With its fully equipped leisure club, swimming pool and Health and Beauty Salon, the Preston Marriott has unrivalled leisure facilities in the area. Local membership is available.

The Broughton Park Restaurant has been justifiably celebrated in the North West for many years as one of the region's best restaurants. It has been one of only four establishments so honoured in Lancashire.

The 98 bedrooms are pleasantly decorated in a traditional style with many having fine views of the gardens and the surrounding Lancashire farmland.

All rooms have TV, free SKY channels, radio, hair drier, direct telephone, tea and coffee making facilities and trouser press. For business or pleasure we look forward to welcoming you in a professional yet friendly manner.

Preston Marriott Hotel
Garstang Road, Broughton
Preston, Lancashire, PR3 5JB
Telephone: 01772 864087
Fax: 01772 861728

AA
★★★★

BACUP
Golf Club

Maden Road, Bacup,
Lancashire OL13 8HY.

Secretary: J. Garvey
01706-874485.
Clubhouse: 01706-873170.

ALTHOUGH the Bacup club is set in hilly countryside along the 1,000-foot contour, the course is predominantly flat and not too taxing. There are great views of the Rossendale Valley.

It's a nine-hole course that exceeds 6000 yards when played as 18 holes.

The course is tight with narrow fairways and small greens. Each hole has an individual character and together they provide a good test of golf.

The Bacup club was formed in 1910 after members of the Bacup Bowling Club called a meeting to discuss the possibility. It appears that several local residents were travelling to Lobden and Rossendale clubs to play golf.

The groundsman at the bowling club, an expert on greens, estimated the cost at £10 per green - and the course was laid out for just £100.

Local newspaper archives show that the course was established at Cowfoot Farm and was in play by July, 1910.

Six years later the club moved to its present site and for seven years a rented cottage served as the clubhouse.

In 1923 a two-storey clubhouse was built and the club progressed until fire destroyed the clubhouse in January 1939. Only 15 months later the present clubhouse was opened on the corner of the course near Bank Side Lane.

At an auction in 1946, the club paid £1,850 for the 54 acres on which the course is located.

Facilities have been improved over the years with the most recent project being a new snooker room in 1990. Members have a busy diary of competitions.

FACT FILE

A moorland course of 9 holes, 6008 yards. Par 70. SSS 69. Record 72.

Restrictions: Visitors welcome Tuesday to Friday. Societies must apply in writing.

Fees: £9 to £12.

Dress code: Usual golf attire.

Facilities:

TO THE CLUB

On the west side of Bacup, off the A671.

Course Information

Hole	Yards	Stroke	Par
1	283	15	4
2	183	11	3
3	354	13	4
4	500	5	5
5	380	9	4
6	389	1	4
7	424	3	4
8	365	7	4
9	134	17	3
10	283	16	4
11	183	12	3
12	354	14	4
13	500	6	5
14	380	10	4
15	389	2	4
16	400	4	4
17	365	8	4
18	142	18	3
OUT	3012		35
IN	2996		35
TOTAL	6008		70

1) Drive up the hill over the marker to play the second shot to a green guarded by two bunkers.

2) A straightforward par three with a green guarded on the right by grass mounds.

3) The fairway is tree lined and two bunkers guard the green.

4) A par five with tree-lined fairways and out-of-bounds on the right. The green is elevated.

5) Driving from an elevated tee, take account of the water hazard at about 220 yards.

6) A slight dogleg to the left. The green is narrow.

7) Tree-lined most of the length and needing two good shots to reach the green.

8) Another elevated tee and a dogleg, this time to the right.

9) A short par three from an elevated tee to a green guarded by a bunker.

Lancashire

Recommended Facilities

THE Grant ARMS HOTEL

The Grant Arms Hotel, situated in the heart of Ramsbottom, Lancashire, is steeped in history. Originally named Top o'th'Brow it became 'Grant Lodge' when the famous Grant Family adopted it as their family home.

The Grant arms provides 14 beautifully appointed recently refurbished en suite bedrooms, colour television with satellite channels, direct dial telephone and tea & coffee making facilities.
Our Function room is superbly appointed, offering an attractive setting for up to 80 diners.
We have an exclusive a la carte restaurant offering attractively priced dishes or you can simply enjoy a pint and a plate of pub food served in the warm and welcoming bar areas.

Market Place ● Ramsbottom ● Lancashire BL0 9AJ
Telephone: 01706 823354 ● Fax: 01706 823381

BAXENDEN
Golf Club

Top o'th Meadow, Wooley Lane, Baxenden, Lancashire BB5 2EA.

Secretary: Len Howard
01706-213394.
Clubhouse: 01254-234555.

ONE of five golf clubs in the East Lancashire borough of Hyndburn, Baxenden and District, to give its full name, is one of the county's highest courses. The golfer has fine views of the Pennines.

The club was founded in 1913 on a nearby site at Gallows Halland and moved to Top 'o th Meadow in 1927-1928, when those early members were fortunate enough to purchase the land.

It's a nine-hole course that runs out at 5717 yards when played as 18, although not all the back nine are played from different tees.

Two notable differences are the 11th, which reduces from a par five of 479 yards to a par four of 440 yards and earns stroke index one as a result; and the 16th, which goes from a par four to a par five by gaining more than 100 yards.

A programme of improvements at the Club has maintained a loyal following of local golfers.

The loyalty of just a few members is what kept the club in existence after World War Two, when they returned home to find the course partly ploughed up. Only three fairways and four greens were playable.

Secretary Len Howard, who took office in 1947 and has served continuously, recalled that there were few members and the club was broke.

Three years of hard manual work by these stalwarts brought the nine holes back into fair condition.

Improvements were made slowly over the next 25 years until the Baxenden club, in common with hundreds of smaller clubs across the country, began to gain the benefit from the increased interest in golf and - more recently - the VAT windfall received by non-profit sports clubs.

The club was able to install an irrigation system with pop-up sprinklers for the tees and greens and some smaller projects are in train. Baxenden members take pride in the success of Kim Rostron, who joined the club at the age of eight in 1982 and won the Northern Women's Championship at Seaton Carew in May, 1996.

Kim is still a member at Baxenden but her nominated club in competitions is Clitheroe.

FACT FILE

A moorland course of 9 holes, 5717 yards. Par 70. SSS 68. Record 63.

Restrictions: Societies apply to the Secretary. No visitors at weekends. Ladies' day Mondays.

Fees: £15 - £8 with member.

Dress code: Usual golf attire.

Facilities:

TO THE CLUB

1½ miles S.E. of Baxenden off the A680.

Course Information

Hole	Yards	Stroke	Par
1	199	9	3
2	479	4	5
3	114	15	3
4	272	17	4
5	360	7	4
6	283	11	4
7	426	2	4
8	408	5	4
9	281	13	4
10	199	10	3
11	440	1	4
12	114	16	3
13	272	18	4
14	360	8	4
15	283	12	4
16	538	3	5
17	408	6	4
18	281	14	4
OUT	2819		35
IN	2898		35
TOTAL	5717		70

1) A par three to open. It's not too short but it's a straightforward shot to a flat green.

2) The par five hole is uphill with out-of-bounds left and thick rough on the right near the undulating green.

3) A short par three - over a valley to an elevated green with bunkers front and back.

4) With out-of-bounds to the left, the green is reachable with a good drive. There's a bunker at the front left.

5) Downhill, with out-of-bounds on the left and a bunker to the front left of a sloping green.

6) Going back uphill to a medium sized green with bunkers front left and right.

7) The well guarded green is in good driving distance but the out-of-bounds is to the right and there are trees on the left.

8) Downhill with out-of-bounds to the left. Again, a good drive will reach the green, which is quite undulating.

9) Playing back uphill, there is a pond at driving distance on the left and the green is well guarded.

Holes 10, 12-15 and holes 17-18 as per first nine.

11) Hole two loses 39 yards and becomes a par four.

16) Hole seven gains 112 yards and becomes a par five.

Recommended Facilities

BEACON PARK
Golf Course

Beacon Lane, Up Holland,
Wigan, Lancashire WN8 7RU.

Phone 01695-622700 for:
The Clubhouse
Secretary: Peter Frodsham
Professional: Ray Peters.

THE Beacon Park course was designed by Donald Steel for West Lancashire Council and was opened in 1982.

The course and the adjoining driving range are situated in rolling pastures and mature woodland high above the Lancashire plain. There are views of the Welsh hills and, swinging round to the north, Blackpool Tower is visible.

The 18-hole hillside course is a challenge to all golfers whatever their handicap may be.

In fact tuition and improvement is a major feature at Beacon Park. The professional, Ray Peters, and his qualified PGA staff give advice and tuition and there is a 24-bay driving range that is open in almost any weather from 9am to 9pm seven days a week.

The golf course and range is serviced by the Beacon Park Visitor Centre.

Beacon Park organises fund-raising competitions for local charities and has supported the Ormskirk Children's Ward and the Cystic Fibrosis charity.

FACT FILE

An undulating/hilly parkland course of 18 holes, 5996 yards. Par 72. SSS 69. Record 68.

Restrictions: Societies apply in advance. Visitors may book in advance for weekends and Bank Holidays.

Fees: £3.70 to £7.20 (pay-and-play municipal course).

Dress code: Casual.

Shop opening: 7am to 8.30pm.

Facilities:

TO THE CLUB
On Beacon Lane, Dalton, Up Holland. From junction 26 of the M6 follow the signs for Up Holland.

Course Information

Hole	Yards	Stroke	Par
1	361	11	4
2	400	5	4
3	132	15	3
4	495	1	5
5	319	9	4
6	322	7	4
7	334	13	4
8	494	3	5
9	122	17	3
10	265	10	4
11	295	12	4
12	169	14	3
13	440	2	4
14	396	4	4
15	157	16	3
16	486	8	5
17	298	18	4
18	511	6	5
OUT	2979		36
IN	3017		36
TOTAL	5996		72

1) A gentle opener; a downhill dogleg with one greenside bunker.

2) One of the hardest holes, playing uphill and very tight with a ditch on drive length.

3) This short hole needs an accurate shot. Trouble waits if to the left.

4) A tree-lined fairway demands accuracy from the tee.

5) A dogleg hole. It's possible to go over the trees.

6) The fairway slopes severely to the right. A good tee shot sets up a short iron to the narrow green.

7) An easy par four. Keep the tee shot to the left.

8) A severe slope and a ditch make this a testing hole.

9) A straightforward par three, played slightly uphill. There are two greenside bunkers.

10) Trees and a water hazard will catch anything hit to the right.

11) Playing downhill, the tee shot must be kept left to find the best approach.

12) A tough par three. Only part of the green can be seen from the tee.

13) A long par four towards the church with a blind second shot.

14) This hole normally plays longer than its yardage. A par is good.

15) A short uphill hole with a narrow entrance to the green.

16) A demanding uphill par five with a smallish green.

17) A good tee shot sets up a short approach to the big green.

18) A difficult driving hole. Trees cut into the fairway and the hole doglegs to the left.

Recommended Facilities

BLACKBURN
Golf Club

Beardwood Brow,
Blackburn, Lancashire BB2 7AX.

Secretary: R. B. Smith
01254-51122.
Professional: Alan Rodwell
01254-55942.

EXTENSIVE improvements over recent years have made the Blackburn course one of the most visited in East Lancashire. A vast improvement in drainage has given the course an envied standard of lush greens and fairways, while the maturing of hundreds of trees and shrubs has given shape and interest in many places.

It was this series of improvements in the 1980s, including the creation of water hazards, that began to attract more visiting parties and boosted the club's revenue, to be followed by the building of a new pro shop and the resurfacing of the car park in time for the 1994 centenary.

The result is a healthy club in pristine condition. The history of the club was written by the secretary (and centenary captain) R. B. Smith in 1993, in which he gave some fascinating details of the conditions that existed when the club was formed.

Golf was in its infancy in Lancashire and developing slowly from seaside links to inland courses, at the behest of the gentry and the newly-wealthy industrialists and professional men.

The nearby Wilpshire club had opened in 1889 and Pleasington in 1891. In Blackburn, a group of enthusiasts leased some farmland for a nine-hole course and were ambitious enough to invite the great Harry Vardon to be their professional. He declined.

Conditions were primitive. Cows and sheep roamed the fairways and local rules advised that if the ball fell in a cow-pat, the player could recover it and clean it!

Gutta-percha balls were in use and 'sang' in flight. They were said to improve with use.

In 1908, the course grew to 18 holes and the steady acquisition of adjoining farmland led to longer and better holes. Today the club owns most of its course; just three holes are leased.

Improvements are ongoing and all the greens can be used in winter.

Parties are welcomed but early inquiry is advised.

FACT FILE

A parkland course of 18 holes, 6144 yards. Par 71. SSS 70. Record 63.

Restrictions: Societies and groups on weekdays. Members only 12.30 to 1.30pm. Ladies' day Tuesday.

Fees: £19.50 to £23.

Dress code: Usual golf attire.

Shop opening: Summer 8.30am to 6.30pm (weekends 7.30am to 6pm). Winter 8.30am to 4pm (weekends 7.45am to 4pm).

Facilities:

TO THE CLUB

Junction 31 of the M6 to Blackburn. Go straight on at the Moat House and turn left at the next lights. Turn left at Beardwood Brow.

Course Information

Hole	Yards	Stroke	Par
1	279	15	4
2	400	1	4
3	405	5	4
4	481	7	5
5	182	9	3
6	289	17	4
7	381	13	4
8	301	3	4
9	191	11	3
10	505	12	5
11	365	6	4
12	135	18	3
13	563	8	5
14	420	4	4
15	370	14	4
16	147	10	3
17	435	2	4
18	295	16	4
OUT	2909		35
IN	3235		36
TOTAL	6144		71

1) An easy uphill hole if you avoid the out-of-bounds.

2) With out-of-bounds right and the need to carry a cross-dyke, this hole is difficult to score.

3) A cross-dyke at drive length causes problems on this short par four.

4) This uphill par five needs length and accuracy.

5) This par three to an elevated green needs good club selection.

6) Trees on the right and the elevated green are the main concerns.

7) A blind hole downhill looks easy until you try the tricky green.

8) Back uphill to an elevated green. It looks much shorter than it is.

9) A par three with left-sloping ground needs an accurate tee shot.

10) An elevated tee makes this a tremendous visual hole. Beware the out-of-bounds right and a dyke just short of the green.

11) A straight par four slightly uphill.

12) A short, tricky par three. Choose the right club!

13) This hole doglegs first to the right, then to the left - and the green is well protected.

14) The tree-lined fairway needs length and accuracy.

15) Don't drive too long here due to the cross-fairway ridge.

16) A dyke and greenside bunkers make accuracy the key.

17) Avoid the trees on the right and the pond on the left to score here.

18) A short par four to finish - but watch out for the sloping fairway and out-of-bounds to the right.

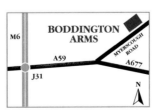

BLACKPOOL NORTH SHORE
Golf Club

Devonshire Road, Blackpool,
Lancashire FY2 0RD.

Secretary: Mike Nuttall
01253-352054.
Professional: Brendan Ward
01253-354640.

ALTHOUGH North Shore has staged the Penfold tournament and has been a qualifying course for the Open Championship at nearby Royal Lytham and St. Annes, the greatest day in the club's history came in 1963 with a match between Britain and the Rest of the World for the Duke of Edinburgh Trophy.

Prince Philip flew in by helicopter and watched much of the action on a day when Arnold Palmer beat Dai Rees, and Peter Alliss halved with the new American sensation, Jack Nicklaus.

Gary Player edged ahead of Bernard Hunt and Eric Brown suffered a rare defeat at the hands of Peter Thomson.

Christy O'Connor also lost - to a tall, slim New Zealander with a magical putting touch who was to have his own moment of history nine days later.

Bob Charles went from North Shore to Royal Lytham, where he became the only left-hander to win the Open Championship, after a 36-hole play-off against the American Phil Rodgers.

Although founded in 1904, Blackpool North Shore moved to its present location in 1928. The course is one of the highest points on the Fylde Coast with views across Morecambe Bay to the Lakeland hills and to Bleasdale Fell in the east.

Parkland in nature but with few trees on the exposed parts, the feature of the course is the naturally undulating terrain.

The three par fives are all more than 500 yards, with the green of the rebuilt 10th being closely guarded by a pond.

There are several testing par fours which use the undulations to good effect and the par threes all play long off the back tees. The green at the closing hole, just over 400 yards, is approached through a narrow neck of fairway and has three bunkers to protect it on each side.

Although open to the wind on all sides, the relatively mild Fylde Coast climate keeps the course open through most winters.

In 1963, when he won the Prince Philip Trophy, Harry Weetman went round in 66 but four years later, in the Penfold, Christy O'Connor set the current record at 63.

FACT FILE

An undulating parkland course of 18 holes, 6431 yards. Par 71. SSS 71. Record 63.

Restrictions: Societies make contact in advance. Ladies' day Thursday, members only Saturday.

Fees: £25 to £30. With member £10.

Dress code: Usual golf attire.

Shop opening: Summer 8am to 8pm; winter 9am to 4pm.

Facilities:

TO THE CLUB

Off Devonshire Road (A677) about a mile north of Blackpool centre. Turn off left at the road's highest point.

Course Information

Hole	Yards	Stroke	Par
1	436	4	4
2	400	10	4
3	524	6	5
4	367	14	4
5	429	2	4
6	385	8	4
7	175	12	3
8	303	16	4
9	196	18	3
10	533	7	5
11	435	1	4
12	178	15	3
13	296	17	4
14	341	13	4
15	537	5	5
16	309	11	4
17	172	9	3
18	415	3	4
OUT	3215		35
IN	3216		36
TOTAL	6431		71

1) A tough opener needing a long iron into a narrow protected green.

2) A long drive uphill to see the green, protected left by a deep pit.

3) A pond at the right collects a sliced drive and another pond near the green makes this a difficult par five.

4) Out-of-bounds right and problems with a narrow green entrance.

5) A long par four needing an accurate drive and a green affected by sloping ground and deep bunkers.

6) A long drive to clear cross bunkers and a long iron shot uphill.

7) A short hole, normally into wind, with cross and greenside bunkers.

8) Out-of-bounds right is the only danger on this short par four.

9) An accurate shot to the green; but the saucer shape is tricky.

10) The third shot to the green needs to clear the water.

11) The hardest par four needing two long shots to a sloping green.

12) A downhill shot of 135 yards over trees and a pit, to a narrow, well protected green.

13) Being alongside the main road makes this difficult and there are cross bunkers just before the green.

14) A blind driving hole at first - then an accurate shot to the green is required.

15) A dogleg right. Drive uphill then drop to the sloping green.

16) A long blind drive uphill is needed to carry a ridge and is rewarded by a short pitch to the green.

17) A long and accurate shot is dictated by cross and green bunkers.

18) The most difficult hole on the course. Two long shots are needed to clear two pits short of the largest green.

Lancashire

BLACKPOOL
Stanley Park
Golf Course and
Blackpool Park
Golf Club

North Park Drive, Blackpool,
Lancashire FY3 8LS.
Secretary: Diane Woodman
01253-397916.
Professional: Brian Purdie
01253-391004.
Bookings: 01253-393960.

STANLEY Park's great claim to fame is that it was designed by Dr. Alister Mackenzie, the only Fylde course to be created by the master golf architect, before he went on to do his greatest work in the United States.

The course was laid out in 1926 on 101 acres as part of a huge Blackpool Council development that included the much larger Stanley Park, which borders the course.

Although not part of the park, it is a public course managed by the council and played over by the Blackpool Park Golf Club. The professional Brian Purdie, is known as 'the park pro.'

The park course is long and challenging for a municipal course. The section near the clubhouse falls away steadily down to East Park Drive, which golfers cross to reach the second section

As might be expected from a Mackenzie course, there are some large greens and because it was designed as a public course some of the fairways are rather wide. The hazards include some large grassy pits and ponds.

An average golfer will take about three and a half hours to go round.

The course is open year-round from first light to dusk.

FACT FILE

An undulating parkland course of 18 holes, 6060 yards. Par 70. SSS 69. Record 66.

Restrictions: Individuals may book up to seven days in advance on 01253-395349. Party bookings are available Monday to Friday for a minimum of 20. Phone 01253-694604

Fees: £9 weekdays, £11 at weekends and Bank Holidays.

Dress code: Smart and casual.

Facilities:

TO THE CLUB

At the bend of North Park Drive on the north west corner of Stanley Park.

Course Information

Hole	Yards	Stroke	Par
1	421	5	4
2	186	17	3
3	481	9	5
4	285	13	4
5	169	15	3
6	439	1	4
7	428	7	4
8	334	11	4
9	505	3	5
10	126	16	3
11	335	12	4
12	354	10	4
13	442	4	4
14	442	2	4
15	360	6	4
16	155	18	3
17	264	14	4
18	334	8	4
OUT	3248		36
IN	2812		34
TOTAL	6060		70

1) The fairway draws slightly to the bunkers on the right on this fine opening hole, popular with big-hitters.
2) Playing down from a ridge, the 'punchbowl' green is reachable.
3) An honest, hard-hitting par five with a dyke all along the right.
4) A diagonal ditch and plantations left and right beckon the mishit.
5) A short hole, uphill over a ditch and bunker with a pit at the right.
6) A dogleg left with out-of-bounds all along the left on this longest hole where a big drive counts.
7) Two very good shots are needed to the semi-plateau green, with a ditch crossing 100 yards in front.
8) A drive slightly left gives a straight approach to the guarded green.
9) Take care with the second shot on this 505-yard par five.
10) The shortest hole but 'the kidney trap' is long on trouble.
11) A short par four, dogleg slightly right, calls for an approach from the left. Out-of-bounds behind the green.
12) A straight drive up the middle sets up the second shot.
13) A blind drive downhill over a brow. The more open shot to the green is from the left.
14) A difficult par four with gorse on the left to claim a pushed-out second shot and a pond wide of the green at the right.
15) Drive downhill and pitch up to a plateau green on a ridge.
16) A short hole with the ground sliding away to the right.
17) A well-hit shot should carry the grassy dip to leave a chip shot.
18) A bunker is awkwardly sited short of the green on the right and the green itself is tightly guarded.

Lancashire

BURNLEY
Golf Club

Glen View, Burnley,
Lancashire BB11 3RW.

Secretary: Geoffrey Butterfield
01282-451281.
Professional: William Tye
01282-455266.

FORMED in 1905, the club's Glen View course was originally a nine-holer and was extended in 1914. It is rated as one of the stiffest in East Lancashire.

It stands on the edge of the moors overlooking Burnley and makes good use of the rolling countryside.

The altitude gives the added challenge of wind - and although the course has only one par five, at least four other holes often seem to be in that class.

The wind farm on the hill at nearby Cliviger is testament to the strength and frequency of the wind.

Many local golfers rate the fifth hole - a long par four - as the hardest, with out-of-bounds all down one side, a ditch on the other and a blind tee shot to make matters uncertain.

Another tough one is the 18th. In spite of being classed easy by the stroke index, it's a downhill hole needing a good tee shot and a good approach shot. Many a good player has hit two, three or even more tee shots into the huge out-of-bounds field on the right.

The Burnley club has a strong competition diary, a good junior section and a thriving social side.

FACT FILE

A moorland course of 18 holes, 5899 yards. Par 69. SSS 69. Record 65.

Restrictions: Societies make contact in advance. No visitors on Saturdays.

Fees: £10 to £25.

Dress code: Usual golf attire.

Shop opening: 8.30am to 7.30pm

Facilities:

TO THE CLUB

One and a half miles south of Burnley on the A646.

Hole	Yards	Stroke	Par
1	322	9	4
2	159	17	3
3	402	5	4
4	333	11	4
5	446	1	4
6	298	15	4
7	204	13	3
8	519	3	5
9	421	7	4
10	330	10	4
11	130	16	3
12	389	4	4
13	324	8	4
14	168	14	3
15	439	2	4
16	368	6	4
17	300	12	4
18	347	18	4
OUT	3104		35
IN	2795		34
TOTAL	5899		69

Course Information

1) A steep but wide fairway to a tricky green, sloping back to front.

2) With the green ringed by bunkers, an accurate tee shot is needed.

3) A blind tee shot makes this a difficult hole. There's a ditch about 265 yards from the tee.

4) Uphill makes the hole play longer than it is; long approach shots hit trouble behind the green.

5) The toughest hole, with another blind tee shot and out-of-bounds on the right.

6) A short dogleg with out-of-bounds along the right.

7) A longish par three down a valley from an elevated tee.

8) The green is reachable in two on the course's only par five.

9) The fairway slopes towards rough on the left, needing a well placed tee shot and tricky second to a tight green.

10) A hard, blind tee shot with a 180-yard carry to a falling fairway.

11) A tough par three with a tricky green ringed by bunkers.

12) Only a good second shot will hold the green, sloping to the back.

13) A tough hole where the pin is usually tucked behind two bunkers.

14) When windy, a particularly good tee shot is needed here.

15) A long dogleg right and two large bunkers call for accuracy.

16) A slight uphill reasonably easy approach shot with only one greenside bunker.

17) The long green needs a good second shot to the pin.

18) A card-wrecker; the toughest drive on the course.

Lancashire

Recommended Facilities

CHARNOCK RICHARD
Golf Club

Preston Road, Charnock Richard, Chorley, Lancashire PR7 5LE.

Secretary: Lee Taylor
01257-470707 (Fax 01257-794343).
Pro Shop: 01257 470707.

ONE of the new golf courses of Lancashire, Charnock Richard was established in 1994.

The 18-hole course winds its way into the small, scenic village of Charnock Richard, near Chorley. To the east of the course is Winter Hill.

The ground is relatively flat parkland with plenty of water to contend with. Designer Chris Court took care to blend the course into the natural landscape, retaining the mature trees and hedges where possible, and 2,000 new trees were planted. "We have tried to make every hole different," secretary Lee Taylor pointed out.

The objective was to produce a course that could be enjoyed by the beginner and the scratch golfer alike. The tees and greens were built to a high standard and most of the greens can be played in winter.

The signature hole of the course is the 512 yard sixth - daunting to all golfers - with three ponds and an island green. A large man-made lake is used to full effect at the end of the course.

In the short time the club has been open, ladies' and junior sections have been formed and there are weekly competitions.

The club has established an annual charity competition, played in September.

The Charnock Richard venture was started by business partners John Ross and Martin Turner on the site of John's farm. Work began in 1991 and the final phase - the building of the clubhouse - was undertaken in 1996. It is on the site of the old farm buildings.

The course is only five miles from the Camelot theme park. Golfers joining the club receive a family pass for Camelot.

Course Information

Hole	Yards	Stroke	Par
1	411	5	4
2	290	18	4
3	477	9	5
4	190	12	3
5	231	7	3
6	512	1	5
7	486	11	5
8	420	3	4
9	316	13	4
10	357	15	4
11	159	17	3
12	477	8	5
13	433	6	4
14	329	16	4
15	372	10	4
16	226	4	3
17	138	14	3
18	410	2	4
OUT	3333		37
IN	2901		34
TOTAL	6234		71

1) An opening par four on which most of the trouble is on the left - plus water at the back of the green.

2) A good birdie hole if the shot keeps clear of the pot bunker.

3) A par five dogleg left. A ditch runs across the fairway and left.

4) A bunker guards the right of the green on the first par three.

5) A demanding par three across water with bunkers left and right.

6) Stroke index one - a long, tough hole with water everywhere!

7) Another par five, over a lake. Out-of-bounds all down the right.

8) A difficult and long par four with water lapping the fairway.

9) A modest par four. It's recommended not to take the driver to avoid the trees along the fairway.

10) A short par four but it's a tricky green to hit with water lapping at the base.

11) A straightforward par three. A bunker guards the left of the green.

12) A tricky and narrow par five needing accuracy. A sharp dogleg to the right.

13) You need to hit the fairway to have a chance at the green. There's a pond just short.

14) Take note of the pin placement on this straight uphill par four.

15) The problem on this par four is the battery of green bunkers.

16) A long par three to a small green. Out-of-bounds on the right.

17) A short and sweet par three. Note the water behind the green.

18) A hard finishing hole with a dogleg right and water to avoid in the middle of the fairway.

Recommended Facilities

CHORLEY
Golf Club

Hall o'th Hill, Heath Charnock,
Chorley, Lancashire PR6 9HX.

Secretary: A. K. Tyrer
01257-480263.
Professional: Mark Tomlinson
01257-481245.

THE Chorley club is known as Hall o'th Hill after the three-story 1724 hall that forms most of the clubhouse.

Golf has been played on the site since 1898 but Chorley Golf Club did not move there until 1926.

The moorland course was designed by J. A. Steer and can prove a very tough test when the wind blows.

There are panoramic views across to Southport and the Fylde Coast, with Longridge Fell directly north and - much closer - the Yarrow Valley and Anglezarke/Rivington.

In the last few years a great deal of improvement work has been done to the course, including better bunkers and tees, new footpaths and a programme of tree planting.

The clubhouse was extended in 1989, allowing the club to convert the downstairs bar and dining area into a new restaurant.

The new building also houses a large bar-lounge and a separate snooker room and mixed lounge.

The club is proud of its facilities on and off the course and visitors are welcome by prior arrangement.

Chorley Golf Club's most successful product is Laura Fairclough, one of Britain's top lady golfers, who won the European Ladies' Championship in 1995.

Laura joined Chorley at the age of 11 and made astonishing progress.

She was given a handicap of 45 and told she would play off 36 when she was 12. But by the time her birthday came round, Laura was playing off eight and the next year she became the youngest player to earn a handicap of less than one.

As an amateur, Laura represented Great Britain at all levels and won the European Junior Championship in 1988.

As a professional her successes included the Swedish Open in 1993, membership of the British team in the Solheim Cup in the United States, and winning the 1995 Ford Classic at Charthills, Kent.

FACT FILE

A moorland course of 18 holes, 6307 yards. Par 71. SSS 70. Record 65.

Restrictions: Visitors and societies make contact in advance. Handicap certificates required.

Fees: £25 - £10 with member.

Dress code: Usual golf attire.

Shop opening: Dawn till dusk.

Facilities:

TO THE CLUB ▶

Two miles south of Chorley, on the A673 near the A6 junction.

Course Information

Hole	Yards	Stroke	Par
1	362	9	4
2	477	15	5
3	146	13	3
4	398	3	4
5	472	1	4
6	364	7	4
7	163	11	3
8	339	17	4
9	388	5	4
10	311	18	4
11	415	6	4
12	380	2	4
13	513	14	5
14	331	10	4
15	384	8	4
16	163	12	3
17	496	16	5
18	205	4	3
OUT	3109		35
IN	3198		36
TOTAL	6307		71

1) Positioning on the green is vital as it slopes severely to the front.
2) The plateau green and large bunker make this one difficult.
3) Miss the green here and you face a tricky pitch.
4) A tight tee shot with the fairway sloping right, towards out-of-bounds. A blind second shot can be aimed left to use the large bank.
5) Two very good shots are needed to find the green because of the valley in front.
6) Aim just right of the mound to leave a mid-iron to a guarded green.
7) A well bunkered Mackenzie green can often lead to three putts.
8) The slope at the front of this green can cause a 'run through.'
9) A good drive uphill towards the clubhouse will leave a long iron to a large green sloping left to right.
10) A relatively easy par four but watch the sloping green.
11) Drive down the left to open a second shot to the green.
12) A good drive just right of the marker leaves a middle iron to the green - another one sloping to the right.
13) Take account of the fairway sloping towards the out-of-bounds. A straight second leaves a comfortable pitch to the green.
14) Hit the right of the fairway to leave a mid/short iron to a raised green, bunkered left and right.
15) A downhill second shot has to be very well judged.
16) Bunkers left, right and short - and another sloping green.
17) Reachable in two for long hitters. But watch the slope again!
18) A tough finishing hole. Out-of-bounds right and bunkers each side of the green. A par three is always a good score here.

Recommended Facilities

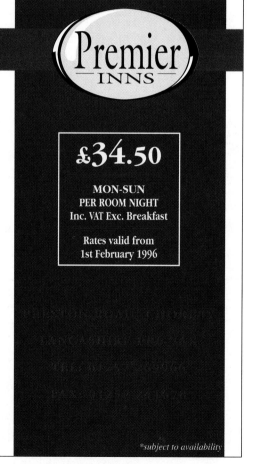

CLITHEROE
Golf Club

Whalley Road, Pendleton,
Clitheroe, Lancashire BB7 1PP.
Secretary: Geoff Roberts
01200-22292.
Professional: John Twissell
01200-24242.

CLITHEROE'S story over more than 100 years has been one of constant improvement with the most recent development being a handsomely extended clubhouse, completed in 1994.

Founded in 1891, the club had to move twice in its first few years and made a great step in 1932 of buying land and engaging James Braid to design the present 18-hole course.

In 1937 the club organised an exhibition match between the American Ryder Club captain, Walter Hagen and local golfing legend Jimmy Rothwell.

The match enhanced the club's name and confirmed the status of the new course.

The golf boom of the 1960s heralded a new era with the appointment of Peter Geddes as the club professional/greenkeeper.

Land was bought from a neighbouring farmer to create two new holes - the present ninth and 17th - which were opened in 1965 with another great occasion, an exhibition match involving three Walker Cup captains, Joe Carr, Michael Bonallack and David Marsh.

In 1977, Clitheroe hosted its first Lancashire County Championship, bringing recognition of the high regard in which the club and the course were held.

The purchase of more land in 1984 gave the club a new practice ground and seven years later the centenary was celebrated in style, from the flag-raising ceremony in January to the EGU Tournament of Champions in September.

It was a fitting climax to the club's first 100 years.

FACT FILE

A parkland course of 18 holes, 6326 yards. Par 71, SSS 71, Record 67.

Restrictions: Societies apply in writing. Other visitors make contact in advance.

Fees: £27 to £32.

Dress code: Usual golf attire.

Shop opening: Dawn till dusk.

Facilities:

TO THE CLUB

Two miles south of Clitheroe on the A671.

Course Information

Hole	Yards	Stroke	Par
1	464	7	5
2	346	11	4
3	447	3	4
4	298	13	4
5	144	17	3
6	345	9	4
7	434	1	4
8	172	15	3
9	379	5	4
10	372	12	4
11	406	6	4
12	445	2	4
13	518	10	5
14	187	16	3
15	379	4	4
16	317	14	4
17	151	18	3
18	522	8	5
OUT	3029		35
IN	3297		36
TOTAL	6326		71

1) An enticingly short par five; trees each side and a guarded green.

2) The fairway falls to the right and if two well-placed bunkers don't collect the drive, a magnificent oak tree can block the second shot.

3) A ditch prevents all but the longest hitters taking a driver and the long second shot has to be accurate.

4) A deceptively short dogleg right invites hitters to cut the corner.

5) With a pond in play, choose the correct club and hit the ball well.

6) A well guarded green demands good position near the railway.

7) Two good shots are needed to hit the two-tiered green.

8) This uphill par three plays one club more than you may think.

9) Out-of-bounds left and a narrow entrance to a raised green.

10) Dogleg right. Cut too much corner and a ditch awaits. Place the tee shot in the left half of the fairway.

11) Between the two big trees then slightly left. The dip disguises the distance to the green.

12) The fairway is generous but every shot requires accuracy.

13) Fairway bunkers pose all kinds of problems here.

14) A slightly uphill par three to a well guarded green.

15) Out-of-bounds right, this dogleg right invites a risky drive. Anyone short must play out left to see the green.

16) A good drive down the middle should clear the unseen ditch.

17) A picturesque par three that's maybe a club longer than you think.

18) Big hitters should guard against running out of fairway on this dogleg left back to the clubhouse.

Recommended Facilities

COLNE
Golf Club

Law Farm, Skipton Old Road,
Colne, Lancashire BB8 7EB.

Secretary: J. T. Duerden
01282-863391.
Clubhouse: 01282-863391.

COLNE Golf Club was founded in 1901 and is regarded as one of North Lancashire's prettiest courses.

The moorland course has a picturesque and tranquil location only a mile or so from the town centre.

It has improved almost out of recognition in recent years. An opinion that trees would not grow on the course has been proved false and an ambitious planting programme has made a marked difference.

Renovations and extensions to the original clubhouse have resulted in an attractive bar and lounge area with separate ladies room, snug bar and a snooker room with two full-size tables. Catering is available with the exception of Mondays.

The nine-hole course provides an excellent test of golf. The first hole, a 399-yard dogleg, can lay claim to being one of the county's most testing opening holes.

The out-of-bounds on the right and the guarded green makes the shot to the green a daunting challenge.

Opinions differ as to the toughest hole on the course. The 437-yard second with trees dominant on one side and a stretch of out-of-bounds on the other, is perhaps justifiably stroke one on the card.

However, the eighth hole - with trees on both sides and bunkers at the entrance to the green - is considered by many Colne members to be the most difficult.

Different tee positions change the distances on the second nine holes.

FACT FILE

A moorland course of 9 holes, 5961 yards. Par 70. SSS 69. Record 63.

Restrictions: Societies make contact in advance. Visitors ask first about weekends. Ladies' day Thursday.

Fees: £15 to £20; £7 to £10 with member.

Dress code: Usual golf attire.

Facilities:

TO THE CLUB

One mile east of Colne on the A56.

Course Information

Hole	Yards	Stroke	Par
1	399	5	4
2	437	1	4
3	496	9	5
4	368	7	4
5	187	11	3
6	296	17	4
7	154	15	3
8	362	3	4
9	320	13	4
10	404	6	4
11	421	2	4
12	478	10	5
13	368	8	4
14	172	12	3
15	300	18	4
16	142	16	3
17	350	4	4
18	307	14	4
OUT	3019		35
IN	2942		35
TOTAL	5961		70

1) A difficult opening drive to make position for the dogleg to the right. Out-of-bounds to the right and bunkers guarding the green.

2) An accurate drive and second shot are needed to avoid trees and out-of-bounds.

3) An excellent par five driving hole. A grass cross-mound can collect the second shot and make the third to the green difficult.

4) A slight dogleg to the right with out-of-bounds at the back of the green.

5) A short hole to a green guarded by bunkers. The tee shot has to carry over a beck. A difficult par three.

6) This hole requires a very accurate second shot to avoid a bunker in front of the green.

7) There's a steep drop to a beck on the right of the green and a lateral water hazard on the right-hand fairway.

8) Considered by many members to be the most difficult. A slight dogleg to the left and a tree-lined fairway require an accurately placed drive.

9) This sharp dogleg left requires another accurate drive. The second shot is to a guarded elevated green with a quarry just feet away on the right.

Lancashire

Recommended Facilities

DARWEN
Golf Club

Winter Hill, Darwen
Lancashire BB3 0LB.

Secretary: Jim Kenyon
01254-704367.
Professional: Wayne Lennon
01254-776370.
Clubhouse: 01254-701287.

NOT many clubs can boast of an Open winner from their membership. Fewer can claim a champion who rolled up his sleeves and helped build part of the course.

But Darwen can also point out that Dick Burton, their British Open Champion of 1939 - at St. Andrews, no less - was born on the original course. And that's not all. There were three Burton brothers, Dick, Tom and John, weavers in a local mill who were caddies and learned their golf at Darwen. Remarkably all of them did a spell as the club professional and Dick became a Ryder Cup player.

Their association with the club is recognised in the annual Burton Trophies competition involving 45 teams of three men, with half the teams coming from other Lancashire clubs.

An even bigger event in the calendar is the Darwen Senior/ Junior Open, which has had a waiting list for several years.

Darwen Golf Club was founded in 1893 with a nine-hole course on rented pasture. Until 1901 the 'clubhouse' was a pair of rented rooms in a farmhouse.

A reporter with the Darwen News made an astute observation in 1896. He advised readers: "Never marry a woman until you have watched her play a round. Be unobtrusive as you do so; the lady's character may well be an open book."

Darwen was one of the many clubs to call on George Lowe, the Lytham St. Annes professional, for advice on how to improve the course, in 1898.

In 1903 the course had expanded to 12 holes and by 1923 it was becoming so busy that the committee sanctioned an increase to 18 holes. It was completed in 1926, with Dick and John Burton doing most of the work, helped by two labourers.

Land was gradually acquired but there was a calamity in 1958 when the National Coal Board started to prospect for open cast coal. Luckily, the idea faded two years later.

Tree planting and other improvements have made the course more attractive and in 1992 a sprinkler system was installed for the greens and approaches.

The course is unusual in that it has only three bunkers. The biggest challenge is on the six par threes.

The club's representation at higher level continues with John Grimshaw, who plays off scratch and is a regular member of the Lancashire team.

FACT FILE

A hilly parkland course of 18 holes, 5727 yards. Par 68. SSS 68. Record 63.

Restrictions: Societies contact the Secretary. No visitors on Monday. Ladies Day Tuesday.

Fees: £13 to £24 - with member £6 and £10.

Dress code: Usual golf attire.

Shop opening: Summer 9am to 7pm; winter 9am to 4pm.

Facilities: (No catering Mondays).

TO THE CLUB

From the M6 via the A59 Blackburn and A666 Darwen, turning right at Lynwood Avenue and left at Duddon Avenue.

Course Information

Hole	Yards	Stroke	Par
1	353	3	4
2	473	6	5
3	332	14	4
4	360	8	4
5	368	12	4
6	131	17	3
7	347	5	4
8	155	16	3
9	363	11	4
10	216	9	3
11	399	1	4
12	155	13	3
13	420	4	4
14	167	18	3
15	395	2	4
16	168	15	3
17	530	7	5
18	395	10	4
OUT	2882		35
IN	2845		33
TOTAL	5727		68

1) A drive slightly left of centre sets up a second shot to the green.

2) Aim the drive to the right - the contours throw shots to the left.

3) Tee shots will again drop to the right. The approach to the three-tier Mackenzie green must be well on or well left.

4) A slight dogleg. Drives to the right will fall left, opening the green.

5) Water is visible from the tee. The shot to the guarded green is usually blind. This becomes No. 6 in 1997 and a new No. 5 opens.

6) A new 'Augusta-style' short hole. Safer to miss on the right. The slope makes putting difficult. This hole becomes No 7. in 1997.

7) Aim to the indicator cross with both shots to the crowned green. This hole becomes No. 8 in 1997.

8) A short, steep uphill par three. It shares No. 1 green until 1997.

9) Drive straight down the left. A deep cleft guards the green on the right.

10) A longish short hole with a green tucked into a corner.

11) A long dogleg par four. A good drive can clear the corner and hit the middle of the fairway.

12) An uphill par three with an obviously difficult bunker on the right.

13) Aim to finish in the bottom right corner of the fairway. The green needs an approach well to the left and is hard to hold.

14) To hold this green tee shots are best slightly left.

15) Two good straight shots are needed. All the problems are visible.

16) Tee shots tend to move forward from the 'steps' before the green.

17) Trees on the right can foul many shots. Keep everything left, particularly the approach to the green.

18) A wide fairway but the drive must clear the water hazard.

Recommended Facilities

SPRINGBANK

WHITEHALL

DARWEN BB3 2JU

TEL: 01254 701595/6

The Whitehall Hotel and Restaurant, one mile south of the town of Darwen and two miles south of Darwen Golf Club, is conveniently situated between the West Pennine Moors and the towns of Bolton and Blackburn. It is ideally placed for access to the Ribble Valley, Lake District, Fylde Coast and North Wales.

The fifteen elegant bedrooms are individually appointed and offer a high standard of personal comfort.

The intimate restaurant compliments traditional English and French cuisine and is a delightful place to dine whatever the occasion.

To add further enjoyment, relax and unwind in our indoor pool with sauna and solarium, or enjoy our three and a half acres of garden and woodland.

A special tariff is offered to golfers of £35.00 single room B & B or £57.00 double room B & B.

DEAN WOOD
Golf Club

Lafford Lane, Up Holland,
Skelmersdale WN8 0QZ.

Secretary: Alan McGregor
01695-622219.
Professional: Tony Coop
01695-622980.

VISITORS never fail to comment that Dean Wood is a course of two distinct halves.

The first nine holes are rolling parkland.

The second nine are more hilly and more varied in character, with some delightful views in summer.

Dean Wood may not claim to be a challenging championship course but the majority of it was the work of James Braid. The constant variety in the holes gives players a full test of their skills.

The popularity of the course is proved by the large proportion of visiting parties who make Dean Wood a permanent entry on their fixture lists.

The club was founded in 1922 but the clubhouse was built in 1989. Members are proud of its welcoming atmosphere and high catering standards.

Just as important to visiting parties is the convenient location. The club is only five minutes from the junction of the M6 and M58.

FACT FILE

An undulating parkland course of 18 holes, 6137 yards. Par 71. SSS 70. Record 66.

Restrictions: Societies contact in writing and visitors phone in advance.

Fees: £24 to £30. With member £8.

Dress code: Usual golf attire.

Shop opening: Dawn till dusk.

Facilities:

TO THE CLUB

From exit 26 of the M6, one and a half miles on the A577 towards Up Holland.

Course Information

Hole	Yards	Stroke	Par
1	367	11	4
2	389	3	4
3	335	13	4
4	157	17	3
5	368	5	4
6	338	15	4
7	514	9	5
8	522	1	5
9	337	7	4
10	157	16	3
11	398	2	4
12	343	14	4
13	358	10	4
14	371	4	4
15	206	12	3
16	192	8	3
17	279	18	4
18	506	6	5
OUT	3327		37
IN	2810		34
TOTAL	6137		71

1) The tee shot must be safe; play to the right.

2) A good driving hole. Play right of the bunker for the best approach to the green.

3) A long, well positioned drive gives an easier approach to the green.

4) This hole needs a precise iron shot to avoid the green bunkers.

5) A straight drive is required on the tree-lined fairway.

6) A good drive is needed on this short par four. Out-of-bounds right.

7) A straight par five with trees both sides of the fairway.

8) Two good wood shots and a short iron to a raised green.

9) Position is needed off the tee; there's a ravine at about 200 yards.

10) Play a good iron shot here. It's out-of-bounds left of the green.

11) A good drive here will set up a long second shot to a raised green.

12) Carry the ravine with a good drive and follow with a mid-iron.

13) This hole demands a straight drive over the guide pole and a second shot over the stream to a raised green.

14) A long drive is called for. There's out-of-bounds left and the second shot is longer than it looks.

15) A good short hole. Out-of-bounds left of the green.

16) The tee shot should carry to the raised green. Any player coming off with seven for 15 and 16 has done well.

17) Seek position off the tee for an easier second shot to a green on the side of a hill.

18) Drive over the guide stick left, to make the second shot easier.

Recommended Facilities

33

DUXBURY PARK
Golf Course/Club

Duxbury Hall Road, Chorley, Lancashire PR7 4AS.

Secretary: Reg Blease
01257-241634.
Professional: Dave Clarke
01257-265380.
Clubhouse: 01257-241378.

DESIGNED by Hawtree and Son and opened in 1977, this municipal course is set in parkland and mature woodland.

The club which plays over the course was formed to coincide with the opening and has grown in status. They are members of the East Lancashire Golf Association, the Lancashire Golf Union and the Manchester Alliance.

In the early years the club held meetings in the local hotel or the cafe adjoining the pro's shop. In 1987 the club leased the old rural studies building in the park and members created a small but welcoming clubhouse.

Duxbury Park is one of the finest municipal layouts in the country and at 6390 yards it offers a good challenge for seasoned players.

To play a course of this standard at modest municipal fees is a real discovery for players not familiar with the area.

The contours, elevated tees and greens, the bunkers and the water hazards on several holes give constant interest and challenge, particularly around the turn when the woods come into play.

The 10th to the 12th offer the hardest challenges with the 17th not far behind in upsetting the card.

The course boasts a practice ground, putting green and cafe.

FACT FILE

An undulating parkland course of 18 holes, 6390 yards. Par 71. SSS 70. Record 66.

Restrictions: Societies may play on weekdays and should first contact the Secretary.

Fees: £6.60 to £8.90.

Dress code: Smart casual.

Shop opening: Summer 7.30am to 8.30pm; winter 7.45am to dusk.

Facilities:

TO THE CLUB

From the M61 exit at junction 6 and follow the A6 to Chorley. Turn left at Wigan Lane and then first right.

Course Information

Hole	Yards	Stroke	Par
1	374	15	4
2	493	7	5
3	231	11	3
4	380	3	4
5	345	13	4
6	513	1	5
7	363	9	4
8	359	5	4
9	164	17	3
10	372	6	4
11	182	14	3
12	387	2	4
13	477	10	5
14	408	8	4
15	187	16	3
16	310	18	4
17	419	4	4
18	416	12	4
OUT	3222		36
IN	3168		35
TOTAL	6390		71

1) A testing par four for any golfer.
2) Most golfers will be happy with a six on this long semi-dogleg.
3) A gentle par three with traps to the left of the green entrance.
4) A semi-dogleg right with two ponds and a guarded green.
5) Beware the two trees left of the fairway and traps right of the green.
6) A long par five with a pond at the end of the second shot.
7) Stay to the left of the fairway. The green is in a cul-de-sac of trees.
8) A good hole for the long hitter.
9) A gentle par three to end the front nine.
10) The Trial. It's not easy for the high handicapper to get across the pond.
11) Ponds left and right so a straight shot is required here.
12) A dogleg left with ponds each side. A marker guides the tee shot.
13) Another dogleg left, with a ditch all along the left of the fairway.
14) A straightforward hole. The practice ground is out-of-bounds left.
15) Fairly easy with a Mackenzie green.
16) Bunkers left and right - and the green slopes.
17) The tee shot is important on this undulating fairway with trees left.
18) A bunker sits at the end of most drives. A pond right and trees to the left.

Recommended Facilities

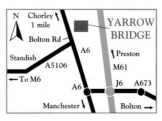

EUXTON PARK
Golf Centre

Euxton Lane, Chorley,
Lancashire PR7 6DL.

Proprietor: Tim Evans
Professional: Mark Tomlinson
01257-261601.

E UXTON Park promotes itself as a centre 'fore all the family' and the slogan neatly sums up the nature of the organisation.

It was conceived as an accessible and fully equipped venue for the first-time golfer.

The first phase, a 30-bay driving range, was opened in 1989. It is floodlit, fully covered and carpeted and also has outdoor tees and grassed practice areas including a bunker.

Alongside the range is an interesting par-three golf course of nine holes, opened in 1993.

The course has features like open ditches, other water hazards and trees. The course is run on a pay-and-play basis with tee-off times bookable at busy periods.

The golf centre has a team of qualified P.G.A. professionals headed by Mark Tomlinson (the Golf World instructor) assisted by Jon Haines, the teaching professional.

Individual tuition is available to golfers of all ages and abilities and there are also group classes for juniors, seniors, ladies, beginners and intermediate golfers. Video tuition is also available.

Another popular feature, aimed at companies, is the fun evening with coffee and biscuits, tuition and a show of trick shots.

A fully stocked golf shop and the Tee-Time cafe are conveniently located for both the driving range and the course. The enterprise was designed and established by father and son Richard and Tim Evans.

FACT FILE

A parkland course of 9 holes, 1181 yards. Par 27.
Restrictions: None.
Shop opening: Weekdays 9.30am/9.30pm, Weekend 7.30am/7.30pm.
Facilities:

 PG DR

TO THE CLUB

M6 motorway junction 28, turn right onto A49, turn left into Euxton Lane.

Course Information

Hole	Yards	Stroke	Par
1	127	4	3
2	182	1	3
3	88	9	3
4	136	2	3
5	140	5	3
6	115	8	3
7	101	7	3
8	142	6	3
9	150	3	3
TOTAL	1181		27

1) A good opening shot is needed to carry the water.

2) The longest hole on the course requires a long, straight shot.

3) A tricky short hole not to be overshot.

4) Carry the ditch and use the greenside bank to advantage.

5) Stay left to avoid the water hazard.

6) A tee shot too long will bring trouble at the back of the green.

7) Water and the greenside bank are the main hazards here.

8) Through the trees, over the ditch and land on the green.

9) There's water at the greenside - and it's not as far away as it seems.

Recommended Facilities

EUXTON PARK is one of the North West's leading practice ranges. It offers all the facilities for the novice golfer to be introduced to the game, plus an ideal facility for established players to develop their skills.

EUXTON LANE, CHORLEY, LANCASHIRE PR7 6DL
TELEPHONE: 01257 261601 OR 01257 233500

OPENING TIMES
WEEKDAYS:
9.30 am. (7.00 am. SUMMER) UNTIL 9.30pm.
WEEKENDS:
8.30 am. (7.00am. SUMMER) UNTIL 7.00 pm.
GOLF COURSE 7am. UNTIL DUSK

EUXTON PARK GOLF CENTRE

FACILITIES

- 30 FLOODLIT BAYS
- PRIVATE TUITION
- TARGET GREENS
- CRAZY GOLF AND PUTTING GREEN
- GOLF SHOP
- HIRE AND TRIAL CLUBS AVAILABLE
- P.G.A. INSTRUCTION INCLUDING VIDEO ANALYSIS
- O.A.P. AND JUNIOR DISCOUNTS
- MEMBERSHIP DISCOUNTS
- CAFE/LOUNGE AREA
- T.V. & VIDEO, GOLF LITERATURE

Lancashire

Brook House Hotel

Set in half an acre, this tastefully modernised 150 year old property offers the visitor

a choice of 20 high standard comfortable rooms all of which enjoy:-

direct dial telephones, satellite TV and video channel, tea/coffee making facilities,

radio, en-suite bath/shower rooms, residents' lounge bar, large private car park.

The hotel is in a semi-rural area within a mile of two golf courses

RAC
Highly
Acclaimed

662, Preston Road, Clayton-le-Woods PR6 7EH
Tel /Fax: 01772 36403

AA
Premier
Selected

FAIRHAVEN
Golf Club

Hall Park Drive, Lytham St. Annes,
Lancashire FY8 4JU.

Secretary: Harold Fielding
01253 736741.
Professional: Brian Plucknett
01253 736976.

THE Fairhaven club, situated a mile from the sea midway between the twin towns of Lytham and St. Annes, recently secured its future by raising £1 million from members to purchase the course from Guardian Assurance.

Established as a golf club in 1895, Fairhaven had two other courses - the first of them sited alongside Fairhaven Lake and the sandhills - before moving to its present location on the edge of Lytham Hall Park in 1924.

The course was originally designed by J. A. Steer and James Braid and was updated by Dave Thomas in 1977. Steer was the professional with the old Blackpool Squires Gate club and Braid had become one of the most prolific golf course designers.

Fairhaven is an 18-hole championship course in an inner and outer nine with the ninth hole adjacent to the clubhouse. This gives players the chance to play only nine holes without any inconvenience.

Basically a flat course, it is not physically demanding, a fact that appeals to many visitors but which also makes it difficult to judge distance. The problem is increased by the pattern on several holes of having bunkers across the fairways some 20 to 40 yards in front of the greens.

There is wildlife on the course, including pheasant, and only two houses are visible - the clubhouse and the well-stocked halfway house donated by Malcolm Hawe in the club's centenary year.

Although the fairways are generous, they are flanked by numerous mounds - sandhills that have become grassed-over - calling for accurate drives to avoid having difficult shots to the well bunkered greens.

The course is normally playable through the winter and has hosted local PGA events both in winter and the playing season.

Qualifying rounds for the Open Championship are held at Fairhaven and, in 1995, there was a full amateur international for the English Golf Union.

Fairhaven's clubhouse, officially opened in 1925, has been kept in character in spite of many improvements. The lounges, dining room, balcony and patio all have unobstructed views of the course and countryside.

Course Information

Hole	Yards	Stroke	Par
1	520	9	5
2	188	7	3
3	508	15	5
4	451	1	4
5	189	17	3
6	381	5	4
7	353	13	4
8	400	3	4
9	362	11	4
10	216	10	3
11	503	12	5
12	381	6	4
13	383	4	4
14	371	2	4
15	500	16	5
16	501	14	5
17	161	8	3
18	515	18	5
OUT	3352		36
IN	3531		38
TOTAL	6883		74

1) A straightforward par five if you can avoid the bunkers.
2) Only a good straight hit with the correct club will do.
3) A drive favouring the right of the fairway shortens this hole.
4) A good drive will still leave a demanding shot to the green.
5) An interesting par three requiring a longish iron.
6) Two good shots will set up a birdie chance at this par four hole.
7) A birdie chance - but this hole is no pushover.
8) One of the best par fours on the course.
9) A drive and a short iron presenting a birdie possibility.
10) A long and testing par three.
11) A good driving hole with out-of-bounds on the right.
12) Again it is the out-of-bounds that presents the main problem from the tee.
13) Judging the approach shot can be tricky on this straightforward hole.
14) This hole also has a difficult approach shot to a green sloping away from the golfer.
15) A good par five with trouble possible on both sides of the fairway.
16) Two good hits should set up the chance of a birdie.
17) Played from a sheltered tee, note should be taken of the wind direction.
18) A good finishing hole that long hitters can reach in two.

Lancashire

Recommended Facilities

FISHWICK HALL
Golf Club

Glenluce Drive, Farringdon Park,
Preston, Lancashire PR1 5TD.

Secretary: R. R. Gearing
01772-798300.
Professional: Steve Bence
01772-795870.

ONE of the Preston area's five golf courses, Fishwick Hall is a parkland course on two levels alongside the River Ribble, handily situated only half a mile from junction 31 of the M6 motorway.

There are fine views up the Ribble Valley and north to the Bowland hills.

A combination of mature woodlands, ponds, streams and the river along its southern boundary make this a picturesque course.

But although easy on the eye, there are some deceptively challenging holes on this course, which has a competition length of 6092 yards.

The club was formed in 1912 and had a nine-hole course until the extension to 18 in 1975.

A recent work programme has seen improvements to several fairways, greens and tees. Early in 1996 the club started a planting programme of 3,600 trees to improve the character of the course.

A well-remembered former professional of the club, Bill Spence, who was at Fishwick Hall for 10 years from the late 1970s, won the PGA Seniors Championship in 1977.

FACT FILE

An undulating parkland course of 18 holes, 6092 yards. Par 70. SSS 69. Record 66.

Restrictions: Visitors and societies contact the Secretary in advance.

Fees: £20 to £25.

Dress code: Usual golf attire.

Shop opening: 8.30am to 7pm. Weekends from 8am.

Facilities:

TO THE CLUB

From junction 31 of the M6 onto the A59 towards Preston for one mile.

Course Information

Hole	Yards	Stroke	Par
1	371	9	4
2	548	13	5
3	416	3	4
4	378	7	4
5	346	11	4
6	140	17	3
7	347	15	4
8	388	5	4
9	450	1	4
10	329	10	4
11	143	16	3
12	346	2	4
13	353	8	4
14	426	6	4
15	517	4	5
16	173	12	3
17	288	14	4
18	143	18	3
OUT	3384		36
IN	2718		34
TOTAL	6092		70

1) A good opening par four bending from left to right.

2) The tee is some 100 feet above the fairway. The shot must carry the first 125 yards. A burn crosses the course and the green is protected.

3) Beware the burn at 260 yards. The elevated green is hard to hit.

4) A dogleg right with a burn at 240 yards and a dangerous green.

5) A carry of 170 yards is needed to set up the second shot.

6) A challenging par three. Bunkers and a pond say: Don't be short!

7) A straight tree-lined par four. Probably the easiest on the course.

8) A testing par four. A good drive leaves a mid-to-long iron approach to a green protected by overhanging trees and bunkers.

9) Stroke index one. A long par four by the river. Don't hook it!

10) A short but dangerous par four. It's better to hit a long iron or short wood leaving 150 yards to the flat green.

11) If you miss the green a par is almost impossible.

12) A difficult tee shot up to the fairway. Watch out for the burn and the awkward Mackenzie green.

13) A split-level fairway makes for a difficult tee shot. Stay right.

14) Drive over a gully to a fairway sloping to the right, leaving a long iron or wood to a long narrow green with bunkers each side.

15) The second shot is critical. It's better to play for the 150 yard marker, leaving a straight approach. A deep gully circles the green.

16) Don't miss this raised green to the left!

17) The chance of a birdie. A good hitter can drive the green.

18) Play an iron over the out-of-bounds to a small Mackenzie green, sloping back to front.

Lancashire

Recommended Facilities

FLEETWOOD
Golf Club

The Golf House, Prince's Way,
Fleetwood, Lancashire FY7 8AF.

Secretary: Roy Yates
01253-773573.
Professional: Stephen McLaughlin
01253-873661.

DESIGNED by James Steer, the Fleetwood course is a typical links and the only one on the Fylde Coast next to the sea.

The 18-hole course was opened in 1932 and is a 'must' for keen golfers.

It offers a challenge with the prevailing winds being a major factor on how the course plays from day to day.

Situated at the end of Fleetwood's Esplanade, it is a very dry and long course with large greens and bunkers galore.

The club is open all year and has a healthy list of visiting players who are attracted by the course and the friendly atmosphere.

The club's open week in August is a popular event, with eight competitions ranging from men's singles to mixed foursomes.

Fleetwood takes pride in the organisation, bringing players from all over the country. There is the great convenience of hundreds of hotels on the Fylde Coast, making the event an ideal tie-in with a family holiday.

The town has many attractions including a famous indoor and outdoor market, the highly acclaimed new Freeport shopping village, a new marina, a pier and other seafront attractions, with summer entertainment at the Marine Hall.

Blackpool's tourist attractions are only ten miles away and will keep families occupied for hours.

FACT FILE

A championship-length links of 18 holes, 6723 yards. Par 72. SSS 72. Record 64.

Restrictions: Societies make contact in advance. No visitors on competition days. Ladies' day Tuesday.

Fees: £20 to £25.

Dress code: Usual golf attire.

Facilities:

TO THE CLUB

At the west end of the Esplanade, a mile from the town centre.

Course Information

Hole	Yards	Stroke	Par
1	315	17	4
2	392	9	4
3	189	11	3
4	416	5	4
5	468	1	4
6	160	15	3
7	443	3	4
8	179	13	3
9	546	7	5
10	530	8	5
11	148	16	3
12	481	10	5
13	430	2	4
14	367	14	4
15	498	12	5
16	431	6	4
17	396	4	4
18	334	18	4
OUT	3108		34
IN	3615		38
TOTAL	6723		72

1) With out-of-bounds left, play safe up the right.
2) Miss the fairway off the tee and you could be approaching a well-bunkered green with a wood.
3) Plays longer than it looks. The sea wall provides some shelter.
4) A new hole and green, this needs an accurate approach.
5) A long par four with a hidden bunker off the tee.
6) Short but well bunkered. The wind dictates the choice of club.
7) A lovely hole with a sandy green to stop the approach shot quickly.
8) Picturesque and well bunkered, with a sloping green.
9) Out-of-bounds left and plenty of bunkers. Green in front of the clubhouse.
10) Sloping fairway, lots of bunkers and a small green with trouble at the back.
11) Miss the green and you're in trouble.
12) An extra 10 yards converted this former par four to a five.
13) Blind tee shot and dogleg left. Pond on the right and well bunkered green.
14) Between the bunkers off the tee. The ground falls away to the right.
15) Ridges on the fairway; humps and hollows each side.
16) A tough par four needing a very good tee shot.
17) The raised green can play longer than it looks.
18) A not-too-long dogleg but accuracy is still needed. Well protected green.

Lancashire

Recommended Facilities

GARSTANG
Golf Club

Garstang Road, Bowgreave,
Garstang, Lancashire PR3 1YE.

Secretary: M. C. Ibison
01995-600100.

ONE of the recent Lancashire golf enterprises, the Garstang course was designed by Richard Bradbeer, the professional at Royal Birkdale. Owned by Tom Ibison, it is a pay-and-play course and is attractively priced.

Designer Bradbeer has allowed the golfer no safety from the River Wyre until the ninth. The sixth green for instance, is tucked into the angle of the River Wyre and the River Calder.

With the two rivers, plus several ponds and a canal to contend with, a fishing net would seem to be an essential part of the big-hitter's golf bag on this course!

If the first nine holes seem to lack length, this is made up from the 11th onwards, starting with the only par five (540 yards) and four par fours of 380 yards or more.

A recent planting programme of more than 8,000 trees and shrubs promises to make it very picturesque and more difficult to play.

The greens are good and not short of interesting features. The final green must be one of the biggest in Lancashire, with fine views of the course.

The Garstang course is part of the Garstang Country Hotel and Golf Course development, which includes a driving range.

As a pay and play course it is accessible to beginners as well as more experienced golfers looking for a change of scene.

The only restriction is that a nine-hole round is not permitted on Saturdays or on Sunday mornings.

FACT FILE

A parkland course of 18 holes, 6050 yards. Par 68. SSS 71.

Restrictions: Societies make arrangements by phone.

Fees: Pay and play £10 and £12. Twilight ticket £6.50.

Dress code: Usual golf attire.

Shop opening: Dawn till dusk.

Facilities:

TO THE CLUB

The course is on the B6430 at Bowgreave, Garstang, reached via the A6 if leaving the motorway at junctions 32 or 33.

Course Information

Hole	Yards	Stroke	Par
1	350	12	4
2	375	8	4
3	180	14	3
4	370	6	4
5	165	18	3
6	425	2	4
7	175	10	3
8	380	4	4
9	320	16	4
10	330	13	4
11	385	9	4
12	540	3	5
13	185	17	3
14	380	11	4
15	445	1	4
16	155	15	3
17	425	7	4
18	465	5	4
OUT	2740		33
IN	3310		35
TOTAL	6050		68

1) A good warm-up hole - straight and open with a two-tier green.

2) A dogleg right with a big tree in the wide fairway.

3) A river on the left and trees on the right converge on the green, giving no margin for error.

4) Tough when windy. The river is still there and the green is small.

5) A very open plan and a small green. The river is on the left.

6) Two rivers join at the big green with two bunkers each side. It's a strong dogleg left and very hard.

7) Another hole that's hard to par, playing across water.

8) A fairly straight hole with a wide fairway and slightly raised green.

9) A straightforward hole with a wide fairway.

10) There's no margin for error on this dogleg left to a corner green.

11) A good hole, dogleg left, with trees and a pond to be negotiated.

12) The only par five, achievable on the wide fairway but - as on many other holes - the trees will eventually change it.

13) A straightforward undemanding hole to enjoy.

14) The river is in play on the left for the last time but it's hard to see until splashdown. The picturesque green is guarded by two bunkers.

15) Stroke index one and hard to par, this hole has an interesting green, wide with two tiers.

16) Some relief after the last hole. Probably the easiest par three.

17) A long uphill par four that some may find as hard as 15.

18) The green is right by the clubhouse. Be careful not to hit the cars or the bystanders!

GATHURST
Golf Club

Miles Lane, Shevington,
Wigan WN6 8EW.
Secretary: Mrs Isabel Fyffe
01257-255235.
Professional: Dave Clarke
01257-254909.
Clubhouse: 01257-252811.

THE upheavals that hit Gathurst Golf Club in the 1950s and 1960s made life difficult for members. But at the same time this Wigan course was producing players who were to bring great credit to the club.

No fewer than five professionals emerged from the junior ranks: David Clarke (currently the pro at Gathurst and also at Duxbury Park); Ian Lee (Haigh Hall), Mark Tomlinson (Euxton Park) and Brian Sharrock.

Pauline Cheetham achieved many successes in amateur golf and Peter K. Abbott became the Lancashire Golf Union first team captain.

Gathurst's 18-hole parkland course is partly a product of the territorial upheavals of the 1950s and 1960s, when the M6 motorway was driven through the old course, followed less than 10 years later by a gas main. The first indication of the road project came from the Ministry of Supply in 1947, the year in which electricity was installed in the clubhouse. The club was struggling to restore the course after the war years and simply stay in existence. Two nearby clubs, Appley Bridge and Standish Park did not survive into the 1950s.

In 1955 it became known that the motorway would bisect every hole except one. Work began in 1959 and compensation of £13,500 was paid, enabling the club to buy some adjoining farmland.

With land on each side of the motorway, the club did a land swap with a neighbouring farmer, who was similarly affected, and the golf designer J. A. Steer, of Blackpool, was engaged to plan a new 12-hole course.

After recovering from the trauma, during which time the members were given the courtesy of the course at Ashton-in-Makerfield Golf Club, the Gathurst club formed itself into a limited company in 1963.

The second bombshell came five years later when the North West gas Board ran a 24-inch main down the entrance drive and through the side of the course, affecting three tees and forcing the seventh green to be moved. Compensation was paltry, so the club sued for loss of profits, settling for £2,000 five years after the event.

Drainage became a problem after the construction work and much remedial work had to be done.

Gathurst was in the news yet again in 1976, when part of the sixth tee vanished down an old mine shaft. There were no casualties - but there is believed to be a second mine shaft in the vicinity.

Gathurst Golf Club was formed in 1913 and for the first nine years existed on a pitifully short nine-hole course until extensions to most holes became possible with a succession of leases and land purchases.

Until the extension to 18 holes in 1995 by golf architect Neville Pearson, the club played over 12.

FACT FILE

A parkland course of 18 holes, 6011 yards. Par 70. SSS 69.

Restrictions: Societies by arrangement with the Secretary except Monday, Wednesday, Saturday and Sunday.
No individual visitors at weekends.

Fees: £20; with member £10.

Dress code: Usual golf attire.

Shop opening: Summer 8am to 6.30pm. Winter 9am to 3pm.

Facilities:

TO THE CLUB

Miles Lane, Shevington is about a mile from junction 27 of the M6.

Course Information

Hole	Yards	Stroke	Par
1	321	17	4
2	439	3	4
3	180	9	3
4	380	7	4
5	492	13	5
6	350	12	4
7	493	11	5
8	155	15	3
9	442	1	4
10	352	6	4
11	316	14	4
12	283	10	4
13	369	8	4
14	188	4	3
15	295	18	4
16	137	16	3
17	377	5	4
18	442	2	4
OUT	3252		36
IN	2759		34
TOTAL	6011		70

1) A tight drive is required to leave a short shot to the green.
2) Again, it's a tight drive downhill, out-of-bounds right and a pond left.
3) A tough uphill par three to a heavily guarded green.
4) An uphill par four with a semi-blind tee shot and a pond short of the green.
5) A downhill dogleg needing a tight tee shot to a green ringed by trees.
6) Uphill - with yet another pond.
7) Trees line the fairway and bunkers are well-placed all the way.
8) A short par three over a pond and through a tunnel of trees.
9) Downhill par four needs accuracy.
10) A good carry over the hill and then a good second shot to the small green.
11) The long-hitter has a chance to drive the green - but don't be wide!
12) Straight between the trees to a small green with one front bunker.
13) An accurate tee shot is vital here.
14) A short par three to a green that slopes away on each side.
15) The fairway slopes to the right and the green is set into the slope.
16) A short par three that must be hit precisely to the right length.
17) A good shot down a tree-lined fairway leaves a mid iron second.
18) A very tough final hole needing two long, accurate shots.

Lancashire

Recommended Facilities

After a day spent sight-seeing, there's no better place to relax or meet up with colleagues and friends than our lounge bar.

Later on perhaps, you can enjoy a meal in Almonds Restaurant, which offers a wide choice of brasserie meals as well as a popular carvery.

MOAT HOUSE

CLUB HEALTH & FITNESS CLUB

WIGAN STANDISH MOAT HOUSE

There is a combination of 122 double, twin, triple, executive and disabled bedrooms. Each comfortable bedroom is provided with, en-suite bathroom/shower, TV with in house movies, hairdryer, trouser press, hospitality tray, laundry and dry cleaning service.

tel: 01257 499988
fax: 01257 427327

Club Moativation, our health and fitness centre is an ideal place to rest, unwind, or tone up a few muscles with:
Heated indoor pool, gym, sauna, sunbeds, steam room, jacuzzi.

GHYLL
Golf Club

Ghyll Brow, Skipton Road,
Barnoldswick, Lancs BB8 6JQ.

Secretary: John Gill.
Clubhouse: 01282-842466.

NOVELS have been written about situations similar to that which exists at this 11-hole club on the border of Lancashire and North Yorkshire.

Nine holes are on the Yorkshire side of the boundary and two recently constructed holes are in Lancashire.

The postal address (shown above) is in Lancashire, via the sorting office at Blackburn. But the club's stationery gives the address as Thornton-in-Craven, Skipton, North Yorkshire.

It could have been worse! When county boundaries were reorganised in 1974, it was intended to transfer the entire club to Lancashire.

Representations were made and a compromise resulted in the new county boundary being drawn along a watercourse named Ghyll Syke, leaving the course on the Yorkshire side.

A dilemma arose in 1994 when the club had the chance to extend the course by two holes on reclaimed land.

Yorkshire members swallowed their pride and accepted the fact that the new land was officially in Lancashire.

They now have the fortunate situation of having 11 holes on the card. The recent holes are listed as 2a and 2b.

Two holes can be taken out of play for repairs or improvements and still leave members with the choice of playing nine or 18 holes.

Ghyll is a small private members' club, founded in 1907, which does not encourage visitors. There is a waiting list for adult membership.

The course is set in scenic country with fine views of the Pennines and Pendle Hill.

FACT FILE

A parkland course of 11 holes with variable yardage. In 1996 played over 5422 yards as 18 holes.

Restrictions: Societies apply in writing. No visitors Tuesday am; Friday after 4.30pm; all day Sunday.

Fees: £14.

Dress code: Usual golf attire.

Facilities:

TO THE CLUB

Opposite the Rolls Royce factory on the road from Barnoldswick to Thornton-in-Craven.

Course Information

Hole	Yards	Stroke	Par
1	188	6	3
2	492	5	5
2a	308	7	4
2b	156	8	3
3	398	2	4
4	430	1	4
5	135	11	3
6	572	3	5
7	219	4	3
8	319	9	4
9	142	10	3
TOTAL	3359		41

1) An uphill hole, with trees each side, to a mounded green.

2) A difficult tree-lined hole with nearly 500 yards of out-of-bounds on the right.

2a) Fairly easy with only a pond left of the green to cause concern.

2b) This one looks easy but watch that stream all down the right side.

3) From the tee it's out-of-bounds on the left and it's not easy to land on the green.

4) Usually played into the wind, this hole has a well bunkered fairway and green.

5) Uphill and fairly easy. Bunkers guard the green.

6) Drive off out of trees for 180 yards, with out-of-bounds right.

7) Uphill and difficult with out-of-bounds left and right.

8) Downhill to a green that slopes to the rear. The out-of-bounds is on both sides.

9) Continuing downhill to a difficult green sloping to the right.

Recommended Facilities

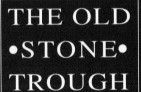

LYTHAM GREEN DRIVE

Golf Club

Ballam Road, Lytham,
Lancashire FY8 4LE.

Secretary: R. Kershaw
01253 737390.
Professional: Andrew Lancaster
01253 737379.

GREEN Drive is an attractive parkland course at Lytham, and is used as a qualifying course for the Open Championships whenever they are held at Royal Lytham and St. Annes.

It is an old established club with excellent facilities which have been enhanced by investment programmes in both course and clubhouse.

Located in 'leafy' Lytham, Green Drive is one of four courses in the area and complements its more illustrious neighbour Royal Lytham, with Fairhaven and St. Annes Old Links giving added variety for golfers.

Green Drive is less than three miles from the M55 motorway. It is within easy reach of Blackpool, whilst offering a tranquil alternative to the hurly-burly of the seaside resort. The course provides a stern challenge for even the most accomplished golfer.

Tight fairways, strategically placed hazards and small, tricky greens are the trademarks.

Meandering through pleasant countryside and flanked by woods, pastures and meadows, the visitor can feel he has arrived in a golfing heaven. But don't be misled by the relatively flat terrain; this course demands accuracy and provides reward or trouble accordingly.

The clubhouse has been the subject of much development in recent years and has extensive bar, lounge and catering facilities.

Green Drive welcomes small and large parties with special all-inclusive golf days available for parties of six or more.

Lytham St. Annes is well served with hotels, guest houses and self catering accommodation and has some fine eating places.

FACT FILE

A parkland course of 18 holes, 6157 yards. Par 70. SSS 69. Record 64.

Restrictions: Visitors and societies enquire in advance. Handicap certificates required. No visitors at weekends.

Fees: £24 to 35, with member £12.

Dress code: Usual golf attire.

Shop opening: Summer 8am to 7pm; winter 8am to 5pm.

Facilities:

TO THE CLUB

The course is on Ballam Road (B5259) a mile inland from Lytham shopping centre.

Course Information

Hole	Yards	Stroke	Par
1	399	6	4
2	274	17	4
3	283	13	4
4	358	7	4
5	519	3	5
6	181	15	3
7	335	11	4
8	354	9	4
9	405	4	4
10	468	2	4
11	345	10	4
12	338	14	4
13	205	16	3
14	443	1	4
15	147	18	3
16	403	5	4
17	201	12	3
18	499	8	5
OUT	3108		36
IN	3049		34
TOTAL	6157		70

1) First tee nerves can bring trouble with out-of-bounds tight right.

2) A medium iron off the tee, laying up short of the stream, leaves a full wedge.

3) A medium to long iron off the tee leaves a full shot to a tiny green.

4) Drive as close to the stream as possible to leave an easier second shot.

5) Trees left and right - so straight driving is needed to tame this hole.

6) A long tricky par three. The onus is on hitting enough club to carry the bunkers.

7) Drive down the left to open up the green for an easier approach shot.

8) Tee to green is easy. The problems lie on a fast sloping green.

9) Drive down the right to have any chance of hitting the green on this dogleg left hole.

10) A long, difficult hole with a tiny green. Play for a bogey and leave happy!

11) A straightforward par four. All the trouble is on the left but the wind can affect the approach.

12) Once the trees on the left and right have been negotiated, the hole becomes easy.

13) A long, tough par three, plays nothing less than a three iron to a well protected green.

14) The toughest on the course. It's a dogleg right with two streams and more than 440 yards.

15) A medium iron, but if you miss the well guarded green, you're dead!

16) Out-of-bounds tight right along to the green. So keep left.

17) Another long par three, always affected by the wind and usually from the left.

18) A great par five with a massive bunker to carry from the tee. There's out-of-bounds tight right and then it gets harder.

Recommended Facilities

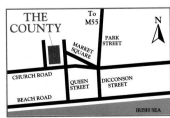

GREAT HARWOOD
Golf Club

Harwood Bar, Whalley Road,
Gt. Harwood, Lancashire BB6 7TE.

Secretary: Alan Clewer
01254-233756.
Clubhouse: 01254-884391.

THE club celebrated its centenary in 1996. But it would have gone out of existence in 1927 but for the enterprise of several members.

For the first 31 years the club occupied land leased from 'the ladies of the manor' at Belmount, to the west of the town.

The original title was Great Harwood and Rishton Golf Club but it was changed in the early 1920s.

The big crisis came in 1927 when the lease was not renewed. A meeting was called to wind up the club but some members asked for a postponement to check out the availability of land at Harwood Bar. The land was acquired and a limited company was formed, 100 shares being issued at £5 and £2,000 was raised through the sale of debentures.

A nine-hole course was laid out on the long-established coal mine of Martholme Pit, owned by Altham Colliery. It was ready for play in July, 1928. The mining connection is remembered in the name of the second hole - Cock Pit.

The Great Harwood course has spectacular views of Pendle Hill and the Forest of Bowland. Its degree of difficulty can be assessed by a par of 73 and SSS of 71. Until recently it was the longest course in the East Lancashire Golf Association.

Every hole is affected by mature trees and the out-of-bounds is present on 12 holes. It is not the course for a hooker of the ball!

The club's first pro, local golfer Maurice Ormerod, who had been the professional at Peel Golf Club, in the Isle of Man, was appointed in 1936.

In June, 1936, an exhibition match was arranged between Maurice Ormerod, Phil Rogers (St. Annes Old) R. Cox (Blackpool North Shore) and Alf Padgham.

The match had been arranged months in advance but as Alf Padgham had won the British Open at Hoylake the day before, it was thought he might not keep the appointment.

Not only did Padgham turn up; he brought the famous Claret Jug and proceeded to break the course record, which still stands.

The photograph of the Open champ with his trophy has pride of place in the clubhouse.

In the 1950s disaster twice hit the club when water pipelines were laid across the course. The fairways were recovering nicely when the process was repeated in 1971.

The club was among the pioneers, in 1965, when holes 4/13, 6/15 and 9/18 were altered so that players drove from different tees. The same was applied later on holes 1/10.

FACT FILE

A flat parkland course of 9 holes, 6411 yards. Par 73. SSS 71. Record 68.

Restrictions: Societies apply in writing. No visitors on Tuesdays or competition days.

Fees: £16 to £22, half with member.

Dress code: Usual golf attire.

Facilities:

TO THE CLUB

The club is on the east side of Great Harwood, on the A680.

Course Information

Hole	Yards	Stroke	Par
1	358	11	4
2	328	15	4
3	378	3	4
4	431	1	4
5	480	7	5
6	184	16	3
7	341	5	4
8	501	9	5
9	186	13	3
10	358	12	4
11	328	14	4
12	378	2	4
13	383	4	4
14	480	8	5
15	169	17	3
16	341	6	4
17	501	10	5
18	286	18	4
OUT	3187		36
IN	3224		37
TOTAL	6411		73

1) This straightforward opener has out-of-bounds down the left and a well bunkered green found through a gap in a line of trees.

2) Out-of-bounds left and a fairway bunker and trees down the right.

3) A dogleg with wooded areas most of the way.

4) A difficult par four due to the large wood out-of-bounds left, a lateral water hazard, trees and a tight green.

5) There's a water hazard at 250 yards and a heavily bunkered green.

6) A longish par three with a big grassy mound catching poor shots.

7) Trees to the left and heavy rough and woods at right demand a good tee shot. Then there's a large dip before the green.

8) A dogleg par five with a large bunker at the elbow. It's out-of-bounds at the left and there are trees all down the right.

9) After a tree-lined fairway there's a heavily bunkered green.

10) This hole is played from a different tee level with the first tee.

11) Similar to the second hole.

12) Similar to the third.

13) This is played from a tee some way forward of the fourth

14) Same as the fifth.

15) A completely different hole due to the change of tee.

16) Same as the seventh.

17) Same as the eighth.

18) The ninth becomes a par four because of the different tee, which makes the drive all-important.

Recommended Facilities

GREEN HAWORTH
Golf Club

Off Willows Lane, Accrington,
Lancashire BB5 3SL.

Secretary: Kevin Lynch
Clubhouse: 01254-237580.

ON a plateau above Accrington, this nine-hole moorland course has a fine panoramic view of the Ribble Valley, the Lancashire Plain, Pendle Hill and the Rossendale Valley.

But although the course is above the 900ft level it is remarkably flat, giving a good test of golf without being physically demanding.

The club was formed in 1914 with 35 members and took on the formidable task of laying out a course on a site that had been used for quarrying stone. The remains of the quarry dominate the course and provide natural hazards that are unique in the East Lancashire area.

The quarry excavation is now a small lake (pictured below) that attracts wildfowl such as mallard and moorhen. In 1995 a pair of Canadian geese took up residence and they returned in 1996 and reared five young.

When played for 18 holes there are alternative tees on four holes.

All the holes are named.

The two best holes on the course are the fourth and fifth. The fourth, named Bedlam, is a short par three, only 129 yards, but it calls for a special tee shot over the lake.

Stroke index one is the fifth, the par four Friarhill which is one of the most difficult in East Lancashire.

A local talking point is the new alternative tee bed at the 17th, nicknamed Fort Apache for its built-up timber base.

In 1995 the club started a tree planting programme and as they mature they will form, along with the heather, a most attractive course. The heather is plentiful and is a sight to behold in August, when it is in full purple bloom.

The club is proud of its new clubhouse, opened in 1992, with a full range of facilities including the ability to cater for up to 180.

The club has received many compliments on the new facilities, which some visitors have rated as the best in East Lancashire.

A leading amateur golfer who learned to play at Green Haworth is Trevor Foster (now a member at Accrington) who had a moment of glory in the 1988 Open Championship when he shared an early lead with Seve Ballesteros, the eventual winner.

FACT FILE

A moorland course of 9 holes, 5556 yards. Par 68. SSS 67. Record 67.

Restrictions: Societies apply in writing. Weekdays before 5pm. No visitors Sundays from March to October.

Fees: £12 to £15, with member £6.

Dress code: Usual golf attire.

Facilities:

TO THE CLUB

Two miles south of Accrington on the A680, turn into Willows Avenue.

Course Information

Hole	Yards	Stroke	Par
1	316	12	4
2	120	18	3
3	422	3	4
4	129	17	3
5	425	1	4
6	185	11	3
7	490	8	5
8	340	6	4
9	367	5	4
10	316	13	4
11	142	15	3
12	402	4	4
13	132	16	3
14	425	2	4
15	185	10	3
16	490	9	5
17	333	7	4
18	337	14	4
OUT	2794		34
IN	2762		34
TOTAL	5556		68

1) An unassuming hole but beware the hazards on this par four opener.

2) A short par three where accuracy is essential.

3) A tight fairway demands a very accurate drive.

4) Another short par three; this one has an intimidating tee shot over the lake, where wildfowl can be seen.

5) The tough one. With hazards left and right, it is difficult to make the par four on Friarhill.

6) A tough hole into the prevailing wind. Out-of-bounds left and right.

7) A good drive on this 490-yarder can bring a birdie chance to the big hitter.

8) A tight green demands accuracy of the second shot.

9) A testing par four with a precise second shot needed to an elevated green.

Lancashire

Recommended Facilities

HERONS REACH
Golf Course

East Park Drive, Blackpool,
Lancashire FY3 8LL.

Manager: Derek Smith
01253-766156.
Professional: Richard Hudson
01253-766156.

BLACKPOOLS first new golf course for 70 years, Heron's Reach was designed by Peter Alliss and Clive Clark. It was opened in 1994 and became part of the De Vere group in 1996.

The golf course and the De Vere Hotel are situated in 236 acres of parkland next to Stanley Park, just over a mile from the resort's famous promenade.

The 18-hole, par 72 championship course of 6431 yards (6257 from the white tees) was built to exacting standards with special USGA green construction promising all-year play. Stroke one is the 14th, not long from the white and yellow tees but calling for an excellent long second shot into the well guarded green.

Stroke two is one of the holes on which the golfer has the novelty of aiming a drive at Blackpool Tower, into the prevailing wind that seems a fixture on the Fylde Coast, and having a couple of lakes to contend with. The layout incorporates 10 lakes and has the scenic backdrop of the lush Fylde countryside, with two windmills in view and the Bleasdale Fells in the distance.

Attached to the development are an 18-bay driving range, putting green, chipping green and golf and leisure shop. There is a wide choice of leisure facilities at the De Vere, including a 21-metre swimming pool, jacuzzi, sauna, aerobic studio, gymnasium and squash and tennis courts. The addition of Heron's Reach to the local golfing scene has certainly gone some way to balancing the resort's inferiority to its illustrious neighbour, Lytham St. Annes.

FACT FILE

An undulating links-style course of 18 holes, 6257 yards. Par 72. SSS 70. Record 68.

Restrictions: Societies must book in advance

Fees: £20 to £30.

Dress code: Usual golf attire.

Shop opening: Summer 7am to 7pm, winter 8am to 6pm.

Facilities:

TO THE CLUB

From junction 4 of the M55, follow the signs for Blackpool Zoo.

Course Information

Hole	Yards	Stroke	Par
1	372	6	4
2	254	18	4
3	486	8	5
4	184	14	3
5	504	16	5
6	397	10	4
7	395	4	4
8	174	12	3
9	445	2	4
10	482	11	5
11	387	9	4
12	153	17	3
13	308	13	4
14	372	3	4
15	424	1	4
16	167	5	3
17	277	15	4
18	476	7	5
OUT	3211		36
IN	3046		36
TOTAL	6257		72

1) The lake on this hole hides behind the right hand fairway bunkers. Keep the drive down the left.

2) This is a difficult green to read; the birdie chance that got away?

3) A par five will please all but the longest hitter.

4) The uphill tee shot requires one more club than many think.

5) A fine hole with a narrow fairway. Par here will satisfy most.

6) One for the big hitter to relish. But the green's hidden slopes have to be overcome to gain the par.

7) Three well sited bunkers make this a most challenging hole.

8) The lake dominates this par three hole. A well struck shot with plenty of carry must hit the green first time.

9) Aim a drive at Blackpool Tower! The big hitter has the advantage.

10) A long, straight hole with a narrow fairway.

11) Downhill but beware. A 220 yard drive to the corner of the dogleg is what is needed.

12) A three-tier tee! But a controlled shot is a must on this short hole.

13) With two lakes on the left an accurate drive is required.

14) The toughest hole. 200 yards of water in front of the tee. A long second shot to the guarded green. Get a par and feel like a pro!

15) Accuracy and length from the tee are paramount. It's out-of-bounds right and there's a lake for the last 100 yards on the left.

16) Another lake and out-of-bounds. This hole can be short and bitter.

17) A big ditch crosses the fairway at 180 yards. Decision time!

18) Out-of-bounds right but this par five has a generous green.

Recommended Facilities

— THE —
DE VERE
BLACKPOOL
★ ★ ★ ★

East Park Drive, Blackpool, Lancashire FY3 8LL
Tel: **01253 838866** *Fax*: **01253 798800**

The De Vere Hotel, Blackpool, is for anyone who takes their leisure seriously. Indoors is the Leisure Club, with snooker, 21m pool, gym, squash, fitness and aerobics studio, spa, sauna, steam room and sun shower. Moving outdoors there are floodlit tennis courts, 18 bay driving range and of course Heron's Reach - our famous par 72 championship golf course designed by Peter Allis and Clive Clark. One of the UK's great golfing experiences, the testing layout incorporates 10 lakes while the USGA green construction promises superb all year round play.

HEYSHAM
Golf Club

Trumacar Park, Middleton Road,
Heysham, Lancashire LA3 3JH.

Secretary: Fred Bland
01524-851011.
Professional: Ryan Done
01524-852000.

ALTHOUGH it is only a short distance from the sea, the Heysham course is not a links but a very fertile grassland.

It does, however, have one of the challenges of the typical links - the almost ever-present prevailing wind coming off the water, in Heysham's case from the south west.

The course was laid out in 1929 by the noted firm of Hawtree and J. H. Taylor Ltd., under the supervision of Alec Herd.

It is a fair course, with all the greens visible for the second shot.

The clubhouse was built in 1936 and has been enlarged over the years to include changing rooms and a dining room with catering available seven days a week.

From the front of the clubhouse there is a panoramic view of the Lune Estuary and Lune Deeps.

Blackpool Tower shows up prominently to the south.

From the elevated part of the course there are magnificent views across Morecambe Bay to the Lakeland hills in the north and the Pennines in the east.

On clear days the North Wales coast is visible to the south west.

Rather more dominating is the Heysham nuclear power station, which makes a massive backdrop to the fourth green and looms into view elsewhere.

An unusual feature of Heysham is the number of par four holes of more than 400 yards, there are seven.

The club has an on-going policy of tree planting and tee improvements. In the last two years about 4,000 trees and shrubs have been put in, making it much more picturesque.

On the playing side, the club has strong juniors' and ladies' sections.

Course Information			
Hole	Yards	Stroke	Par
1	429	4	4
2	321	12	4
3	144	18	3
4	495	9	5
5	166	16	3
6	432	2	4
7	381	8	4
8	335	14	4
9	331	10	4
10	416	3	4
11	127	17	3
12	420	7	4
13	194	11	3
14	431	5	4
15	447	1	4
16	157	15	3
17	332	13	4
18	423	6	4
OUT	3034		35
IN	2947		33
TOTAL	5981		68

1) Aim towards the shed for the best route into the hole.

2) The green is ringed by trees with a picturesque approach. Don't go too far left.

3) A short par three with a tilting green. Bunkers and bumps abound.

4) A classic 500-yarder uphill with a large green to land on!

5) The tee shot is over water onto a fairly open fairway. Be straight!

6) Fairly open but pay regard to the slope, which takes the ball towards the out-of-bounds at the left.

7) A nice long green to aim at. If you hit wires, play the shot again.

8) Up to the highest point on the course, with fine views.

9) It's out-of-bounds to the right and the back of the green.

10) A long, cruel par four! Aim high and right from the tee shot.

11) At last a short hole! It has a rising, double-terraced green with bunkers on each side.

12) Downhill to a lake, then up to the hole. The green is reachable in two if you want to get wet.

13) A long par three with a raised green but little trouble.

14) A slight dogleg left. Take one club more on the second shot.

15) Without doubt the hardest on the course. Don't expect to reach in two.

16) Watch out for that small pond to the left of the green.

17) In the prevailing wind, be wary of the bunkers short of the green.

18) A testing hole to finish; the seventh par four of more than 400 yards.

Lancashire

Recommended Facilities

HOUGHWOOD
Golf Club

Billinge Hill, Crank, near
Wigan WN5 7UA.

Secretary: Mrs. Trish Valentine
01744-894444 (Fax same).
Professional: Dave Clarke
01744-894444 (Fax 894440).

THERE are not many golf courses in the North of England with south-facing views like the panorama from Houghwood.

On a clear day, ships can be seen entering and leaving Liverpool, while the Welsh mountains form the back drop a little to the east.

Houghwood Golf Club opened on May 1, 1996, and due to the excellent natural drainage and the high specification of course construction, the grass quickly matured.

The course was planned by Neville Pearson of ADAS, with the greens being built on the guidelines of the USGA. The greens are designed to absorb much heavier rainfall than is usual in the north of England.

The contouring of the putting surfaces is extremely creative and is in perfect contrast to the undulating site.

This course is one of the few recent developments that allows the average golfer the chance to make a few pars, whilst at the same time testing his ability to position the ball and test his nerve. Off the back tees, holes seven and 13 are colossal, requiring the most accurate of shots.

The clubhouse is centrally located within the course and therefore has fine views from the bar, restaurant and society room. There is no 'collar and tie' rule in the clubhouse but smart casual dress is necessary.

The number of members has been limited in order to allow some high quality 'pay as you play.' It should be stressed that Houghwood is not a beginner's course and anyone not able to play to a respectable standard is asked to remain at the local municipal course.

The element of 'pay as you play' here is reserved for discerning golfers who are tired of poor etiquette and five-hour rounds!

FACT FILE

A parkland course of 18 holes, 5902 yards. Par 70, SSS 70.
Restrictions: Societies and vistors phone in advance.
Fees: £12 to £15.
Dress code: Usual golf attire.
Shop opening: Dawn till dusk.
Facilities:

TO THE CLUB

From Junction 23 of the M6 take the East Lancashire Road (A580) to the A570 and then follow the signs.

Course Information

Hole	Yards	Stroke	Par
1	367	16	4
2	122	15	3
3	324	10	4
4	147	12	3
5	366	7	4
6	337	14	4
7	341	6	4
8	165	11	3
9	409	2	4
10	169	9	3
11	525	4	5
12	308	18	4
13	524	1	5
14	355	5	4
15	437	3	4
16	186	13	3
17	505	8	5
18	315	17	4
OUT	2578		33
IN	3324		37
TOTAL	5902		70

1) A drive and pitch hole.
2) A subtle par three hole with superb shaping round the green.
3) A good drive and a simple mid iron second shot into a two-level green.
4) An attractive par three.
5) One of the medium length holes where there is a bit of space off the tee.
6) Stay out of trouble down the right and a birdie is for the taking.
7) A difficult par four.
8) Probably the easiest par three - you should make par here.
9) A good tee shot down the right will run and you can reach the green in two.
10) A par three that must be played from the left to avoid big trouble.
11) What a par five! Be sure to keep the second shot up the left.
12) You may get up with a tee shot. If not, there are 17 bunkers waiting.
13) Another cracking par five. Even the pros won't try it in two.
14) Favour the right and try to chase the ball along a bit.
15) The toughest on the course. Anyone who gets up in two should tell the pro.
16) Think carefully about club selection on this downhill par three.
17) A steep dogleg left. Watch those bunkers near the green.
18) A dogleg to the right - with water stick high on the left near the green.

Recommended Facilities

HURLSTON HALL
Golf Club

Hurlston Lane,
Scarisbrick,
Lancashire L40 8JD.

General Manager (Clubhouse):
01704-840400 (Fax 01704-841404).
Bookings and Shop:
01704-841120.
Director of Golf: Gerry Bond.

THE newest golf club in the West Lancashire area, Hurlston Hall's undulating parkland course was designed by Donald Steel and opened in 1994.

Hurlston Hall has been designated the official Regional Training Centre for Juniors by the English Golf Union. The adjacent golf centre has an 18-bay driving range and separate teaching bays.

Set in 135 acres of beautiful parkland six miles from Southport, the 18-hole course has the focal point of a luxurious Colonial-style clubhouse.

The course is gently undulating and has views across the Lancashire plain to the Pennines and the Bowland Fells.

Two brooks meander across the course. The main brook, the Hurlston, creates a shallow valley through the course and is in play on seven holes, with three greens set on its banks. The second brook joins Hurlston close to the first green and water presents a challenge in the form of seven lakes.

The course has three par fives of more than 500 yards and none of the short holes are actually short!

All the holes are named and some are local talking points - such as Jim's Billabong, Cromwell's Table, Diglake Creek and Bane of Hurlston.

The course record of 70 was set by Mike Hollingworth, the Denton pro, in June 1995.

All the seven and five-day playing memberships were soon full but house, social and corporate memberships are available.

FACT FILE

A parkland course of 18 holes, 6746 yards. Par 72. SSS 72. Record 70.

Restrictions: Only registered societies can book to play the course. Visitors book in advance. Handicap certificates required.

Fees: £25 to £35; with member £12.50.

Dress code: Usual golf attire.

Shop opening: 8am to 8pm in summer.

Facilities:

TO THE CLUB

On the A470, two miles from Ormskirk, six miles from Southport.

Course Information

Hole	Yards	Stroke	Par
1	414	6	4
2	170	18	3
3	355	12	4
4	379	14	4
5	422	8	4
6	463	2	5
7	211	16	3
8	507	4	5
9	407	10	4
10	429	7	4
11	552	1	5
12	206	15	3
13	383	5	4
14	359	13	4
15	430	3	4
16	172	17	3
17	377	11	4
18	510	9	5
OUT	3328		36
IN	3418		36
TOTAL	6746		72

1) Sweeping gently right, the fairway narrows into a sloping green.

2) A nice par three, over the largest lake and Hurlston Brook, to a three-tier green with bunkers front left and right.

3) A small lake in front of the green makes this a short par four.

4) With fine views from the tee, the hole sweeps left to an undulating green protected by mounds.

5) Spectacular! A brook enters half-way and meanders up the fairway.

6) A tight fairway with gorse and broom both sides. Play for safety.

7) A very hard par three. Bunkers dictate you must hit the green.

8) A great par five, downhill over a brook and two lakes into a huge but narrow green.

9) Hurlston Brook is in front of a narrow green, sloping backwards.

10) A gap in the trees, two lakes, a huge raised, sloping, undulating green. Everyone will remember this hole.

11) A good drive to the right is needed on the longest par five.

12) A par three to challenge all. A deep valley runs around the rear and left of a large green that demands good putting.

13) Mounds block out the green from the tee and bunkers stand guard.

14) There's a ditch at 200 yards and the fairway switches right and left into the fiercely guarded green.

15) You could have a 45 yard putt on this green!

16) Another massive green that could become a legend with its slopes.

17) A tight dogleg right through trees and uphill to a sloping green.

18) This is Ruth's Surprise. A finishing hole to remember.

Lancashire

Recommended Facilities

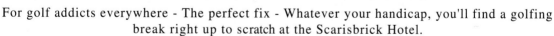

INGOL
Golf Club

Tanterton Hall Road, Ingol,
Preston, Lancashire PR2 7BY.

Secretary: Peter Marshall:
01772-734556.
Professional: Peter Laycock
01772-734556.

INGOL'S course is set in 250 acres of lovely parkland and yet it is only five minutes from junction 32 of the M6 and 25 minutes from the bright lights of Blackpool.

The club was opened in May 1981, by golfing legend Sir Henry Cotton, who was co-designer with Michael Bonallack.

Originally built as a championship course, it is now reduced to around 6300 yards due to the proximity of houses to some of the early holes.

A major development programme was under way in 1996 with better drainage and new tees due to be followed by work to improve the bunkers.

Greenkeeper Andrew Turnbull, a former assistant greenkeeper at Wentworth, reckons Ingol is the most challenging course in the Preston area. It is a meandering loop with a tough front nine, very tight at the third and fourth, and a picturesque back nine 'out in the country' where the 15th and 17th cause the most concern.

Accurate tee shots are called for throughout as there are expanses of rough and many mature trees.

Ingol is geared to welcome societies and corporate groups and the facilities include a driving range, a practice ground and two squash courts.

The complex was acquired from the original management by Tee Jay Leisure Ltd., who own Lingfield Park racecourse and golf course.

Ingol members enjoy reduced fees when visiting Lingfield.

FACT FILE

A parkland course of 18 holes, 6300 yards. Par 72. SSS 70.

Restrictions: Societies apply in writing; visitors by phone.

Fees: £15 to £25, with member £10.

Dress code: Usual golf attire.

Shop opening: Dawn till dusk.

Facilities:

TO THE CLUB

The course is on the B5411, one mile south west of junction 32 of the M6 (M55).

Course Information

Hole	Yards	Stroke	Par
1	364	13	4
2	400	1	4
3	353	11	4
4	164	17	3
5	273	15	4
6	513	3	5
7	545	5	5
8	382	7	4
9	465	9	5
10	360	12	4
11	291	16	4
12	157	18	3
13	394	4	4
14	188	14	3
15	527	2	5
16	214	6	3
17	356	10	4
18	354	8	4
OUT	3459		38
IN	2841		34
TOTAL	6300		72

1) Drive at the large tree right. Out-of-bounds all along the left.

2) A straight drive is needed here. It's out-of-bounds left and right.

3) The brave take a driver; but for safety play an iron off the tee.

4) The distance on this par three is deceiving. Ignore the great view!

5) A new tee has made this hole more challenging. Beware of the ditch.

6) A long hole that needs to be played left to centre.

7) The longest hole on the course. Aiming left can give the shortest line but be careful of the out-of-bounds on both sides.

8) The tee shot must be straight to set up the long second shot.

9) Play for safety with a long iron off the tee and there may be the chance of a birdie.

10) Concentrate on hitting the fairway. To miss could be expensive.

11) This par four is driveable in one, but for safety it's better to take the left hand route.

12) The correct choice of club should avoid disaster on this par three.

13) Drive left of the bunker. Try to carry the second shot all the way.

14) A straightforward hole but there are many fours taken here.

15) Drive at the steeple in the distance and be careful of the out-of-bounds all along the right.

16) Miss the green at your peril! A bunker waits on the right and it's out-of-bounds all down the left.

17) Aim left of the big tree to gain an easy approach.

18) A good finishing hole. Drive just short of the large trees and beware the pond with your second.

Lancashire

Recommended Facilities

KNOTT END
Golf Club

Wyreside, Knott End, near
Blackpool, Lancashire FY6 0AA.

Secretary: Keith Butcher
01253-810576.
Professional: Paul Walker
01253-811365.

IT may be off the beaten track, out on the end of the peninsula on the northern side of the River Wyre, but Knott End is well worth the trip.

Out on the estuary the wind seems ever-present and that's the challenge of Knott End, coupled with the guile of the legendary golf course architect James Braid, who was engaged in 1921 to reshape the course, which suffered from having too many short par fours.

Braid sized up the course by going round with a mashie - today's five iron - and instinctively knew what was needed.

He asked the club to buy a piece of adjacent land, known as the bottom field, which enabled him to relocate the 11th and 12th holes and re-jig half the course, adding about 400 yards in the exercise.

A focal point is Braid's Bunker, a large sandtrap sitting between the third and 16th fairways.

The course was partly redesigned in 1975, when three new greens were put in under the supervision of the club's technical consultant Jim Arthur, who was also an agronomist employed by the R. and A.

Knott End's third, fourth and fifth holes run alongside the river, which provides the ultimate punishment for a sliced shot if the tide is in.

The best views are from the third tee where the panorama from left to right takes in Morecambe Bay, the Furness Peninsula and Lakeland mountains, the flat top of Ingleborough and the Pennine chain.

The club has taken a commercial stance in providing a first class golf day out for visitors and societies.

The club professional, Paul Walker, was runner-up in 1995 in the Vaux Sunderland Masters, one of the north's top events.

FACT FILE

A links/parkland course of 18 holes, 5789 yards. Par 69. SSS 68. Record 63.

Restrictions: Societies and visitors contact the Secretary by phone.

Fees: £20 to £26, with member £9 and £10.

Dress code: Usual golf attire.

Shop opening: Summer 7.30am to 8.30pm; winter 9am to 5pm.

Facilities:

TO THE CLUB

From the M55 exit at junction 3 and follow the A585 and A588. From the Blackpool area the A586 and A588. From the Lancaster area the A588.

Course Information

Hole	Yards	Stroke	Par
1	328	17	4
2	216	5	3
3	334	11	4
4	268	15	4
5	393	3	4
6	530	7	5
7	548	1	5
8	152	13	3
9	310	9	4
10	371	6	4
11	119	18	3
12	341	10	4
13	340	8	4
14	179	14	3
15	186	12	3
16	415	2	4
17	306	16	4
18	453	4	4
OUT	3079		36
IN	2710		33
TOTAL	5789		69

1) A good test to start, with the river at right and the green in a hollow.

2) A par three playing towards a raised green with the river behind.

3) The river is on the right and the sloping green makes this hole more difficult than it looks.

4) A short uphill par four hole with the river still to the right.

5) On this last hole alongside the river, a good accurate drive is needed to set up the approach to a raised green.

6) A par five downhill with trouble waiting behind the green.

7) With out-of-bounds right and a pond at driving range, this is a difficult one.

8) A short par three with cross bunkers before the green.

9) A good drive over the fairway ridge leaves a short iron to the green.

10) From an elevated tee, drive between tall trees to a guarded green.

11) A hole to remember! A very short iron to a green that has a stream and out-of-bounds behind it.

12) Keep left of the lateral water hazard. The green is nice and flat.

13) Drive up to a slight rise. The green is partly hidden.

14) An uphill par three needing accuracy and good club selection.

15) A downhill par three over scrub to a sloping green.

16) A difficult par four. Keep well clear of the wood at the right.

17) A downhill par four - one of the easiest for the average player.

18) Only a long accurate drive will get you up in two.

Recommended Facilities

Singleton Lodge

COUNTRY HOUSE
—— HOTEL ——

Lodge Lane, Singleton,
Nr. Blackpool. FY6 8LT
tel.: 01253 883854
fax.: 01253 894432

Alan and Anne Smith extend you a warm hearted welcome to their country house, built in 1702 and set in five acres of peaceful gardens.

Sample our superb new a la carte menu, or select from our excellent table d'hote.

Singleton Lodge is the ideal venue for your conference, offering secluded privacy and excellent accommodation. Golfing parties, Wedding receptions, Christenings and private functions are given meticulous attention.

Each comfortable bedroom is individually styled and tastefully furnished.

For the golf minded, you will find fourteen 18-hole golf gourses (including Royal Lytham) that are only 20 minutes drive from our front door.

LANCASTER
Golf and
Country Club

Ashton Hall, Ashton-with-Stodday, Lancaster, Lancashire LA2 0AJ.

Secretary: Duncan Palmer
01524-751247.
Professional: David Sutcliffe
01524-751802.

THERE can't be many more historic or impressive club-houses in the country than the one that dominates this club.

Ashton Hall, with its medieval tower and adjoining Gothic-style main building, is steeped in tradition and history and has played host to many a royal visitor down the centuries.

James I held court here one night in August 1617, and bestowed knighthoods on two of his citizens.

The tenth Duke of Hamilton got into debt gambling and had to sell the estate in 1853. Three years later the new owner, a Mr. Starkie, rebuilt the hall in Gothic style.

In 1884 the property was bought by James Williamson, the MP for Lancaster who later became Lord Ashton.

When he died in 1931 the Pye family bought the property, and leased it to the Lancaster Golf Club the following year, when the course was laid out to James Braid's meticulous design.

After many unsuccessful attempts, the golf club finally purchased the hall and course in July 1993, securing the future.

The club had three courses before moving to Ashton Hall. The first was opened in 1889 at Cockerham, six miles south west of Lancaster, but the club moved in 1901 to Scale Hall, between Lancaster and Morecambe.

Only four years later a syndicate of local golfers financed the rental of a farm known as Dolphinlee, just north east of Lancaster. This is now the home of Lansil Golf Club.

Ashton Hall is set in lovely parkland on the Lune estuary, two miles south of the city.

The northern backdrop to the course is provided by the Lakeland hills, with heather clad hills to the east. It is perfectly situated to enjoy the changing seasons.

The course demands maximum concentration, especially on the superb dogleg ninth hole and on the daunting elevated 18th tee to the final green below.

The setting lends itself to the grand occasion and the club plays host each year to the regional finals of the Famous Grouse Shotgun Foursomes and the Benson and Hedges Club Champions.

From March to October, Dormy House facilities are available in the wonderful ambience of Ashton Hall.

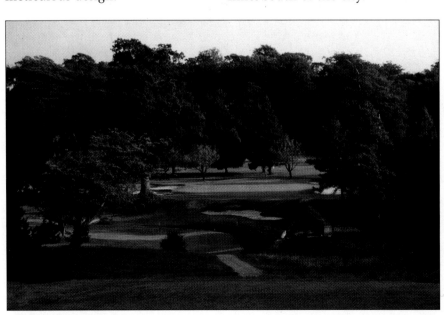

FACT FILE

A parkland course of 18 holes, 6465 yards. Par 71. SSS 71. Record 66.

Restrictions: Visitors and societies Monday to Friday only by prior arrangement. Must have handicap certificates.

Fees: £28 - with member £10.

Dress code: Usual golf attire.

Shop opening: Dawn till dusk.

Facilities:

TO THE CLUB

From junction 33 of the M6 to the A588, two miles south of Lancaster.

Course Information			
Hole	Yards	Stroke	Par
1	419	3	4
2	508	11	5
3	425	1	4
4	166	17	3
5	358	9	4
6	175	15	3
7	365	13	4
8	415	5	4
9	385	7	4
10	397	6	4
11	482	12	5
12	396	4	4
13	142	18	3
14	528	10	5
15	388	8	4
16	300	14	4
17	437	2	4
18	179	16	3
OUT	3216		35
IN	3249		36
TOTAL	6465		71

1) This tough opening hole, a gradual uphill dogleg right, demands two first class shots to reach the green.

2) Uphill after the drive with plenty of trouble along the way.

3) A drive downhill to the left of the fairway, which slopes right.

4) An accurate mid-iron shot is vital to the heavily guarded green.

5) A drive to the right opens the dogleg to a sloping green, which needs more club than it appears.

6) Normally played down wind. Miss the green and hit sand!

7) A gentle dogleg right needs a tee shot to the left of the fairway to avoid strategically placed bunkers.

8) Beware the out-of-bounds and heavily bunkered green.

9) A magnificent hole. A blind drive over the marker post will prevent the golfer being cut off to the green, above and beyond the stream.

10) A solid second shot is a must on this gradual uphill par four.

11) A moderate par five, also slightly uphill, with sand and trees.

12) A fine hole with panoramic views. A straight drive along the hogback leaves a medium iron to a green where the trouble is at the front.

13) A tricky short hole not to be taken lightly.

14) The longest hole, played along a sloping fairway. Avoid those bunkers before descending slightly to the green.

15) A charming tree-lined hole. The green needs some reading!

16) Drive at the marker post. Trouble is out of sight, on both sides.

17) A central drive escapes the fairway bunker. So far, so good!

18) One of the finest par threes anywhere in the country, with a daunting view from the tee. No prizes for being short.

Recommended Facilities

LANSIL
Golf Club

Caton Road, Lancaster,
Lancashire LA1 3PD.

Secretary: Jim McIntyre
01524-823732.
Clubhouse: 01524-39269.

THE Lansil club inherited the 18-hole course vacated by Lancaster Golf Club in their move to Ashton Hall in the early 1930s.

But today, Lansil has only nine holes. The other nine were lost in the building of the M6 motorway and although the club hopes to expand if an opportunity arises, there is nothing currently in prospect.

The golf course, beautifully mature for many decades, has recently seen improvements to tees and a general enhancement of the course.

It has some excellent holes and if the majority of the greens are quite small they are also firm and in pristine condition.

The second hole is the most talked-about. It is tight all the way from the tee and the 500 yards will seem a long haul if wayward shots are made.

The most spectacular is the seventh, along a ridge at the highest point, with fine views down the River Lune and across to the Lake District.

Lansil is not only a golf club; it also has bowling, fishing and football sections.

Course Information

Hole	Yards	Stroke	Par
1	305	13	4
2	507	3	5
3	111	17	3
4	320	9	4
5	219	7	3
6	308	11	4
7	502	1	5
8	141	15	3
9	391	5	4
10	305	14	4
11	507	4	5
12	111	18	3
13	320	10	4
14	219	8	3
15	308	12	4
16	502	2	5
17	141	16	3
18	391	6	4
OUT	2804		35
IN	2804		35
TOTAL	5608		70

1) A tee shot across a football pitch to an elevated green with bunkers and a steep bank to the left that can ruin an approach shot.

2) The par five, slight left dogleg, tree-lined all the way, ends on a sloping green with sand traps front and trees at the back.

3) A very short hole cut through trees to a fast, undulating green.

4) Built into a hill and sloping severely to the right, the green can only be seen if the tee shot clears the huge depression.

5) A long par three with out-of-bounds tight along the left and the terrain sloping away to the right.

6) Relatively straightforward but the ground drops away steeply at the right of the green.

7) Out-of-bounds all along the left for this long hole, with the ground again sloping away to the right

8) A downhill drive to an elevated green with no chance of a par if too long or off line.

9) A good driving hole to finish but the fairway slopes towards the canal at the left.

Recommended Facilities

The Channings

The Channings is a tastefully modernised Victorian building. 20 en-suite rooms all with colour TV and tea/coffee making facilities. Well stocked bar.

The Channings is situated on the Promenade directly opposite Bare Pool and close to Happy Mount Park, where various sports can be enjoyed, and of course, the adjacent golf club only 500 yards from the hotel. The Lake District is on our doorstep with Lake Windermere a 40 minute drive away.

Promenade, Bare, Morecambe Bay, Lancashire LA4 6AD.
Telephone: 01524 417925

LEYLAND
Golf Club

Wigan Road, Leyland,
Lancashire PR5 2UD.

Secretary: John Ross
01772-436457.
Professional: Colin Burgess
01772-423425.

THE Leyland club was started in 1923 by a group of local business people who won support at a public meeting.

About 60 acres of marshy farmland was rented between the A49 and Bryning Brook and hundreds of tons of burnt foundry sand was dumped into the wetter sections.

Voluntary labour shaped the first three holes, followed by two more groups of three.

Four ex-army huts were bought cheaply and assembled on the crosslock principal.

But Leyland's arrival in the world of golf was problematic. The club struggled to keep the course and the clubhouse going.

They met the problem by inviting a limited number of artisans to use the course in return for maintenance work.

This arrangement continued until 1939 when the course was taken over by the military. After the war the club encouraged younger people who brought in a more competitive attitude.

The youngsters took off their jackets and helped improve the course and replaced the old army huts. Membership rocketed and for the first time the club had a waiting list.

The course was extended to 15 holes in the late 1950s, and finally, to 18 holes in the early 1970s.

Although they were not involved in the design, Peter Alliss and Dave Thomas formally opened the 'new' course in 1974 and played an exhibition match with two of Leyland's low-handicap players, Harry Parr and George Norris, who won the day.

Development of the club continued with the handsome new clubhouse in 1994 and further projects are being considered by the club for the 75th anniversary in 1998.

Course Information

Hole	Yards	Stroke	Par
1	405	2	4
2	412	4	4
3	153	18	3
4	169	14	3
5	511	10	5
6	375	8	4
7	365	6	4
8	279	16	4
9	330	12	4
10	170	17	3
11	451	1	4
12	382	7	4
13	324	11	4
14	179	15	3
15	343	13	4
16	523	5	5
17	397	3	4
18	355	9	4
OUT	2999		35
IN	3124		35
TOTAL	6123		70

1) A tough starter; out-of-bounds right and a hard-to-hit plateau green.

2) A 412-yarder usually played against the wind, with out-of-bounds near the green.

3) Just 153 yards going downhill. Don't go through the back.

4) This hole plays longer than it looks and is heavily bunkered.

5) Beware the dreaded ditch! If your drive is not long, lay up short of the green.

6) The fairway slopes right to left. A short to medium iron second shot.

7) On this sloping, elevated green two putts from past the flag is good.

8) Lay up short of the ditch or go for it with a driver.

9) Avoid the ditch and bunkers down the right and it's easy!

10) A downhill par three to a Mackenzie green.

11) Two big hits to the green - then try to judge the slope.

12) On this good par four aim the tee shot at the fairway bunker with draw on.

13) A short par four. A three iron off the tee leaves a seven or eight to a large green.

14) Trees down the right and a pond left of the green demands a good shot but don't be big.

15) A dogleg best played with a three iron off the tee.

16) A long hole against the wind with out-of-bounds on the left.

17) Another hard hole in the wind. Avoid the ditch on the right at tee shot distance.

18) Lay up short of the pond leaving a seven iron to the long green.

Lancashire

Recommended Facilities

LOBDEN
Golf Club

Whitworth, Rochdale,
Lancashire OL12 8XJ.
Secretary: N. Danby
01706-43241.

GOLF has been played at Lobden since 1888. It is the second oldest nine-hole course in England.

Situated on high moorland over-looking Rochdale, after which it was first named, the club claims to have the highest tee-bed (the sixth) in Lancashire.

On fine days there are outstanding views from the course.

The original meeting to form the club was held in February, 1888, but 18 years later there was a split.

A group of members took the club name of Rochdale Golf Club to start a new course while the remaining members kept the nine-hole course and changed its name.

The trophies were shared between the two clubs and Lobden, as the original course, kept the minute books. All but the first book still exist.

The two clubs have progressed over the years and while, from time to time, a degree of rivalry has been known, all has settled to a graceful old age.

Today, many learn their golf at Lobden and move on to Rochdale for the challenge of 18 holes or for business purposes.

Both clubs accept that golfers who reach a reasonable standard at Lobden are likely to be six to 10 strokes better elsewhere.

In recent years Lobden has enjoyed a golf boom. The clubhouse has been refurbished and re-roofed and the winding road up to the club has been upgraded.

New tee beds have been laid at the fifth, seventh and 18th with the result that every hole now has a different tee when the course is played as 18 holes.

Sheep graze on the Lobden course and an ancient local law has prevented their removal. It dates back to manorial times when local farmers were given permission in perpetuity to graze their animals there. The farmers have upheld their rights and the greens are ringed by wire fences as seen in the photograph at the foot of the page.

Lobden has an unfortunate event in its history that resulted in a major rule change by the Royal and Ancient.

On Saturday, May 29, 1948, Mr. Albert Hill was killed by lightening whilst playing the 10th hole. A letter was sent to the R and A and a reply from the Rules of Golf Committee stated that provision was being made within the rules for cessation of play when lives of players were threatened by lightning within the area.

FACT FILE

A moorland course of 9 holes, 5697 yards. Par 70. SSS 68. Record 66.

Restrictions: Societies contact the Secretary. Tuesday, ladies' from 3pm; Wednesday pm, nine-hole competition; Thursday pm, juniors priority; Saturday, competition day.

Green fees: Not stated.

Dress code: Usual golf attire.

Facilities:

TO THE CLUB

On the Burnley road four miles north of Rochdale.

Course Information

Hole	Yards	Stroke	Par
1	281	14	4
2	390	3	4
3	191	12	3
4	325	10	4
5	274	16	4
6	396	2	4
7	481	7	5
8	414	5	4
9	120	17	3
10	302	9	4
11	323	13	4
12	201	8	3
13	325	11	4
14	238	18	4
15	396	1	4
16	481	6	5
17	414	4	4
18	145	15	3
OUT	2825		35
IN	2872		35
TOTAL	5697		70

1) A short par four to begin. It's a straight hole with out-of-bounds on the left, to a plateau green.

2) Another straight hole, this time uphill with a lateral water hazard.

3) This par three hole has a blind tee shot.

4) A long carry uphill is required with an out-of-bounds and two bunkers to contend with.

5) Played into the prevailing wind, this par four is a dogleg to the left.

6) The highest tee in Lancashire. The hole is a dogleg right with out-of-bounds right. The green can't be seen from the fairway.

7) The longest on the course. For the first two shots the player can't see the green, which runs to the right.

8) From the elevated tee a carry of 195 yards is needed to the fairway. The hole doglegs to the right.

9) A short uphill par three with a bunker in front of the green. Playing a second nine, the second plays shorter by 67 yards and four other holes have slightly changed yardage.

Recommended Facilities

LONGRIDGE
Golf Club

Fell Barn, Jeffrey Hill,
Longridge, Lancashire PR3 2TH.

Secretary: David Wensley
01772-783291.
Professional: Neil James
01772-783291.

THE reference books state that the Longridge club was founded in 1877, making it the oldest club in the county of Lancashire and one of the oldest in England.

But the club's centenary booklet made no reference to golf having been played at Longridge at that time.

The centenary story related how it was originally a cycling club and the first reference to golf was when the wheelers set up their headquarters in an old house at Broad Fell, Scorton, near Garstang, in 1892.

The laying out of a nine-hole golf course, at a time when the game was taking root in the county, changed the nature of the club.

The club was there until the hot summer of 1911, when fire destroyed the house. After finding a temporary home they moved to Broad Fell, Longridge, in 1915.

In 1917 the Preston Cycling Club paid £550 for the 16th century Fell Barn and 29 acres of land and two clubs merged under the joint title of Longridge Golf Club and Preston Cycling Club.

The Longridge Golf Club of today was forged in 1963 with the building of a dining room, bar and ladies' room. An adjoining site of 56 acres was bought and Fell Barn was extended.

With the help of a 50 per cent grant from the North West Sports Council, and much voluntary labour, a new 18-hole course took shape.

After about 6,000 tons of rock had been carted away, 1,000 tons of cinders and 5,000 tons of topsoil were brought in. Followed by 10,000 square feet of turf and more than 8,000 field tiles.

The new course opened on August 28, 1971, and a new era began for Longridge. The roof of the 400-year-old barn had to be replaced before it was developed into a luxurious clubhouse.

The development of the club has continued into the 1990s with a clubhouse extension, providing new changing rooms, a pro shop, and an irrigation system with pop-up sprinklers fed from the club's own bore-hole.

Course Information

Hole	Yards	Stroke	Par
1	323	15	4
2	255	11	4
3	507	9	5
4	414	5	4
5	186	13	3
6	427	1	4
7	415	3	4
8	218	7	3
9	254	17	4
10	370	4	4
11	488	6	5
12	123	18	3
13	165	16	3
14	419	2	4
15	369	12	4
16	335	10	4
17	285	14	4
18	309	8	4
OUT	2999		35
IN	2863		35
TOTAL	5862		70

1) A steep downhill hole and almost driveable.

2) A steep uphill hole needing the correct club for the second shot to the green.

3) The magnificent views are the great feature of this par five played along a ridge to a sloping green.

4) A good drive keeping to the right to allow for the sloping ground sets you up to a long green.

5) A medium par three needing accuracy and good club selection.

6) A long par four to a raised double green. Stroke index one.

7) Keep your drive clear of the out-of-bounds at the right.

8) This hole is set into the side of a hill. Out-of-bounds to the right.

9) This short par four is almost driveable but the green is tricky.

10) Alongside a wall, over a deep hole - and you are set up!

11) Fairway bunkers and out-of-bounds on the left cause the problems.

12) A par three to a blind green makes club selection paramount.

13) Another par three to a tricky, sloping green.

14) Keep as close to the out-of-bounds on the left, as you dare.

15) A good drive will do it - but beware the double Mackenzie green.

16) A nice par four needing a short iron to the green.

17) Avoid the field at the right and the cross-stream on the downhill fairway of this short par four.

18) Back uphill, needing a good drive and a precise shot to the green.

Lancashire

Recommended Facilities

MARSDEN PARK
Golf Course/Club

Townhouse Road, Nelson,
Lancashire BB9 8DG.

Secretary: Brian Goodwin
01282-614094.
Professional: Nic Predolac
01282-617525.

MARSDEN Park is a municipal course in the Borough of Pendle and has a reputation for having some rather tough holes.

The course was opened with nine holes in 1968 and extended to 18 in 1976. The Marsden Park club was formed in 1969 and later assumed responsibility for the clubhouse, which was refurbished in 1995.

The course is a centre of tuition in the area and has attracted scores of newcomers to the game, many of whom have joined East Lancashire clubs and achieved very respectable handicaps.

The original nine holes at Marsden Park have a couple of open ditches and several out-of-bounds, making them more difficult than might be assumed from the yardages on the card.

The back nine steps up the pressure and demands accuracy, for there are several tight layouts.

The longest hole is the par five third but the 16th earns top rating for its difficult uphill challenge.

Marsden Park's two biggest diary dates are the Municipal Trophy in August and the Memorial Trophy in October. It is a measure of the club's enthusiasm that they have an annual match against an Australian club for the Alcoa Trophy.

FACT FILE

A parkland course of 18 holes, 5806 yards. Par 70. SSS 68. Record 66.

Restrictions: Societies apply in writing. Visitors phone in advance for weekends.

Fees: £7.20 to £8.45. Nine holes £4.70 to £5.50

Dress code: Smart casual.

Shop opening: Dawn till dusk.

Facilities:

TO THE CLUB

One mile east of Nelson town centre off the A56.

Course Information

Hole	Yards	Stroke	Par
1	388	2	4
2	138	18	3
3	477	7	5
4	252	16	4
5	350	4	4
6	307	13	4
7	193	14	3
8	323	9	4
9	367	10	4
10	382	3	4
11	319	15	4
12	476	8	5
13	375	5	4
14	175	12	3
15	144	17	3
16	390	1	4
17	373	6	4
18	377	11	4
OUT	2795		35
IN	3011		35
TOTAL	5806		70

1) A ditch runs across the fairway on this dogleg right hole with a two-tier green.

2) A fairly easy par three. A bunker guards the sloping green.

3) Straight uphill with a ditch at driving range.

4) A modest par four, lay up short for a pitch to the elevated green.

5) The drive is uphill on the dogleg right with out-of-bounds right.

6) Trees to the right and out-of-bounds to the left.

7) A tough par three. The green slopes to the right.

8) Two ditches cross the fairway and the green is hard to hit.

9) Keep down the middle to avoid the large bunkers placed each side of the green.

10) This hole is a dogleg left and drops down to the left with a stream next to the green.

11) Straight downhill. No bunkers and the green is almost flat.

12) Tee off over a ravine. It's out-of-bounds all down the right.

13) It's still out-of-bounds right. Play short of the green or the ball could roll off.

14) A tough hole going uphill. A ravine runs down the left and there are houses to the right.

15) The elevated green slopes viciously to the left.

16) Uphill all the way and the approach to the green slopes severely.

17) Trees all along the left and out-of-bounds on the right.

18) Hit straight! Out-of-bounds left and a bunker right of the green.

Lancashire

Recommended Facilities

MORECAMBE
Golf Club

The Clubhouse, Morecambe,
Lancashire LA4 6AJ.

Secretary: Mrs Judith Atkinson
01524-412841.
Professional: Simon Fletcher
01524-415596.

THE course may be short but it was designed by Dr. Alister Mackenzie and the golf is superb.

First-timers at Morecambe are mesmerised by the subtleties of a tight course dominated by the two-tier Mackenzie greens that demand a variety of approach shots in a good test of golf.

The course, which has no par fives, could be described as links, but is more accurately parkland.

It is situated between Happy Mount Park and Hest Bank on the coastal road in Morecambe Bay, with the Lakeland mountains providing a wonderful backdrop to the north and west and the Pennines to the east.

The club was founded in 1904, when members played on a nine hole course at Thornton Road. It soon proved inadequate and the present course was laid out in 1923.

The land was earlier used by the Army as a summer training camp (the promontory adjacent to the second tee having been a World War One gun emplacement) and was bought by the Morecambe and Heysham Borough Council and leased to the golf club.

The lease has recently been converted to a 250-year tenure, ensuring the club's long-term future.

Many visitors make the mistake of passing the course by, in favour of one of the longer courses in the area.

For others, the length of a course is not as important as the condition and the presentation.

Whatever the view, the club's history of professional tournaments and a recommendation by Peter Oosterhuis may tip the balance, he broke the record with a 63 in 1970.

The professional at Morecambe, Simon Fletcher, was a junior at the club before embarking on a career that took him to Heysham and Fairhaven.

The club has recently improved the clubhouse to expand the facilities and has the unusual feature of a patio terrace.

The course is open all year and never has to use temporary greens. Winter packages are offered from November to March and there are special summer rates for parties of more than eight. The more players, the better the discount. Casual visitors are always welcome.

FACT FILE

A seaside parkland course of 18 holes, 5770 yards. Par 67. SSS 68. Record 63.

Restrictions: Societies phone the Secretary. No visitors before 9.30am or from noon to 1.30pm Monday to Friday or before 11.15am on Sunday. Handicap certificates required.

Fees: £20 to £30.

Dress code: Usual golf attire.

Shop opening: Summer 8am to 8pm, winter 8am to 5pm.

Facilities:

PG PN

TO THE CLUB

On the north side of Morecambe on the A5105.

Course Information

Hole	Yards	Stroke	Par
1	339	15	4
2	451	3	4
3	152	17	3
4	443	1	4
5	193	11	3
6	374	5	4
7	388	7	4
8	355	13	4
9	389	9	4
10	191	6	3
11	324	12	4
12	183	16	3
13	362	8	4
14	395	2	4
15	415	4	4
16	175	14	3
17	348	10	4
18	293	18	4
OUT	3084		34
IN	2686		33
TOTAL	5770		67

1) A dogleg right with a bunker 170 yards from the green.

2) A long par four hole parallel to the beach with two bunkers about 75 yards from the green.

3) A large green is an inviting target on this straight par three.

4) One of Morecambe's 'classics' it has doglegs left then right. A stream, out-of-bounds and fairway bunkers call for decisions.

5) From an elevated tee over the stream to a small green.

6) Another challenging hole doglegging right and a stream crossing the fairway about 40 yards short of the green.

7) A narrowing fairway to a large Mackenzie green.

8) A choice between safety and length with a crucial approach.

9) A slight dogleg right and a well protected green calls for a well placed drive to the left of the fairway.

10) The tee shot must carry to the sloping green, banked at the front.

11) Straight uphill with punishing trees and rough to the highest point on the course, with a great panoramic view.

12) A tough par three with a narrow, protected entrance to the green.

13) The key here is judging distance with the downhill shot.

14) Down into a valley and up to an elevated, well guarded green.

15) The tee shot must carry a valley to an uphill landing area, with trees and fairway bunkers to watch, to reach a small green.

16) An excellent par three with a green split by a diagonal ridge.

17) A straight par four over a valley up to a Mackenzie green.

18) A short but deceptively difficult hole with pin placement the key. The green has three areas separated by severe slopes.

Recommended Facilities

MYTTON FOLD
Golf Club

Mytton Fold Farm Hotel,
Whalley Road, Langho,
Blackburn, Lancs BB6 8AB.

Manager: Dave Wright
01254-240662 (Fax 248119).
Professional: Gary Coope
01254-240662 (Fax 248119).

MYTTON Fold is one of Lancashire's newest golf courses and is situated in 100 acres of rolling parkland overlooking the lovely Ribble Valley.

The course is at Langho on the north east side of Blackburn and has fine views of Pendle Hill.

Mytton Fold is part of the golf and hotel complex established by Frank Hargreaves, who decided to switch from farming and join the boom in catering for golfers.

The course was opened in 1994 by soccer personality Kenny Dalglish and as well as attracting business parties it has built a following among local golfers.

There is an ongoing development programme and an irrigation system was installed in 1996.

The club was accepted into the Lancashire Golf Union in April, 1995, and the East Lancashire Golf Association in April, 1996.

As part of a hotel complex the facilities are extensive. The hotel has 29 bedrooms and the banquetting suite can accommodate up to 250.

Societies and corporate golf days are welcomed, with packages tailored to requirements.

As well as a games room the club also boasts a gymnasium on site.

There are nets as well as a practice ground and the golf shop's range of facilities includes electric trolley hire and indoor video tuition.

The course has three holes of more than 500 yards, with the intimidating fourth being rated stroke index one.

The score to beat in mid-1996 was 70, set by the club professional Gary Coope and equalled by amateur player Michael Bardi.

FACT FILE

A parkland course of 18 holes, 6217 yards. Par 72. SSS 72.

Restrictions: Societies and visitors contact the professional.

Fees: £12 to £14, with member £8.

Dress code: Usual golf attire.

Shop opening: Summer 8.30am to 6.30pm; winter 8.30am to 3.30pm.

Facilities:

TO THE CLUB

From junction 31 of the M6, follow the A59 with the Clitheroe sign for 10 miles to Langho.

Course Information

Hole	Yards	Stroke	Par
1	193	5	3
2	272	11	4
3	250	15	4
4	503	1	5
5	528	3	5
6	294	13	4
7	516	7	5
8	335	9	4
9	168	17	3
10	311	8	4
11	352	16	4
12	408	6	4
13	346	14	4
14	408	12	4
15	366	10	4
16	415	2	4
17	327	18	4
18	225	4	3
OUT	3059		37
IN	3158		35
TOTAL	6217		72

1) A very tough opening par three. Take a long iron or wood to the small two-tier green and watch out for the ditches.

2) A three wood off the tee and short iron over the two ponds.

3) A tempter for long hitters but beware the ditch.

4) Don't be intimidated. Three good hits and you'll be near the hole!

5) A tough drive to a narrow fairway. A good second shot will leave a short iron to the pin.

6) An easier hole. Drive down the left and have a short pitch in.

7) A great driving hole. The green is reachable in two for long hitters but it's a small target.

8) Another narrow fairway, a ditch on the right and the second shot is longer than it looks.

9) Beware the three bunkers guarding the front of the green.

10) Not an easy drive over a pond to a tight fairway with out-of-bounds left and a small green.

11) Drive up the right to leave a short iron to a long, narrow green.

12) This is an intimidating tee shot with out-of-bounds right.

13) A straight drive uphill - and a deceptively long second shot.

14) Another good driving hole down to a wide fairway.

15) A dogleg left. The second shot is very deceptive. Take two more clubs than you think.

16) A real card-wrecker. It's safer played as a five.

17) A steady drive will leave a short iron.

18) A long par three to finish. Take a long iron or three wood.

NELSON
Golf Club

King's Causeway, Brierfield,
Nelson, Lancashire BB9 0EM.

Secretary: Barry Thomason
01282-611834.
Professional: Nigel Sumner
01282-617000.

THE Nelson course stands on Marsden Heights, a section of moorland between Brierfield and Nelson, but has many of the characteristics of a parkland course.

Founded in 1902, the club has built a reputation on three fronts - the course itself, the clubhouse and facilities and the success of members in local competitions.

Most successful of the local players since 1970 was Hogan Stott, who represented England at boys' and youths' levels before becoming a full international. He later turned professional.

A famous name at Nelson in the 1970s and 1980s was Australian Test cricketer Neil Hawke, who played for Nelson CC in the Lancashire League and was captain of Nelson Golf Club in 1979.

During his summers in East Lancashire, Hawke arranged several celebrity competitions.

When the Nelson club was founded, it played over a nine-hole course at Kibble Bank and moved a short distance to a larger site at Marsden Heights in 1917.

Local legend has it that the new 18-hole course was designed by Dr. Alister Mackenzie but this has not yet been established with authority. The course certainly has many Mackenzie greens that the master designer would have been proud of.

It is a popular venue with visitors and societies, several of which run charity events. The views from the course are a big plus factor and with its mature trees and water features, several holes are picturesque.

Two major competitions are the Nelson Trophy, a handicap event, and the recently-created Trafalgar Trophy, a scratch event.

The only hole of more than 500 yards, from the back tee, is the 12th but the two most highly-rated are the seventh and 14th, par fours that are played into the prevailing wind. And it can be windy here! The course is challenging and attracts East Lancashire's leading golfers to the open and invitation events.

FACT FILE

A moorland/parkland course of 18 holes, 5967 yards. Par 70. SSS 69. Record 63.

Restrictions: Societies contact the Secretary. Ladies' day Thursday. No catering on Mondays.

Fees: £25 to £30.

Dress code: Usual golf attire.

Shop opening: 8.30am to 6.30pm.

Facilities:

TO THE CLUB

The course is off the A56, two miles east of Brierfield. From the M65 exit at junction 12.

Course Information

Hole	Yards	Stroke	Par
1	354	5	4
2	158	11	3
3	485	17	5
4	310	15	4
5	301	9	4
6	174	13	3
7	430	1	4
8	376	3	4
9	376	7	4
10	415	6	4
11	169	16	3
12	545	4	5
13	147	18	3
14	419	2	4
15	478	10	5
16	184	12	3
17	336	8	4
18	310	14	4
OUT	2964		35
IN	3003		35
TOTAL	5967		70

1) A difficult starting hole with a tree-lined sunken green.

2) A premium on accuracy on this par three with a back-sloping green.

3) A blind drive followed by downhill shots to a flat green.

4) A short par four with out-of-bounds to the left and a green that is difficult to read.

5) This short par four has a narrow Mackenzie green.

6) Another sloping green makes this short par three difficult.

7) The longest of the par fours needs two accurate shots to score.

8) An uphill drive and a problem with club selection for the second.

9) Only an accurate drive on this dogleg left, with out-of-bounds to the left, will be rewarded.

10) A tree-lined fairway makes this par four.

11) An elevated tee on this short par three makes club selection tricky.

12) This long par five needs three excellent shots to have any chance.

13) Again it is club selection that is important for this uphill par three to a well protected green.

14) First a good drive and then an accurate second to a narrow green, which slopes to the front and is ringed by bunkers.

15) This long par five uphill needs length and accuracy.

16) A nice par three, slightly uphill. The green looks nearer than it is.

17) Driving through an avenue of trees leads to a narrow cross green.

18) Avoid the fairway bunkers and the reward is a welcome short iron shot to a raised green.

Recommended Facilities

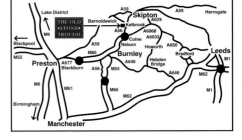

ORMSKIRK
Golf Club

Cranes Lane, Lathom,
Ormskirk, Lancs L40 5UJ.

Secretary: Raymond Lawrence
01695-572227.
Professional: Jack Hammond
01695-572074.
Clubhouse: 01695-572112.

ON the left side of the 16th hole, close to the brook, is a crescent-shaped hollow that is reputed to have been an emplacement for a battery of Cromwell's army when they attacked Lathom House in 1644.

Battle recommenced in a more sporting manner in 1899, when the Ormskirk club established a nine-hole golf course designed by Harold Hilton, of Royal Liverpool, the year before he won the Amateur Championship for the first time. The new Ormskirk course was formally opened on December 2, with the Earl of Lathom driving the first ball.

Success came quickly and in 1901 the club decided to extend the course to 18, which was in play by the spring of 1903. The name of the designer has not been established.

The clubhouse was built in 1914 and has been improved several times, while retaining its original character.

The course was lengthened to 6500 yards, probably just after World War One and, in a booklet

some years later, the supervising architect was named as Major C. A. Mackenzie.

It has not been authenticated but could the architect have been Dr. Alister Mackenzie?

The first green is 150 feet above sea level but it is a fairly flat parkland layout that is not over-taxing. The course is maintained to a high standard and for six years to 1991 was a regional qualifying course for the Open Championship.

The Lancashire Ladies' Championship was held at Ormskirk in 1995 and the English Seniors Championship was co-hosted with West Lancashire Golf Club in 1996.

In 1996, Ormskirk Golf Club had plans to refurbish the locker rooms, changing rooms and showers and intended to follow this scheme with a new car park.

FACT FILE

A parkland course of 18 holes, 6358 yards. Par 70. SSS 70. Record 63.

Restrictions: Societies apply in writing. Visitors phone first and have introductions from their own club.

Fees: £30 to £40.

Dress code: Usual golf attire.

Shop opening: Summer 9am to 7pm; winter 9am to 4pm.

Facilities:

TO THE CLUB

The course is at Lathom, two miles east of Ormskirk.

Course Information

Hole	Yards	Stroke	Par
1	381	13	4
2	372	7	4
3	464	1	4
4	189	17	3
5	368	11	4
6	376	15	4
7	447	3	4
8	448	5	4
9	501	9	5
10	343	10	4
11	360	8	4
12	162	14	3
13	487	4	5
14	142	16	3
15	379	2	4
16	359	12	4
17	154	18	3
18	426	6	4
OUT	3546		36
IN	2812		34
TOTAL	6358		70

1) Avoid the right hand bunkers - but don't go over the wall left - to open up the hole.

2) A similar length as the first and the wall is still there.

3) Commit yourself to a driver to avoid the water on the left.

4) Take note of the prevailing wind on this deceptively long par three.

5) A dogleg left with a hollow just past the elbow and a narrow green.

6) A straight par four. The snag is the slope at the back of the green.

7) This long par four seems to have an elusive green and the bunker on the right 75 yards short of the green is a threat.

8) This dogleg left needs a good carry over the fairway bunkers.

9) Drive left of the water and maybe set up a birdie chance.

10) A straight hit is vital to set up a short iron shot.

11) A dogleg left requiring a long drive to open up the second shot.

12) A short hole calling for good judgement to the green.

13) A sporting chance on this par five if you miss the hidden ditch at the 400 yard mark.

14) A short hole ringed by bunkers and having a wicked left slope.

15) Two good straight shots are needed on this long par four.

16) Drive left to open up an approach and a birdie opportunity

17) A tiny target with all the trouble coming short of the green.

18) A tough finish into the prevailing wind. Watch that big pond on the right.

Recommended Facilities

PENWORTHAM
Golf Club

Blundel Lane, Penwortham,
Preston, Lancashire PR1 0AX.

Secretary: J. Parkinson
01772-744630.
Professional: John Wright
01772-742345.

BELIEVED to have provided sanctuary for Royalist troops put to flight by Cromwell's Roundheads after the Battle of Preston in 1648, the ancient manor of Penwortham was the happy choice of the club's founders when they acquired land there shortly before the First World War.

They had occupied a nine-hole course at Howick Cross on the Preston to Liverpool road.

And that's how the Hutton Golf Club became the Penwortham Golf Club, retaining its original membership but gaining potential for development.

Situated on the wooded promontory overlooking the old Port of Preston and the River Ribble, the course is only a 10-minute drive from the bustling industrial town and not many more minutes from the M6 motorway.

Nature herself carved the undulating slopes and wooded ravines on the breezy plateau overlooked by the river. These, like the woods they divide, figure importantly in a round of golf at Penwortham for all but four of the 18 holes are well above sea level.

The remainder are on low ground beside the river, and being naturally well drained, it is a course that plays all year.

There are two loops of nine holes running east to west and back.

The 10th tee (an alternative starting point when circumstances permit) is conveniently close to the bungalow clubhouse, which was opened the day King George VI was crowned in 1937.

Extended several times, it has two bars, a billiard room with full size table, a spacious dining room and a fine maple dance floor for the party nights that are a regular feature of the club's social calendar.

The late Cyril Race, one of the architects of the course as it stands today, was the club professional and greenkeeper for nearly 30 years.

Now the club has John Wright (ex-Tyne and Wear) whose acclaimed coaching manuals are popular with improvers and established players alike. He has been joined by his brother Tim, an experienced club maker whose special professional skills have enhanced the services of the pro's shop.

Proof of Penwortham's drawing power is shown in the three-year average of 6,000 annual visitors.

FACT FILE

A parkland course of 18 holes, 5915 yards. Par 69. SSS 68. Record 66.

Restrictions: Societies and visitors phone in advance. Visitors must play with a member at weekends. Ladies' day Tuesday.

Fees: Weekdays £25 (£8 with member) weekends £28 (£10).

Dress code: Usual golf attire.

Shop opening: Dawn till dusk.

Facilities:

TO THE CLUB

One mile west of Penwortham centre, off the A59.

Course Information

Hole	Yards	Stroke	Par
1	389	3	4
2	328	13	4
3	178	11	3
4	398	2	4
5	361	8	4
6	480	6	5
7	315	15	4
8	396	9	4
9	157	17	3
10	443	1	4
11	350	10	4
12	135	16	3
13	307	12	4
14	524	5	5
15	148	18	3
16	398	4	4
17	437	7	4
18	171	14	3
OUT	3002		35
IN	2913		34
TOTAL	5915		69

1) A wide tree-lined fairway. Just keep it straight.

2) Same again - but watch that pond 30 yards from the tee.

3) A classic short hole calling for club judgement and a precise shot.

4) A blind uphill drive over a marker post and a direct second shot.

5) For the first time, the chance to have a go down a wide fairway, and a comfortable second to a built-up, bunkered green.

6) A dogleg with out-of-bounds in two places, plus a ditch.

7) A duckpond and two cross-bunkers - but a longish green.

8) Another hole where playing it straight brings its reward.

9) Carry the ravine at half distance and plenty of air to the green.

10) Back over the ravine and up the slope to a well bunkered green.

11) Carry the shallow trough and there's a straight run-in between the bunkers. Hooked shots fall away left.

12) This picturesque short hole needs a well flighted tee shot to a long green protected by overhanging trees and sand traps.

13) A straight drive over the trees in front of the gully and a quiet pitch to a green in a basin by the river.

14) The longest hole, on the flat, and straight up the middle.

15) A cross bunker catches under-clubbed shots on this short hole.

16) Accuracy from the tee and boldness in approach to carry the dyke 30 yards from the green.

17) A first class 'two shot' hole, the second being blind and downhill to a green flanked by a poplar-lined banking.

18) A short finish through an avenue of trees - with a cross bunker and side bunkers demanding accuracy and good weight from the tee.

Recommended Facilities

PLEASINGTON
Golf Club

Pleasington Lane, Blackburn,
Lancashire BB2 5JF.

Secretary: Mrs. Jean Leyland
01254-202177.
Professional: Ged Furey
01254-201630.

ONE of Lancashire's oldest clubs, founded in 1890, Pleasington's name has travelled far and wide by being a favourite for decades of societies and business groups.

The attraction of the course draws visitors back again and again. The Walker Steel event has been held each year since 1973 and the Northern Bar Circuit return every other year for their July meeting - the only society given the privilege of a Saturday booking!

Since 1979 the course has often been chosen as an Open championship regional qualifying course and the Pleasington Pro-Am competition, started in 1987, has grown in popularity.

Pleasington's hallmarks are the 'up hill and down dale' contours and the great variety of greens and bunkers. The course is bisected by a railway line but the scenic qualities compensate for this.

Playing the course demands good form. Two of the par fives are more than 500 yards and two of the par fours seem like fives.

Pleasington's envied position in the north west golf world is, however, quite a long shot from the struggles of the early years and, like most clubs in the first half of this century, a battle with the bank overdraft.

The club was instituted in 1890, soon after Wilpshire Golf Club was founded on the other side of Blackburn. Some local figures were members of both clubs.

The first nine-hole course was laid out by George Lowe, the Scottish professional at the Lytham and St. Annes Golf Club, on land leased from the de Hoghton Estate. The course opened in 1891.

According to Pleasington's centenary history, the club struggled to exist and had only 44 members in 1902. Was declining membership the reason the club voted to admit girls and ladies in 1905?

In 1909, the club leased more land on the other side of the railway and Alex Herd extended the course to 18 holes, the club formed itself into The Pleasington Golf Links Company Limited, and a clubhouse was built (still recognizable in today's much-extended building.

The course was lengthened several times, including a partial re-design by James Braid in 1929, after another 28 acres had been leased.

But, in spite of continued improvement, parts of the original nine-hole course - opened in 1891 - remain as originally laid out by George Lowe. Pleasington's development accelerated in the 1960s and today about half the club's revenue comes from visitors.

The de Hoghton Estate granted a new 75-year lease to the club in the late 1980s. The historic Hoghton Tower is visible from parts of the course.

FACT FILE

A moorland course of 18 holes, 6423 yards. Par 71. SSS 71. Record 65.

Restrictions: Societies contact the Secretary by phone. No visitors at weekends or Tuesdays.

Fees: £30 to £35.

Dress code: Usual golf attire.

Shop opening: Dawn till dusk.

Facilities:

TO THE CLUB

The course is on the western side of Blackburn, off the A674 road to Chorley. From the M6, exit at junction 31.

Course Information

Hole	Yards	Stroke	Par
1	387	7	4
2	350	15	4
3	333	11	4
4	435	3	4
5	344	13	4
6	358	9	4
7	524	1	5
8	167	17	3
9	490	5	5
10	189	12	3
11	559	2	5
12	168	14	3
13	463	6	4
14	391	10	4
15	355	4	4
16	155	16	3
17	370	8	4
18	385	18	4
OUT	3388		37
IN	3035		34
TOTAL	6423		71

1) A good opening hole of nearly 400 yards with the fairway bunker on the right being the main problem.

2) A short par four needing an accurate shot to the protected green.

3) Out-of-bounds right and trees on the left demand an accurate drive.

4) With sloping ground to the right, be accurate with the drive!

5) The railway to the left and the uphill second shot are the problems.

6) After a good drive, the second shot to a raised and protected green needs good club selection.

7) A long drive allows the ball to run down a gully to the fairway.

8) Good club selection is needed to clear the scrubland.

9) This par five begins with a blind drive and the uphill route makes this a difficult hole.

10) A long iron shot to a green protected by cross bunkers.

11) A blind drive and a second shot that avoids the dyke to the right will decide the outcome on the longest hole.

12) Good club selection is vital on this uphill par three.

13) A slight dogleg left needs two good long shots to get in position.

14) An attractive par four from an elevated tee to an elevated green.

15) After a good drive the challenge is a second shot between two sets of trees to find the hidden green.

16) The tee shot must carry the trees on the shortest of the par threes.

17) An accurate second shot is required to the long, narrow green.

18) A very accurate drive is needed to have a chance at the elevated, well protected green.

Recommended Facilities

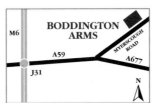

POULTON-le-FYLDE
Golf Course/Club

Breck Road, Poulton-le-Fylde,
Lancashire FY6 7HJ.

Secretary: Eric Astbury (Owner)
01253-893150.
Professional: Lewis Ware
01253-892444.

POULTON'S nine-hole course could soon be extended to 18.

But until the 1970s few local golfers had any hopes of the game returning to the old market town three miles from Blackpool.

A course had existed in the agricultural area to the north of the town but it went out of existence before World War Two.

In 1972 the old Poulton-le-Fylde Urban Council earmarked a golf course as part of a major leisure development for the district. The indoor pool on the adjacent site was part of the scheme, which opened in 1974. The golf layout was virtually on the same site as the pre-war course. In 1982, the Wyre Borough Council, which had taken over the old urban council in the 1974 local government reorganisation, leased the course out to the private sector and work was done to improve the course, particularly with drainage and tree planting.

In 1989, Eric Astbury became the sole leaseholder and after an 18-month building programme, was granted a 30-year lease.

The greens were relaid and the sixth hole was lengthened. Land has been bought to the west with the intention of extending the course to 18 holes.

An indoor driving range, built in 1990, has proved to be a successful attraction. Although the course is open to the public without restriction on a pay-and-play basis, there is also a private members' club. The clubhouse and cafeteria are open all day and professional Lewis Ware is on hand at the pro shop to give advice and lessons.

FACT FILE

A parkland course of 9 holes, 6056 yards. Par 70. SSS 69.

Restrictions: Visitors are welcome without restriction.

Fees: £3.50 to £11.

Dress code: Smart casual.

Shop opening: Dawn till dusk.

Facilities:

TO THE CLUB

Three miles east of Blackpool, turn off the A586 road through the centre of Poulton-le-Fylde, into Breck Road. The course is on the left, just past the car showrooms.

Course Information

Hole	Yards	Stroke	Par
1	147	15	3
2	357	9	4
3	488	7	5
4	398	5	4
5	336	11	4
6	185	13	3
7	409	1	4
8	566	3	5
9	142	17	3
10	147	16	3
11	357	10	4
12	488	8	5
13	398	6	4
14	336	12	4
15	185	14	3
16	409	2	4
17	566	4	5
18	142	18	3
OUT	3028		35
IN	3028		35
TOTAL	6056		70

1) This short par three is a tempting first hole. There are trees to the right and out-of-bounds behind the green.

2) An accurate drive will carry the dyke and avoid the pond on the left.

3) A good drive and accurate second shot over a dyke has a good chance of a birdie.

4) Teeing off in front of the clubhouse and crossing the dyke with the second shot.

5) A dogleg left needs accuracy to view the green.

6) Beware the pond on the left on this extended par three.

7) The view of the green is obscured by a pond surrounded by trees.

8) One of the longest par fives in the country. Keep the drive straight.

9) With trees down the right, an accurate shot finds the green by the clubhouse.

Lancashire

Recommended Facilities

PRESTON
Golf Club

Fulwood Hall Lane, Fulwood,
Preston, Lancashire PR2 8DD.

Secretary: John R. Spedding
01772-700011.
Professional: Pat Wells
01772-700022.

MAJOR improvements at Preston during 1996 saw new locker rooms and offices and a programme of re-laying the greens.

The club celebrated its centenary in 1992 in a happy financial position due to land sales after periods when the future often looked unsure.

Back in the early 1890s, golf was a strange pursuit to the great majority of Prestonians but in the space of two years two clubs were formed and the prime movers of both were James Rigby and Nicholas Cockshutt, a local solicitor.

First to open was the Preston Golf Club with a nine-hole course overlooking the River Ribble at Ribbleton. It was laid out by George Lowe, the professional at Lytham St. Annes.

In 1894 the Fulwood Golf Club was launched with an 18-hole course and the same three names were involved. The following year the two clubs amalgamated on the superior Fulwood course but took the Preston name.

After World War One the club was intent on restoring and improving the course. Dr. Alister Mackenzie, who was later to design many famous courses, submitted three proposals but each was turned down for financial or physical reasons.

It fell to the club's head greenkeeper, George Mackintosh, who had joined them in 1898 as the professional, to produce an acceptable plan.

The club sought expert advice from James Braid, who approved of the greensman's designs and made three visits to supervise the £2,000 scheme. Braid's fees came to £25 and Mackintosh was given a 50-guinea bonus by the club.

Braid was one of the four professionals who played in exhibition matches at the formal opening of the new course in September, 1923. The others were Arthur Havers (who was the current Open champion) Ted Ray and Abe Mitchell. Ray had an afternoon round of 66, which was 11 under par. James Braid was consulted by the club in 1928, 1932 and 1934 to add more bunkers and give better definition to some holes. Consequently, it is the Braid stamp that can be seen on most of the Preston course to this day.

The club secured its future in 1950 by purchasing the site for £7,800 and continued to develop the clubhouse and course. Three new holes were laid out in 1962.

Preston was the scene of many big name exhibition matches up to the time when the major tours took up the pros' time; Max Faulkner, Harry Weetman, Dai Rees, Fred Daly, Bernard Hunt, Peter Alliss and Ken Bousfield to name a few.

The biggest event was the Roosevelt Nine Nations Tournament played in 1964 and won by Bob Charles.

FACT FILE

A parkland course of 18 holes, 6212 yards, Par 71. SSS 70. Record 65.

Restrictions: Societies and visitors phone. Ladies' day Tuesday.
No visitors at weekends. Handicap certificates preferred.

Fees: £22 to £27.

Dress code: Usual golf attire.

Shop opening: Dawn till dusk.

Facilities:

TO THE CLUB

The course is at Fulwood, near the army barracks, East of the A6.

Course Information

Hole	Yards	Stroke	Par
1	147	15	3
2	340	7	4
3	444	3	4
4	440	1	4
5	377	11	4
6	518	5	5
7	501	9	5
8	172	13	3
9	315	17	4
10	361	4	4
11	342	14	4
12	127	16	3
13	311	18	4
14	201	12	3
15	334	8	4
16	419	2	4
17	481	10	5
18	382	6	4
OUT	3254		36
IN	2958		35
TOTAL	6212		71

1) A short par three needing accuracy and good club selection.

2) From an elevated tee, drive down to the valley and uphill through an avenue to a tree-ringed green.

3) Out-of-bounds right and a stream crossing in front of the green.

4) Hit a good drive to clear a deep depression. The green is big.

5) Avoid the fairway bunker and trees each side to obtain par!

6) A slight dogleg left near the green and trees to the right make this a good par five.

7) A long drive is needed to start. The green is protected by trees.

8) A good par three needing accuracy with a mid to long iron.

9) Drive from an elevated tee into a valley and cross a stream to a green set into a hillside.

10) A good drive from the elevated tee and a mid iron to the green.

11) Avoid the trees on the right and there's a chance to par.

12) A short hole, needing to carry the scrub all the way to the green.

13) Keep the drive left here to set up a short iron to the green.

14) A long par three from an elevated tee to a large green.

15) To avoid the stream on the left, drive over the hillock on the right.

16) Avoid the lonesome tree to the right of the fairway for a second shot to the elevated green.

17) On this par five hole, just keep to the left.

18) Two good shots will get to the green on this 390-yard par four.

Recommended Facilities

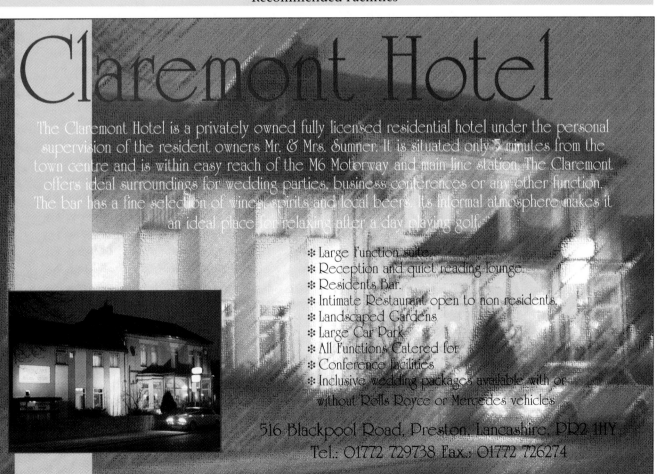

RISHTON
Golf Club

Eachill Links, Hawthorn Drive,
Rishton, Lancashire BB1 4HG.
Secretary: W. Ramsbottom
Clubhouse: 01254-884442.

IN the 1980s the Rishton club survived a major threat to its existence when the M65 was surveyed to slice through the nine hole course.

Fifty years of golf at the Eachill Links on the north east side of Blackburn were in the balance as the East Lancashire motorway scheme progressed.

The course lost two holes - but fortune smiled and the club used the compensation money to buy some adjoining land and commissioned Peter Alliss and Dave Thomas to put in three new holes and improve the remainder of the course.

Evidence that the club was carved up by the motorway is in the location of the clubhouse. It is on the opposite side of the tarmac to the 10-hole course.

The Rishton club's origins go back to the 1920s, when the Great Harwood and Rishton Golf Club separated due to the expiration of a lease on Belmont Farm.

The Great Harwood Golf Club was re-established at Harwood Bar and Rishton signed a lease on the Eachill Links, which opened in 1929.

The first match was against Great Harwood.

The club was converted into a limited company in 1932 and Harold Boswell came from Silloth as professional.

In 1937, Donald McNeil became honorary secretary and began his remarkable link with the club as secretary, captain and - in 1996 - council member.

Mr. McNeil recalled that on his return from war service in 1946, he found there were fewer than 10 members and there was a proposal

to disband. Mr. McNeil and the club's first captain, Neil Halliwell, opposed the move and Rishton Golf Club was re-started on a sound basis.

During his long membership, Mr. McNeil became chairman of Rishton Urban Council, then Mayor of Hyndburn and a member of the Lancashire County Council.

The hard work and steady progress of the nearly 40 years was almost dashed with the arrival of the M65 project, but the club has survived and now has a first class course and a full membership list.

FACT FILE

A parkland/links course of 10 holes, 6097 yards. Par 70. SSS 69. Record 66.

Restrictions: Societies make contact in advance. Visitors at weekends only with a member. Ladies' day Wednesday.

Fees: £13, with member £9.

Dress code: Usual golf attire.

Facilities:

TO THE CLUB

Three miles east of Blackburn at Rishton, signposted from the village centre.

Course Information

Hole	Yards	Stroke	Par
1	329	5	4
2	346	13	4
3	381	1	4
4	244	7	3
5	160	15	3
6	555	11	5
7	314	9	4
8	326	17	4
9	410	3	4
10	321	6	4
11	346	12	4
12	381	2	4
13	181	14	3
14	160	16	3
15	555	10	5
16	352	8	4
17	326	18	4
18	410	4	4
OUT	3065		35
IN	3032		35
TOTAL	6097		70

1) A dogleg to the right with out-of-bounds right. There's a ditch and a pond on the left of the elevated green.

2) The drive must clear the ditch and the second shot must carry two mounds to reach the elevated green.

3) Lay up with the first shot, for a good view of the elevated green.

4) A long downhill par three with the ditch running across.

5) A short uphill par three with a narrow green and entrance.

6) The only par five is this straight 555-yard hole downhill with out-of-bounds right. The green is large.

7) Tree-lined on the left, a short par four with an approach to the green between two trees.

8) Another short par four going downhill with out-of-bounds right and water on the left.

9) The trees on the left force the tee shot right and the second shot is over trees and a dyke.

Note: The club's 'extra' hole is actually an alternative green to hole four and played from a forward tee. It becomes a 181-yard par three and is shown on the card as hole 13.

Recommended Facilities

ROSSENDALE
Golf Club

Ewood Lane, Head, Haslingden,
Lancashire BB4 6LH.

Secretary: J. R. Swain
01706-831339.
Professional: S. Nicholls
01706-213616.

ROSSENDALE has become one of East Lancashire's leading clubs since the course was extended to 18 holes in 1970.

Sam Torrance played his early golf here when his father, Bob, was the club professional in the 1960s.

The course is located between Haslingden and Ewood Bridge and the natural contours of the area are used to give a good mixture of flat and hilly holes.

In the early 1990s a couple of water features were introduced in the form of duck ponds.

The course is acknowledged throughout East Lancashire as a severe test of golf and it is usually windy. Team events of the East Lancashire Golf Association are held there.

The Rossendale club was founded in 1903 with a nine-hole layout that existed, with steady improvement, for nearly 70 years. The present course bears little resemblance.

The first clubhouse was built in 1914 on the site of a farmhouse. It has been extended and improved to meet the needs of a busy membership.

Rossendale's big annual event is the Derek Ingham Memorial Trophy competition, which attracts Lancashire's best golfers. It is a Northern Order of Merit ranking tournament.

FACT FILE

A meadowland course of 18 holes, 6293 yards. Par 72. SSS 70. Record 64.

Restrictions: Societies contact the Secretary; visitors contact the pro. Ladies' Tuesday and Thursday. Saturday play only if accompanied by a member.

Fees: £22.50 to £27.50, with member £9 and £11.

Dress code: Usual golf attire (collar, tie and jacket from 8pm weekends).

Shop opening: 9am to 6.30pm

Facilities:

TO THE CLUB

About two miles south of Haslingden at Ewood Lane, off the A56.

Course Information

Hole	Yards	Stroke	Par
1	163	15	3
2	406	1	4
3	532	3	5
4	518	11	5
5	207	5	3
6	369	13	4
7	393	7	4
8	330	9	4
9	123	17	3
10	363	8	4
11	313	18	4
12	486	6	5
13	150	14	3
14	374	10	4
15	396	4	4
16	530	12	5
17	377	2	4
18	263	16	4
OUT	3041		35
IN	3252		37
TOTAL	6293		72

1) An opening par three needing to clear the trees and a deep hollow in front of the green.

2) A straight par four, rated stroke index one. The hillocks and trees on the left are the problems.

3) The longest hole. Big hitters should avoid reaching the stream.

4) Again, avoid the stream after driving through the avenue of trees.

5) Accuracy and the right club selection are vital here.

6) A straightforward par four, obtainable with a good drive.

7) A dogleg to the right. Long hitters can try to clear the corner - which is a reservoir.

8) A nice downhill par four with out-of-bounds to the left.

9) Be accurate here. There are bunkers in front of the green.

10) This uphill hole needs long shots to reach the green.

11) This downhill par four is an easy hole to score.

12) Back uphill again on this par five. It is a dogleg left with houses out-of-bounds on the left.

13) The shot to the green needs to clear the deep depression.

14) A par four with a duck pond to avoid on the right.

15) A tree-lined fairway on this par four hole.

16) Again, the fairway is crossed by a stream just short of the green.

17) An accurate drive is needed to set up a shot to the protected green on this par four that is rated stroke index two.

18) The slightly elevated green is almost reachable with a driver. But beware - it's a tricky green.

Recommended Facilities

SHAW HILL
Golf and Country Club

Whittle-le-Woods, Chorley,
Lancashire PR6 7PP.

Secretary: Frank Wharton
01257-269221.
Professional: Dave Clarke
01257-279222.

SHAW Hill is spectacular! From the moment the visitor passes through the imposing entrance gates, the estate breathes quality and well-being.

An elegant Georgian mansion rimmed by a tough course in beautiful parkland comes close to the proverbial 'golf heaven.'

The golf club was founded in 1925 as a nine-hole course leased, together with the house, from the Kevill family, of Chorley.

Within five years it had been re-designed and extended to an 18-hole championship course by T. J. McCauley.

The house and course were bought by the Rodwell Group, the mansion being renovated into a sumptuous hotel, country club and a restaurant evocatively named The Vardon.

Out on the par 72 course the golfer soon encounters serious challenges amid the fine landscaping.

It is a course made interesting by the variety, including some American design features. There are lakes on seven holes although two of them shouldn't worry the average golfer.

The 18th is agreed to be the hardest, with a stream and lake at modest driving distance. The ground starts to fall away to the left about 100 yards from the green, which is protected by three front bunkers. But the real problem is the Mackenzie green.

FACT FILE

A parkland course of 18 holes, 6323 yards. Par 72. SSS 70.

Restrictions: Societies contacts the Secretary, visitors contact the pro.

Fees: £30 to £40 - with member £7.50 and £12.50.

Dress code: Usual golf attire.

Shop opening: 8am to 7pm.

Facilities:

TO THE CLUB

At Whittle-le-Woods on the A6, a mile and a half north of Chorley.

Course Information

Hole	Yards	Stroke	Par
1	253	16	4
2	180	8	3
3	369	4	4
4	481	12	5
5	334	6	4
6	159	14	3
7	311	10	4
8	481	18	5
9	382	2	4
10	206	15	3
11	360	9	4
12	405	13	4
13	379	3	4
14	517	5	5
15	468	1	4
16	143	17	3
17	498	11	5
18	397	7	4
OUT	2950		36
IN	3373		36
TOTAL	6323		72

1) A straight drive over the mark will get you near the green.
2) Take enough club to carry those two bunkers fronting the green.
3) The drive must be long and right of the oak tree on the left of the fairway.
4) A stream hides behind the lake at 380 yards so the tee shot must be long.
5) Drive to the right of the fairway to gain a good position.
6) Beware the two bunkers on the left front of the green and one at the back.
7) A fairly easy hole if you avoid the wooded area to the right.
8) A bunker 60 yards short of the green demands a long drive.
9) Go for position rather than length on this acute dogleg left.
10) A straight long iron shot between the two big trees hits the green.
11) Driving true over the marker post leaves a nice mid iron shot.
12) Trees each side - but a long straight drive leaves a mid iron shot to the green.
13) A stream at 160 yards will gather poor shots; out-of-bounds behind green.
14) If the drive fails to carry, play the second shot short of the lake.
15) Same again. The drive and the lake decide the second shot.
16) An attractive prospect at 143 yards but beware the sloping green.
17) A difficult par five with a lake, a stream and a possible downhill lie.
18) On approaching the green take care not to land on the top level.

Recommended Facilities

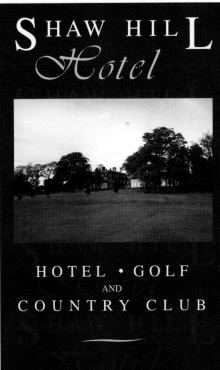

SILVERDALE
Golf Club

Redbridge Lane, Silverdale,
Lancashire LA5 0SP.

Secretary: Peter J. Watts
01524-702074.
Professional: David Wilkinson
Clubhouse: 01524-701300.

THIS is one of the most beautiful golf courses in Lancashire - and it is only just in Lancashire - hidden in the wooded countryside between Lancaster and Arnside.

Silverdale is also one of the most unusual courses in the county. Its first claim to novelty is that the course has 12 holes and second is the way the natural lie of the rock has been made a feature.

It's a difficult layout at the best of times but a first visit is one of the toughest encounters in the north west.

Silverdale Golf Club was formed in 1905 and for most of its existence played over nine holes. In the early 1990s three holes (two, three and four) were added across the road. They are not as hilly as the original holes.

Typical of the original nine is the fifth, the longest on the course, that has to be played through a narrow gorge and finishes with a pitch up to the elevated green.

The eighth can be trickier. After driving to the landing area there is a blind shot up to a rocky plateau to a green that slopes.

FACT FILE

A heathland/rocky course of 12 holes, 5463 yards. Par 69. SSS 67. Record 67.

Restrictions: Societies apply in writing. Weekend play only if accompanied by a member.

Fees: £12 to £17

Dress code: Smart and casual.

Facilities:

TO THE CLUB

Opposite Silverdale railway station.

Course Information

Hole	Yards	Stroke	Par
1	400	3	4
2	156	12	3
3	355	5	4
4	383	1	4
5	480	7	5
6	153	17	3
7	268	15	4
8	312	10	4
9	151	16	3
10	267	14	4
11	306	9	4
12	305	11	4
13	400	4	4
14	156	13	3
15	355	6	4
16	383	2	4
17	480	8	5
18	153	18	3
OUT	2658		34
IN	2805		35
TOTAL	5463		69

1) A quite open first hole with an elevated circular green guarded by a rocky outcrop and two bunkers.

2) The first of the three new holes is a long par three from a high tee. Very tight and there are trees behind the green.

3) An uphill par four needing two moderate hits. The problem is a bank crossing the fairway at 250 yards.

4) Back down the hill from an elevated tee.

5) It's out-of-bounds on the right and a tree blocks the safer shot to the left. Accuracy is paramount but rocks make things unpredictable.

6) From a high tee, over the clubhouse and down to a green surrounded by bunkers, this is a dramatic par three.

7) This short par four is relatively easy if you master the sloping green, which is backed by trees.

8) The green is atop a rocky outcrop and is out of view for that critical shot. A different kind of challenge that needs just a bit of luck.

9) A short downhill par three to a large, flat green gives a good birdie chance.

10) Teeing off down through an apple orchard with a mid-iron is the safest option, leaving a short iron up to another elevated green.

11) Aiming up through the quarry face to a tight, undulating fairway, leaves a short iron to the target.

12) Two options from the elevated tee. The bold can take the right side and risk the out-of-bounds.

Recommended Facilities

ST. ANNES OLD LINKS
Golf Club

Highbury Road, St. Annes-on-Sea,
Lancashire FY8 2LD.

Secretary: Peter Ray
01253-723597.
Professional: G. G. Hardiman
01253-722432.

THE 'Old Links' is situated on the breezy Fylde Coast, renowned for its championship links courses.

Alone among the four Lytham St. Annes clubs, Old Links retains an openness to the sea for part of its length, being separated from the beach by extensive sandhills, a single-track railway and the coast road.

It is the same railway line that runs alongside Royal Lytham and St. Annes.

The prevailing south-westerlies, the springy turf, the matchless greens and the fairways bordered by sand dunes are the memories that stay after a visit to Old Links.

Previous visitors will notice the club's policy of careful improvement. More dunes have been added to the sixth fairway and a natural pond has been re-established in front of the tee to daunt the faint-hearted and make it an outstanding par five hole.

The course is not the actual 'Old Links' from which the club takes its title. That name refers to the club's first course, of nine holes, a small part of which remains, which they took over in 1901.

Four years earlier, the Lytham and St. Annes Golf Club had moved a mile or so to start the now famous championship course at Links Gate.

A few years later, when the 'Old Links' club extended eastwards, becoming an 18-hole course, the name sounded very appropriate and was retained.

The present course holds a special place among Britain's entertainers for it has long been the favourite of the stars who appear in summer shows in nearby Blackpool.

On many days at St. Annes there have been as many famous faces on the course as could be seen at Wentworth or Sunningdale.

Among the several classic Old Links holes is the short ninth. When Bobby Jones visited the course at the time of his 1926 Open victory at Royal Lytham, he took a detailed plan of this hole and it was copied on several American courses.

Old Links is one of the qualifying courses for the Open.

The club requires smart casual dress, with jacket, collar and tie compulsory after 7pm. Unsuitable clothing is not allowed on the course or in the clubhouse.

Offenders are instructed to leave.

FACT FILE

A championship seaside links of 18 holes, 6616 yards. Par 72. SSS 72. Record 66.

Restrictions: Societies write in advance. Other visitors write or phone.

Fees: Not stated.

Dress code: Usual golf attire. Jacket, collar and tie after 7pm. See the report above.

Shop opening: 7.30am to dusk.

Facilities:

TO THE CLUB

On Highbury Road, St. Annes, 400 yards from the traffic light controlled junction with Clifton Drive North.

Course Information

Hole	Yards	Stroke	Par
1	338	13	4
2	393	9	4
3	171	15	3
4	439	1	4
5	544	5	5
6	520	7	5
7	447	3	4
8	366	11	4
9	171	17	3
10	321	16	4
11	335	14	4
12	405	2	4
13	201	8	3
14	374	10	4
15	374	4	4
16	169	18	3
17	552	6	5
18	496	12	5
OUT	3389		36
IN	3227		36
TOTAL	6616		72

1) A drive between two sandhills opens up the rising green.
2) A long drive is needed to clear cross bunkers before the green.
3) An iron shot of 170 yards will hit the well protected green.
4) The first of three successive long holes needs two long and accurate shots. The narrow green entrance is awkward from the wrong angle.
5) A long par five with sandhills left and out-of-bounds right.
6) Clear the pond and sandhills and avoid the line of fairway bunkers to set up your approach on another long hole.
7) Not much shorter but very difficult when played into the wind.
8) Two accurate shots usually succeed on this heavily-bunkered hole.
9) The famous ninth in front of the clubhouse is a narrow corridor between sandhills with a long green.
10) Club selection is important on this short par four.
11) An accurate drive between sandhills followed by a shot to a narrow green that falls away at the sides.
12) Avoid the water hazard at the right to get a good score here.
13) A long par three needs a good carry to the Mackenzie green.
14) A double line of fairway bunkers and cross-sandhills are the main hazards here.
15) Two long shots, particularly the second to clear the cross-bunkers, make a par possible.
16) Normally into the wind, this par three needs accuracy to a narrow, well protected green.
17) A long hole with the railway to the right and a long green to judge.
18) Still alongside the railway, with a high sandhill and blind shot to the green, this is a tough finishing hole.

Lancashire

Recommended Facilities

STONYHURST PARK
Golf Club

The Bayley Arms, Hurst Green, Clitheroe, Lancashire.

Secretary: Max Aitken
01254-826478.

COULD the Walker Cup owe its existence to this nine-hole course set in the sylvan setting of Lancashire's Ribble Valley?

If George Walker had not become such an avid golfer in his teenage years at Stonyhurst College, he may not have reached such high office in the American golf world.

And his grandson, former President George Bush, would not be an honorary member.

George Herbert Walker was sent by his family in the United States to be a student at Stoneyhurst, one of the leading Jesuit schools in Britain, at the turn of the century.

He became a leading amateur player and president of the USGA, donating the Walker Cup in 1922.

The Stonyhurst course was established in 1896 and for 80 years was an exclusive facility for students; a factor that persuaded many parents that this was the place for their boy.

In 1979, approaches were made to the college with the aim of giving local residents access to the course. A licence was granted and the Stonyhurst Park Golf Club came into being.

The move led to the steady development of the course. Larger greens, improved tees and better fairways have brough the layout up to a high standard. A small club-house was opened in 1994 although the 19th hole continues to be the Bayley Arms, where the green fees are payable.

Dinners, presentations and social events have been held at the hotel since the club's early days.

FACT FILE

A parkland course of 9 holes, 5529 yards. Par 69. SSS 66. Record 74.

Restrictions: Societies contact the Secretary. Visitors may play only on weekdays.

Fees: £10, with member £5.

Dress code: Usual golf attire.

Facilities:

🍴 ☕ 🍷 🎱 🚻 PG PN

TO THE CLUB

Hurst Green is on the B6243 midway between Clitheroe and Longridge.

Course Information

Hole	Yards	Stroke	Par
1	484	8	5
2	131	18	3
3	280	4	4
4	337	10	4
5	162	14	3
6	303	12	4
7	293	16	4
8	331	6	4
9	409	2	4
10	423	1	4
11	161	17	3
12	323	5	4
13	337	9	4
14	162	13	3
15	360	11	4
16	293	15	4
17	331	7	4
18	409	3	4
OUT	2730		35
IN	2799		34
TOTAL	5529		69

1) The third shot is the crucial. It's out-of-bounds behind the green.

2) The easiest hole. Just hit the green for a par!

3) A dogleg to the left with a steeply sloping fairway to a tight green.

4) A slight dogleg right. Beware the ditch in front of the green.

5) A par three over rough. Miss the big tree and hit the green for a par.

6) A dogleg left, with a small water hazard left of the fairway at around driving range. The best chance yet of a birdie.

7) Drive over the large pit for another birdie chance.

8) Position is all important here. Out-of-bounds right of the fairway.

9) The second hardest hole. A drive too close to the trees on the left brings problems. There's trouble all round the green.

10) Now for the hardest hole! You must clear the small valley and make an accurate second shot.

11) About 20 yards longer than the second hole.

12) A better driving hole than the third because the tee position is now 40 yards to the right.

13) Same as the fourth.

14) The fifth hole plus 20 yards.

15) The sixth with the tee 30 yards back.

16) Same as the seventh.

17) Same as the eighth.

18) Same as the ninth - so not an easy one to finish with.

Recommended Facilities

TOWNELEY
Golf Course/Club

Towneley Park, Todmorden Road,
Burnley, Lancashire BB11 3ED.

Secretary: Nigel Clark
01282-451636.
Pro shop: D. Garside
01282-38473.
Clubhouse: 01282-451636.

THE finest golf club setting in East Lancashire is Towneley Park, which was benevolently handed to the local council by the Towneley family in 1931.

Remarkable as that may have been in those days of privilege, the family's stipulation was even more unusual. They wanted the working class to be able to play golf!

After Burnley Council laid out a nine-hole course, the Towneley Golf Club was formed in 1932 and has helped develop the facility.

Meanwhile, the focal point of the park, the ancestral home of the Towneleys, became the borough's cultural attraction of art galleries, museum and natural history centre.

Golf at Towneley Hall remained on a modest scale until the course was extended in 1967 to an 18-hole, par 70 layout known as the Towneley course.

When the golf boom of the 1980s arrived, the council met the demand by adding a nine hole layout known as the Brunshaw course, on the other side of the River Calder and more than the Towneleys may have anticipated, the 'ordinary' man took to golf as if to the manor born!

In 1982 a new clubhouse evolved in the conversion, by golf club members, of the old Causeway Farm on the estate. Joint ventures between the club and the borough council have added an upstairs lounge and balcony, games room, pro shop, and locker facilities for 300 members and visitors. The clubhouse is a listed building.

The 18-hole course is a parkland layout with quite wide fairways, allowing some latitude to lesser golfers but there are internal out-of-bounds and some rather small, well guarded greens.

The nine-hole course is a different matter, being very tight and ideal for sharpening the game.

As more golfers are attracted to the courses, with about 80,000 rounds played each year, the golf club has responded by integrating many of them into club life.

FACT FILE

A parkland course of 18 holes, 5811 yards. Par 70. SSS 68. Record 67. An additional course of nine holes, 2229 yards. Par 31.

Restrictions: Societies make initial contact by phone.

Fees: £7.25 and £8.25. Juniors and pensioners £2. Nine hole course £4.10.

Dress code: Usual golf attire.

Shop opening: Summer 7am to 8pm. Winter 8am to 5pm.

Facilities:

TO THE CLUB

Towneley Park is one mile south east of Burnley on the A671.

Course Information

Hole	Yards	Stroke	Par
1	379	6	4
2	380	8	4
3	375	7	4
4	171	13	3
5	297	16	4
6	361	4	4
7	402	2	4
8	132	17	3
9	502	10	5
10	413	1	4
11	297	18	4
12	484	5	5
13	305	14	4
14	371	11	4
15	259	15	4
16	198	9	3
17	173	12	3
18	311	3	4
OUT	2812		35
IN	2999		35
TOTAL	5811		70

1) A 90 degree dogleg left with out-of-bounds all down the left. The 190-yard carry over the corner is only for the brave!

2) A blind second shot is longer than it looks and the green is trouble.

3) Beware the trees all down the right on this long par four.

4) The green is protected by bunkers and lateral water hazard.

5) Big-hitters can go for the green on this straightforward par four.

6) A straight drive is needed to have a chance of reaching in two.

7) A flat fairway for 400 yards but the green is small and tight to out-of-bounds on the left.

8) From a pitching wedge to a five iron, depending on the wind.

9) Par five and uphill with little trouble.

10) Four-putting is not uncommon on this sloping green.

11) Big-hitters can have a go in safety on this easy par four.

12) Think safety on this long par five; out-of-bounds left and right.

13) With a wide fairway the out-of-bounds is not normally a problem.

14) The widest fairway on the course. Think big on this hole!

15) A good birdie hole. Out of the trees to an elevated green.

16) An uphill par three all carry, bunkered left and right. A good drive is required to hit the green.

17) A downhill par three sloping to the right with trees through the green. Club selection is all important.

18) A card wrecker! Out-of-bounds left and right all the way to a heavily bunkered green.

Recommended Facilities

WHALLEY
Golf Club

Long Leese Barn, Portfield Lane,
Whalley, Lancashire BB6 9DR.

Secretary: J. S. Dawson
01254-886313.
Professional: Harry Smith
01254-824766.

THE Whalley club was founded in 1912 on its present site. But the clubhouse dates back to 1751!

It was an old barn that was converted and extended in 1972 when a highway scheme alongside the course made it necessary to find a new clubhouse.

Careful renovation allowed some of the original beams and walls to be featured. Almost the entire course can be viewed from the clubhouse.

The Whalley club can claim to have one of the finest nine-hole courses in the county. It is a nine-hole parkland course with beautifully matured trees and wonderful views of the Ribble Valley and the Lakeland hills.

Alterations have been made over many years, adding to the interest and difficulties for the golfer.

Two of the short holes call for shots over water and several greens are guarded by front and side bunkers. When played as 18, the inward nine have different tee positions.

FACT FILE

A parkland course of 9 holes, 6258 yards. Par 72. SSS 70. Record 69.

Restrictions: Societies initially contact the pro.
Ladies' Thursday pm.

Fees: £15 to £20, with member £8 and £12.

Dress code: Usual golf attire.

Shop opening: Dawn to dusk.

Facilities:

TO THE CLUB

The course is one mile south east of Whalley off the A671.

Course Information

Hole	Yards	Stroke	Par
1	435	3	4
2	485	1	5
3	179	17	3
4	355	7	4
5	525	13	5
6	325	5	4
7	320	15	4
8	333	11	4
9	178	9	3
10	470	2	4
11	470	4	5
12	212	12	3
13	364	6	4
14	518	14	5
15	294	8	4
16	312	16	4
17	333	10	4
18	150	18	3
OUT	3135		36
IN	3123		36
TOTAL	6258		72

1) This long par four has a slight dogleg left. Keep the drive left.

2) A par five uphill seems longer than its 485 yards. A ditch crosses the fairway 70 yards from the green.

3) A well bunkered short par three.

4) A bunker is strategically sited at driving range.

5) A par five running downhill. Entry to the green is tricky.

6) Bunkers to the right and a well guarded green.

7) Same again but with a slight dogleg to the left.

8) A straight drive is needed with trees right and out-of-bounds left.

9) Playing across a pond to a well guarded green in front of the clubhouse.

Lancashire

Recommended Facilities

WILPSHIRE
Golf Club

Whalley Road, Wilpshire,
Blackburn, Lancs BB1 9LF.

Secretary: John Ditchfield
01254-248260.
Professional: Walter Slavin
01254-249558.

WILPSHIRE is the oldest club playing on an 18-hole course in East Lancashire. It was founded in 1890, just ahead of Pleasington and Clitheroe.

The club started with a nine-hole layout, but acquired new land in 1907 and has been playing on its present course since then.

Various great names of golf course design had a hand in the development in the early years. They included James Braid, Dr. Alister Mackenzie and H. S. Colt.

The club's great advantage on the new course was its location between the hub of East Lancashire business and commerce and the sweeter air and wide vistas of the Ribble Valley.

The views from the course are magnificent, extending from the Lancashire coast on the left to the Forest of Bowland, Pendle and the Yorkshire Dales, with Ingleborough, Pen-y-Ghent and Whernside clearly in view.

After the input of famous golf designers, the course has been improved gradually over the years, notably through the planting of many trees, which have softened and sheltered the course.

The latest major alteration was the laying out of a new 17th hole in 1995.

FACT FILE

A semi-moorland course of 18 holes, 5921 yards. Par 69. SSS 68. Record 61.

Restrictions: Societies make initial contact by phone. Ladies' day Tuesday. Handicap certificates required.

Fees: £25 to £30, with member £8 and £11.

Dress code: Usual golf attire.

Shop opening: Dawn till dusk.

Facilities:

TO THE CLUB

Four miles north east of Blackburn off the A666.

Course Information

Hole	Yards	Stroke	Par
1	307	15	4
2	433	4	4
3	400	6	4
4	355	9	4
5	162	13	3
6	300	11	4
7	422	2	4
8	154	18	3
9	500	8	5
10	522	1	5
11	196	12	3
12	373	7	4
13	259	17	4
14	364	3	4
15	192	16	3
16	393	5	4
17	229	10	3
18	360	14	4
OUT	3033		35
IN	2888		34
TOTAL	5921		69

1) A dogleg right. Drive left of the marker post for a relatively easy pitch to the green.
2) A dogleg to the left. Drive just to the right of the big tree.
3) A straightforward drive from an elevated tee - left centre is perfect - but beware the bunkers close to and surrounding the green.
4) Drive through 'the Polo mint' to set up an easy second shot.
5) A devilish par three. There is a bunker hidden on the left and the green is not as flat as it appears.
6) Hug the left of the fairway for a short pitch to a Mackenzie green.
7) Drive slightly right of the bunker, aim the second shot slightly right of the green centre - and be prepared to three-putt.
8) An impish short hole with large green bunkers.
9) A comfortable par five. Drive over the right-hand hump and be careful of the cross-bunkers with the second shot.
10) The drive and second shot must be straight to set up the third.
11) A cruel par three with a long, narrow green in trees.
12) Aim the drive at the end of the wall with a slight fade.
13) A spectacular short par four. A testing tee shot to those who try and drive the green.
14) A long drive, slightly right of the marker post, can give an opening for the difficult second shot to the long green.
15) A long iron or even a wood, depending on the wind.
16) A long drive is a must, in order to play a difficult second shot.
17) The new, shorter par three needs accuracy over water or bunker.
18) A straight drive slightly right of centre is needed here and the second calls for a well struck iron to a cunningly bunkered green.

113

NON-STOP BLACKPOOL

The biggest and most popular seaside resort in Europe, Blackpool offers just about everything a holidaymaker can wish.

Everyone has heard of the Tower and the seven mile promenade but when it comes down to numbers, the Pleasure Beach tops the lot.

The Big One is Europe's tallest roller coaster, standing 235ft at its highest point, and the 40-acre amusement park is Britain's biggest single tourist attraction with six and a half million annual visitors.

Back in Victorian days, Blackpool was the first town in the country to 'go electric.' A century later the resort's love affair with light has taken a new dimension.

Every autumn the town becomes a blaze of coloured lights and tableaux for 'the greatest free show on earth' - the Blackpool Illuminations.

In contrast to the fast-moving fun and entertainment is Blackpool Zoo Park and the adjacent Stanley Park, a haven of green with a large boating lake.

When it comes to accommodation the resort can outnumber its rivals by a Golden Mile. There are more than 120,000 beds in 3,000 hotels, guest houses and holiday apartments.

A PROUD HERITAGE

Lancashire's industrial heritage can be seen in the handsome Victorian architecture and the many centres of interest created from the mills, docks and waterways around the county.

Preston, the county's administrative centre, has developed its old docks into a thriving retail and residential centre grouped round a marina.

The Wyre port of Fleetwood has also been transformed by a marina with the preserved trawler Jacinta, and the Freeport shopping village.

Marsh Mill at Thornton Cleveleys is a beautiful example of a 19th century tower mill, restored to working order, while another fine example stands on

LANCASHIRE'S HILL COUNTRY

Away from the towns and cities of the north west, another world awaits.

The beautiful Ribble Valley and the Forest of Bowland are threaded with quiet byways and silent valleys watched over by the brooding bulk of Pendle Hill, land of the famous Lancashire witches.

The market town of Clitheroe is a popular centre just off the A59, the main route through the valley.

To the south, near Chorley, Anglezark Moor and Rivington Pike, offer spectacular views over the West Lancashire plain to the coastline between the Ribble and the Mersey.

HISTORIC LANCASTER

History appears round every corner in Lancaster, where the skyline is dominated by the 800-year-old castle, open to the public in summer. The Lancashire witches were imprisoned here.

See the maritime museum in the riverside Customs House, designed by Richard Gillow, the renowned furniture maker.

A collection of Gillow pieces is on display at the Judges' Lodgings Museum, reputedly the city's oldest town house.

Williamson Park is set in 38 acres with a commanding view from the Ashton Memorial.

The many other points of interest in the city include the 200-year-old canal, the Grand Theatre - of similar vintage - and the Priory and Parish Church of St. Mary, mostly medieval, on the site of an earlier Saxon church and Roman remains.

the green at Lytham.

Railway fans can ride behind restored steam locomotives on the East Lancashire Railway between Rawtenstall and Bury.

And Britain's oldest electric tramway system remains a vital part of Blackpool's transport system, with several veteran tramcars to be seen among the modern fleet.

Local Facilities

116

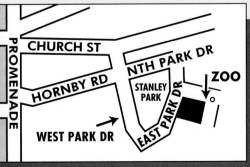

Isle of Man

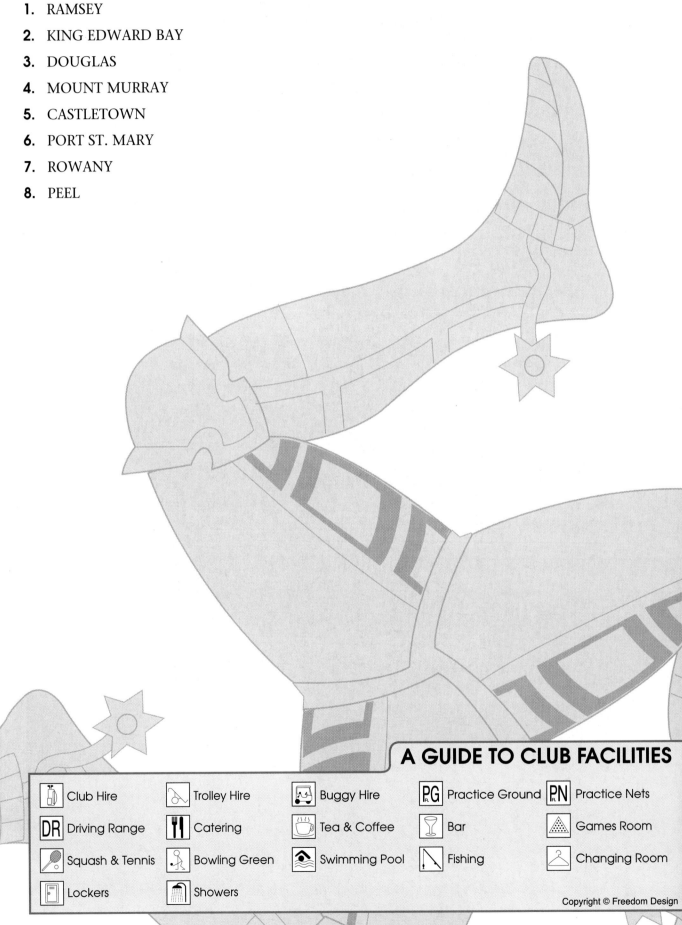

A GUIDE TO CLUB FACILITIES

Club Hire	Trolley Hire	Buggy Hire	PG Practice Ground	PN Practice Nets
DR Driving Range	Catering	Tea & Coffee	Bar	Games Room
Squash & Tennis	Bowling Green	Swimming Pool	Fishing	Changing Room
Lockers	Showers			

Copyright © Freedom Design

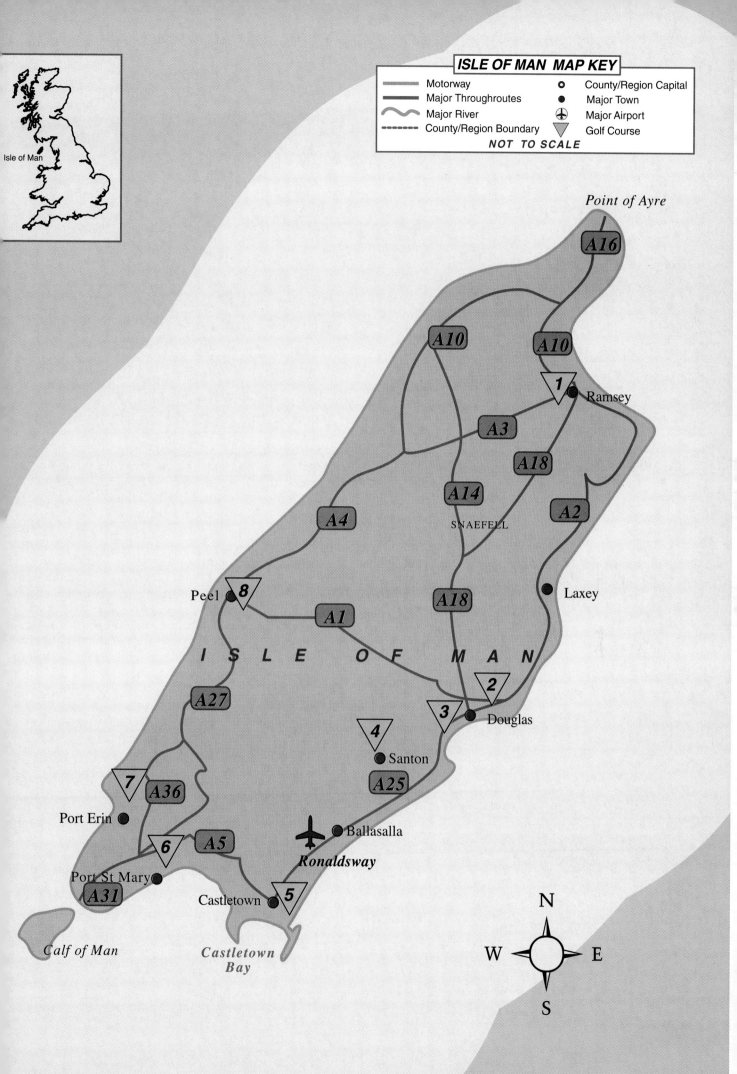

CASTLETOWN
Golf Links

Fort Island, Derbyhaven,
Isle of Man IM9 1UA.

Golf Secretary: Mrs C. M. Kaye
01624-825435 (Fax 824633).
Professional: Murray Crowe
01624-822211.

AT the south eastern tip of the Isle of Man, the Langness Peninsula - better known as Fort Island - pushes out into the Irish Sea.

This triangular peninsula, connected to the mainland by a thin strip of rock, is the location of the magnificent Castletown Golf Links Hotel, a haven of luxury living and superb golf.

The course is a true links of easy-draining turf and fast, smooth greens with most of the holes well above sea level, providing the player with a most therapeutic seascape of cliffs, rocky and sandy coves, sweeping bays, and blue horizons.

The warming effect of the Gulf Stream gives a helping hand to the plentiful gorse and heather.

The original Castletown course was laid out in the 1890s by Old Tom Morris of St. Andrews.

After World War Two the course was restored and partially re-designed by Mackenzie Ross, placing it in the top rank of links courses in the British Isles.

The quality of the course matches the setting. Its hallmark is small greens and few bunkers, with the defence coming from the bumps, dips and gorse of classic links.

The first hole is just one yard over the limit for a par three so there are only three short holes, the 135-yard sixth being the shortest.

Rated stroke index one is the eighth, a 410-yard par four known as Castletown's Road Hole, although it is not in play and only marks the out-of-bounds between the fairway and a lovely sandy cove.

The second nine begins with a testing 550-yard par five which is laid out on the site, reputedly, of the horse race that originally bore Lord Derby's name, before it re-located to Epsom.

But the hole that is usually the main talking point is the 17th - the cliff-top hole that needs a carry of 200 yards over water from the back tee. Lesser mortals can take a safer line! The course does not have a clubhouse, offering golfers the more lavish facilities of the Castletown Golf Links Hotel with its superb restaurant, bars, sauna, solarium and heated indoor swimming pool. This is the Castletown experience.

FACT FILE

A championship links course of 18 holes, 6567 yards. Par 72. SSS 73. Record 65.

Restrictions: Societies apply initially by phone. Ladies' day Wednesday 9.30am til noon.

Fees: £20 to £25.

Dress code: Usual golf attire.

Shop opening: 8am to 6pm.

Facilities:

TO THE CLUB

Signposted from Castletown and Ronaldsway Airport.

Course Information			
Hole	**Yards**	**Stroke**	**Par**
1	251	18	4
2	390	3	4
3	516	11	5
4	367	5	4
5	486	13	5
6	135	17	3
7	350	7	4
8	410	1	4
9	368	9	4
10	550	4	5
11	173	15	3
12	366	10	4
13	345	14	4
14	468	2	4
15	375	6	4
16	193	16	3
17	414	8	4
18	410	12	4
OUT	**3273**		**37**
IN	**3294**		**35**
TOTAL	**6567**		**72**

1) This hole just qualifies as a par four - but birdies are not guaranteed due to the well-guarded elevated green.

2) A simple par four but it can play long into the prevailing wind.

3) On this long par five dogleg, play the tee shot to the right of the wall and keep the second shot right to open up the green.

4) Slightly left off the tee in order to open up the green.

5) A narrow fairway - so drive accurately. The green is well guarded.

6) Short but very tricky with deep bunkers fronting the green.

7) A very tough dogleg. A straight drive will leave about a nine iron second shot but drive off line and there is big trouble left in gorse.

8) The Road Hole - a difficult 400 yards. The sea is on the right and there's thick heathery rough to the left.

9) Thick gorse left, out-of-bounds right. Drive straight!

10) The longest hole and it plays that way. After missing the bunkers the third shot is to a two-tiered green.

11) A good short hole. The trouble is right of the green.

12) You must drive down the left of the fairway on this one.

13) There are lots of gorse and sandy lies on the right of the fairway.

14) A long and troublesome par four. The drive must be accurate.

15) With out-of-bounds on the right and two awkward bunkers left, a well-placed drive leaves a tricky green as the problem.

16) A short hole where club selection depends on the wind.

17) Frightening but picturesque! 200 yards of frothing water.

18) An excellent finishing hole needing a good drive towards the hotel and a good second shot over a ravine.

Recommended Facilities

CASTLETOWN GOLF LINKS HOTEL

FORT ISLAND • DERBYHAVEN • ISLE OF MAN

tel: 01624 822201

fax: 01624 824633

The Castletown Golf Links Hotel, situated on the beautiful Langness peninsula, is internationally famous for its challenging 6000 yard, 18-hole Championship Golf Course.

Best Western

A member of the world's largest group of fine independent hotels

The Course is wholly owned by the Castletown Golf Links Hotel. There are many 'Golf Packages' available at Castletown which include unlimited golf. Please telephone 01624 825435 for more infomation about booking.

Isle of Man

DOUGLAS
Golf Course/Club

Pulrose Park, Douglas,
Isle of Man IM2 1AE.

Secretary: Michael Moyer
01624-675952.
Professional: Kevin Parry
01624-661558.

JUST over a mile from the centre of Douglas, this 18-hole municipal course is invariably referred to as Pulrose.

It has a particularly attractive mature parkland setting. Having been established in 1891, the course was redesigned by Alister Mackenzie in the early 1920s, since when there have been only a few minor changes.

The course covers a large undulating area and is kept in fine condition by Douglas Corporation.

It is operated on a pay-and-play basis. Visitors need only make a phone call to ensure a tee-off time and handicap certificates are not required. The course is also played over by the Douglas Golf Club.

It is an interesting layout and has no fairway bunkers apart from the 18th but some greens are small and call for an accurate approach.

Two excellent holes are the 332-yard second, a par four, and the 214-yard 17th, a par three.

The second requires a well-placed drive in order to get position for the difficult mid-iron second shot into a high and closely guarded green.

The 17th is the signature hole and requires a very accurate shot from a high tee to the green 70 feet below.

There is only one par five hole, the 478-yard 11th but this is not regarded as one of the hardest to play. The last six holes are regarded as a test for a good player, particularly in the breeze that seems ever-present. The Manx Championship has often been played here.

Holidaymakers may find it useful to know there are reduced fees after 2.30pm on weekdays and 5pm on weekends.

FACT FILE

An undulating parkland course of 18 holes, 5922 yards. Par 69. SSS 68. Record 64.

Restrictions: Societies contact the professional by phone.

Fees: £6.80 to £12.50. Reductions for parties of eight or more.

Dress code: Casual.

Shop opening: Weekdays 8.30am to 8pm, weekends 7am to 8pm.

Facilities:

TO THE CLUB

At Pulrose Park, one and a half miles south west of Douglas.

Course Information

Hole	Yards	Stroke	Par
1	283	14	4
2	332	4	4
3	376	5	4
4	162	10	3
5	299	15	4
6	365	9	4
7	399	7	4
8	146	18	3
9	432	2	4
10	377	6	4
11	478	11	5
12	307	16	4
13	177	12	3
14	431	8	4
15	421	1	4
16	447	3	4
17	214	13	3
18	276	17	4
OUT	2794		34
IN	3128		35
TOTAL	5922		69

1) A relatively easy par four with a stream on the left of the fairway, which is shared with the final hole.
2) A tough par four. The green is cut into the hillside with out-of-bounds left. No bail out!
3) Two large trees guard the entrance to this well bunkered green.
4) Hook the ball on this par three and you'll be in the nearby school!
5) A short, hilly par four. Play left from the tee.
6) The highest point on the course. The fairway slopes to the right.
7) A longer hole, usually played into the wind, it needs a good tee shot to stand any chance of the second hitting the green.
8) A good little par three over a valley to a bunkered green. It often plays harder than its stroke index.
9) This difficult par four is a thinker's hole. The fairway slopes sharply. Settle for the par!
10) A dogleg to the left and into the wind. The second shot can play anything from a wood to a wedge.
11) This nice par five over a valley is a birdie chance.
12) A short par four with a sloping green that's a two putt.
13) The start of a great finish to the course, this is a tough par three.
14) A lovely driving hole but beware the tricky approach.
15) The toughest on the course is uphill, 421 yards and it plays longer. It's a par five for most golfers.
16) Another long hole needing a very good drive.
17) The signature hole. Club selection is the key.
18) A short par four with big trouble left and a bunker in the fairway to catch the bail-out drive.

Recommended Facilities

SEFTON HOTEL

HARRIS PROMENADE • DOUGLAS • ISLE OF MAN • IM1 2RW
Tel: 01624 626011   Fax: 01624 676004

HIGHLY COMMENDED

'The Hotel for all seasons'
There are 74 very pleasant en-suite rooms all with teletext/satellite TVs, radio, hospitality tray, hairdryer and direct dial phones. These are divided into 6 budget singles, 35 standard, 30 executive and 3 rooms suitable for the disabled.

The Gaiety Theatre
If you have already decided that we couldn't possibly have a Theatre inside the hotel you would be right...but only just...there is a secret door into the beautifully restored Gaiety Theatre from the hotel.

The Fountain Health & Leisure Club
This luxury club with its pool, poolside bar and reception desk, saunas, steam rooms, sunbed rooms, beauty therapy room, jacuzzi and gym is a great place to relax. There is a club membership too so it's a great place to get to know some lovely local people.

Situated equidistant to all golf courses on the island

KING EDWARD BAY
Golf and Country Club

Howstrake, Groudle Road,
Onchan, Isle of Man IM3 2JR.
Office: 01624-620430/673821.
Course Director: Peter Gough
01624-673821 (Fax. 676794).
Professional: Don Jones
01624-672709.
Secretary: 01624-861430.

KING Edward Bay is the new name given to the former Howstrake Golf Course after it was redesigned and modern clubhouse facilities were built in 1987.

The 18-hole moorland-heathland course, which is noted for its springy turf, has a dramatic location on and around the Onchan headland, to the north of the promenade at Douglas.

Its commanding position gives spectacular views of the capital, the rocky coasts and bays and of Groudle Glen on the other side.

The handsome red brick and cement clubhouse is the focal point for visitors who should expect a moderately hilly course with only the second and 13th holes likely to be over-taxing.

The course was founded in 1893 by Manx entrepreneur Alexander Bruce. Nine holes were laid out by Old Tom Morris of St. Andrews, assisted by George Lowe, the professional at Lytham and St. Annes. It was converted to 18 holes when additional land was acquired in 1914. In 1896 a three-day autumn meeting was held at Howstrake. It attracted several leading professionals. In good conditions on the Wednesday, Ben Sayers, of North Berwick, set a new course record of 69. The next day, in bad conditions, Sayers and Alex Herd, of Huddersfield, both went round in 82 and A. Simpson, of Musselburgh, in 81.

Veteran members of the club remember seeing an up and coming young golfer named Henry Cotton playing in an exhibition match in the early 1930s.

FACT FILE

A heathland course of 18 holes, 5485 yards. Par 67. SSS 65. Record 63.

Restrictions: Societies phone in advance.

Fees: £10 to £12. Societies of 10 or more £8 each.

Dress code: Usual golf attire.

Shop opening: 9am to 6pm.

Facilities:

TO THE CLUB

The course is five minutes north of Douglas seafront.

Hole	Yards	Stroke	Par
1	380	3	4
2	200	9	3
3	432	1	4
4	485	15	5
5	350	11	4
6	355	7	4
7	150	17	3
8	390	5	4
9	198	13	3
10	258	18	4
11	428	4	4
12	156	14	3
13	272	8	4
14	150	16	3
15	390	6	4
16	312	12	4
17	390	2	4
18	189	10	3
OUT	2940		34
IN	2545		33
TOTAL	5485		67

Course Information

1) A good opening hole. Don't be short with the second shot or the ball will fall away to the left.

2) Only a well struck iron will find the green on this par three.

3) A longish par four that doglegs to the right. Watch the out-of-bounds posts on the right.

4) A par five that may offer a birdie chance if the wind is favourable.

5) A good drive over the guide-post will give a short iron approach.

6) A short par four but the tee shot must be accurate.

7) An uphill one-shotter. Nothing for being short here!

8) A pleasant downhill drive but finesse is needed with the second shot.

9) Only a straight shot will find the green below. Spectacular view!

10) A drive and pitch to a small green starts the back nine.

11) A good second shot over the crest of a hill will find the green below. Another spectacular view!

12) A lovely par three but aim right because of the sloping terrain.

13) On this short par four a straight tee shot leaves a high pitch over a steep bank to the green.

14) A soft wedge over the heather. The green is hard to hold.

15) A pleasing hole curving to the left and downhill provides yet another great view.

16) Keep the drive right of centre on this shortish par four because the trouble is mostly on the left.

17) A longer par four with trouble all along the left.

18) A good medium iron will find the green if you avoid the bunker.

Recommended Facilities

Isle of Man

9

MOUNT MURRAY
Golf and
Country Club

Santon, Isle of Man IM4 2HT

Secretary/professional:
Andrew Dyson 01624-661111.

THERE'S a Mediterranean feel to this wonderful development set in 260 acres a few miles south of Douglas.

Mount Murray is a luxurious hotel and conference centre that can accommodate up to 300 delegates, backed by a secretarial bureau and state-of-the-art technology.

Golf and other sporting facilities are an important part of the experience.

The golf course, opened in 1994, skilfully incorporated the natural features of Manx hedging, streams and lakes. It is a challenging 6664 yards from the back tees but the variable teeing allows the moderate player a fairer round.

The opening hole is a pleasant downhill par four. This is followed by a climb from the second tee to the sixth green. On the long seventh hole the views are spectacular, swinging from Douglas down to the south coast of the island.

The hazards on the course are grass and gorse banks, streams and a couple of lakes. The feature hole is the 18th, where two good shots leave the golfer with a memorable approach shot over the point of a lake to the green in front of the clubhouse.

Most of the greens are large and beautifully contoured. The effect can be deceiving when judging distances.

As a new course, Mount Murray has not hosted any major events but this would seem to be only a matter of time.

The golf complex includes a 24-bay driving range and practice ground.

The adjacent fitness centre has a heated indoor swimming pool and steam room suite, floodlit, all-weather tennis courts, and crown green bowling.

FACT FILE

A parkland/heathland course of 18 holes, 6664 yards. Par 72. SSS 72.

Restrictions: Societies make contact by phone.

Fees: Weekdays £18, weekends £24.

Dress code: Usual golf attire.

Shop opening: 8.30am to 8pm

Facilities:

TO THE CLUB

Three miles from Douglas on the road to Castletown.

Course Information

Hole	Yards	Stroke	Par
1	433	5	4
2	445	1	4
3	214	11	3
4	298	15	4
5	278	17	4
6	170	13	3
7	595	9	5
8	572	3	5
9	398	7	4
10	522	4	5
11	435	2	4
12	490	14	5
13	159	16	3
14	367	12	4
15	205	8	3
16	394	10	4
17	155	18	3
18	534	6	5
OUT	3403		36
IN	3261		36
TOTAL	6664		72

1) A pleasant downhill par four with trees to the left and a Manx hedge all the way down the right.
2) Two monster hits are needed to reach this long uphill par four. Most of the trouble is to the right.
3) A three-tiered green awaits a quality hit long iron on this good par three, but try to avoid the four bunkers protecting the green.
4) A good driving hole. A bunker on the right will gather a slice.
5) A short dogleg par four is a real tease for the long hitter but beware of the bunkers protecting both sides of the tricky green.
6) Island View. An uphill par three with the forest to the left and fantastic views.
7) Longest hole on the course. Three sensible shots will get you home in regulation.
8) A par five out of the top drawer. Gorse everywhere. Two straight hits leave an approach shot to a green nestling between the gorse.
9) A tricky par four through the Manx hedging. Avoid the bunker to the right.
10) Long hitters can reach the green in two but the stream in front suggests a more cautious approach.
11) A very tough hole, with the wind often against, a ditch down the right and pond by the green.
12) Keep the tee shot straight, negotiate the fairway bunker and a short third shot to a two-tiered green will give a birdie opportunity.
13) This par three isn't too long, hit the green and the par is safe.
14) How brave do you want to be off the tee? If you fail to cut the corner a stream and gorse awaits.
15) A long iron or wood to reach the two-tiered putting surface. Don't be short and left.
16) More spectacular views. Avoid the fairway bunker.
17) A bunker short left and a grass banking short right can catch an off-centre strike.
18) Get your tee shot away avoiding out-of-bounds left and right, and the real decisions have to be made. A stunning finish.

Recommended Facilities

Isle of Man

11

PEEL
Golf Club

Rheast Lane, Peel,
Isle of Man IM5 1BG.

Secretary: James Cuan
01624-843456.
Professional: Murray Crowe
01624-844232.

THE Peel course on the west of the island is an undulating heathland layout with gorse bushes and pine plantations.

It is not a long course, even from the back tees, and the only par five hole is the 481-yard seventh hole.

But is has plenty of variety and challenge for the golfer. The highlight must be the 11th, a 447-yard par four, which is rated stroke index one. It involves a long carry over gorse bushes.

The Peel club's centenary was in 1995, for which the club built an extension - featuring a clock tower- to the 1977 clubhouse.

Peel Golf Club was founded in 1895 and started to play over a nine-hole course the following May. It was spread over 25 acres of farmers' fields and the encroachment of sheep and ponies caused the club to fence the greens in 1903.

The course was extended to 15 holes in 1921 by George Lowe, the professional at Lytham and St.

Annes. He had been involved in the design of the Ramsey and Howstrake (now King Edward Bay) courses. His love of the island showed in the names of his daughter and son - Peel and Ramsey!

Land for the final three holes was soon acquired and by 1927 the course was considered good enough for the semi-final and final of the Manx Championship.

Although a majority of the members lived in England, the course became an asset to the local holiday industry but struggled to stay in existence.

After World War Two, when 43 acres of cereal were grown on the course, the club was leased to Mr. F. S. Dalgleish, who operated it as the Peel Golf and Country Club until 1959.

The enthusiasm of older members steered the club through the 1960s to the point where the club was able to embark on the long process of purchasing the various parcels of land that make up the course.

The major step of building a new clubhouse, officially opened in 1977 by Peter Alliss, was followed four years later by the appointment of the first paid secretary to cope with the dramatic increase in membership.

FACT FILE

A moorland/heathland course of 18 holes, 5914 yards. Par 69. SSS 68. Record 63.

Restrictions: Societies make arrangements by phone. Ladies' day Thursday.

Fees: £15 to £18.

Dress code: Usual golf attire.

Shop opening: 8am to 6pm in summer; 8.30am to 4pm in winter.

Facilities:

TO THE CLUB

On the Douglas road, east of Peel. Signposted.

Course Information			
Hole	Yards	Stroke	Par
1	315	14	4
2	152	18	3
3	442	2	4
4	369	6	4
5	345	11	4
6	184	9	3
7	481	8	5
8	408	3	4
9	336	12	4
10	143	17	3
11	447	1	4
12	310	13	4
13	413	4	4
14	360	7	4
15	318	15	4
16	321	10	4
17	158	16	3
18	412	5	4
OUT	3032		35
IN	2882		34
TOTAL	5914		69

1) A gentle opening hole but with out-of-bounds on the right.

2) The green on this short hole is out of sight of the tee.

3) A long par four, rated stroke index two. It is played from an elevated tee and has out-of-bounds on both sides.

4) A tricky two-shot hole. A stream guards the steeply sloped green.

5) A short par four with a second shot to a well bunkered green.

6) A mid to long iron is required to hit the 'upturned saucer' green.

7) A fairly short par five. It has out-of-bounds all along the right.

8) A long par four with a tricky second shot to an elevated green.

9) This is a straightforward and modest par four until the steeply sloped green is encountered.

10) A picturesque par three down to a valley green.

11) The toughest on the course, this is a par four doglegging to the right around gorse and ending with a saddle green.

12) A good drive is required over gorse. If successful, it leaves a short iron to a large green.

13) Two long shots are needed on this straight par four.

14) Another straightforward par four but with a tricky green.

15) Only a brave tee shot over the out-of-bounds will leave a good line into this well protected green.

16) The fairway narrows as you near the green. Out-of-bounds right.

17) A short par three to a two-tier green surrounded by bunkers.

18) A tough finishing hole with a second shot to a green tucked in behind out-of-bounds.

Recommended Facilities

Isle of Man

PORT ST. MARY
Golf Club

Kallow Point Road,
Port St. Mary, Isle of Man.
Secretary: Terry Boyle
01624-832274 (Fax 835677).

ONE of the greatest views from any golf course on the island is the highlight of a round played on this nine-hole municipally-owned layout.

It is to be seen from the high tee at the sixth hole and it is truly breathtaking, from Snaefell on the left, round to the Calf of Man.

And the green has a wonderful backdrop of Port St. Mary harbour with its fishing boats and visiting yachts at anchor.

Local history records the existence of several golf courses in the Port St. Mary district but they all vanished under the plough, the gorse or building development.

This course was established on high ground above the village in 1936. It was designed by George Duncan, the 1920 Open champion.

There are no lakes, rivers or stately oak trees and there are only four bunkers but newcomers should

beware. It is rather steep and high.

The course has seven par fours and two par threes. The longest hole is only 374 yards which makes for a relaxed holiday round. Not that this course is a pushover. It is a serious test of golf.

Port St. Mary's eighth hole is reckoned by some to be the most difficult par three on the island. Sitting on the skyline the distance can be deceptive. The local advice is to treat it as a par five.

As George Duncan said when he designed the course: " I can't make it long but I can make it tricky."

The Port St. Mary Golf Club is based on the course and has its own clubhouse.

FACT FILE

A seaside links course of 9 holes, 5418 yards played as 18. Par 68. SSS 66. Record 62.

Restrictions: Societies make arrangements by phone.

Fees: £10.50 to £13.50 per day.

Dress code: Smart casual.

Facilities:

TO THE CLUB

The course is one mile from Port St. Mary, which is well signposted from Douglas.

Course Information

Hole	Yards	Stroke	Par
1	277	15	4
2	342	5	4
3	367	1	4
4	374	7	4
5	289	13	4
6	214	9	3
7	350	11	4
8	213	3	3
9	283	17	4
10	277	16	4
11	342	6	4
12	367	2	4
13	374	8	4
14	289	14	4
15	214	10	3
16	350	12	4
17	213	4	3
18	283	18	4
OUT	2709		34
IN	2709		34
TOTAL	5418		68

1) It's out-of-bounds left but there's plenty of room on the right. An easy opening hole.

2) A blind tee shot and the approach to the green is guarded by two bunkers, requiring a very accurate second shot.

3) It only measures 367 yards but it's all uphill. This is stroke index one on the card and most golfers will be happy with a five.

4) Tee off over the marker post. It's out-of-bounds down the right and slightly doglegged. The green is difficult to hit and hold.

5) A dogleg to the left with out-of-bounds left. Most members play an iron to avoid rough. There's a tricky second shot to a plateau green.

6) Majestic views overlooking the harbour. It needs an accurate and well judged shot to make this par three.

7) A difficult hole with a green protected by a bunker on the left.

8) Port St Mary's highly regarded par three hole. Depending on the wind, anything from a driver to a seven iron.

9) A short par four but the small two-tier green is difficult to hit with the second shot.

RAMSEY
Golf Club

Brookfield, Ramsey,
Isle of Man IM8 2AH.

Secretary: John Mead
01624-812244 (Fax same).
Professional: Calum Wilson
01624-814736 (Fax same).
Clubhouse: 01624-813365.

A magnificent new clubhouse and an extensive tree-planting scheme marked the start of the Ramsey club's second century.

The club was formed in 1891 with a 12-hole course designed by Old Tom Morris at Milntown, part of which comprises the present 11th to 15th holes.

After 15 years the club leased a further parcel of land and a new 18 hole course was laid out by George Lowe, who also designed Royal Lytham and St. Annes, where he was the professional.

In 1925 came the chance to buy the lands comprising the Milntown and Brookfield Estates. A limited company was formed with members taking shares and a mortgage was raised for the balance.

James Braid, the five-times Open champion and prolific designer of golf courses was engaged to redesign Lowe's layout for a fee of 20 guineas. The work was carried out in 1926 by the Glasgow firm of J. R. Strutt,

the leading firm of the day.

Only minor changes have been necessary and aficionados of course design can recognise Braid's work to this day. The pine and mature trees have enhanced it over the years.

The course begins with the most challenging opening hole on the island, a par five bordered by water and other out-of-bounds.

There is a good mixture of challenging par threes and tricky par fours over pleasant parkland with some fine views and - for the greater part - easy walking.

The clubhouse, set in a commanding position, gives the finishing touch to a beautiful course. It replaced a wooden clubhouse that

was second-hand when bought in 1892!

It was finally demolished in 1989 to make way for the handsome new building in time for the centenary. The club then marked the 100 years by launching a planting programme that will be appreciated by future generations.

Famous members of the club include comedian Norman Wisdom, who organises the annual Norman Wisdom Charity Classic, and racing driver Nigel Mansell (an honorary member) who was club champion in 1990.

FACT FILE

A parkland course of 18 holes, 5960 yards. Par 70. SSS 69. Record 64.

Restrictions: Societies make contact by phone (no bookings on Sundays). Ladies' day Tuesday am. No visitors Monday to Friday 10am to noon and 2 to 4pm and Saturday 2.30 to 3.30pm.

Fees: £16 to £20.

Dress code: Usual golf attire.

Shop opening: Dawn till dusk.

Facilities:

TO THE CLUB

On the Douglas to Ramsay mountain road turn off at Ray Motors into Brookfield Avenue.

Course Information

Hole	Yards	Stroke	Par
1	510	3	5
2	303	13	4
3	140	7	3
4	256	17	4
5	373	9	4
6	272	15	4
7	417	1	4
8	388	11	4
9	200	5	3
10	371	10	4
11	524	16	5
12	215	2	3
13	397	6	4
14	497	18	5
15	436	4	4
16	339	14	4
17	178	8	3
18	144	12	3
OUT	2859		35
IN	3101		35
TOTAL	5960		70

1) A card-wrecker! Out-of-bounds both sides with water on the right.

2) The drive must favour the right side on this short uphill par four.

3) The shortest hole - but Augusta would be proud of this green.

4) It looks simple but isn't. An iron off the tee and a short pitch over water and bunkers.

5) With out-of-bounds right and fairway bunkers, drive straight.

6) A short par four with hedges and out-of-bounds behind the green.

7) This needs two good shots. A gorse hedge offers trouble on the right.

8) Hit the drive slightly left to avoid the big fairway bunker right.

9) Trouble waits behind the green if too much club is taken.

10) A straight drive is required. The green doglegs to the left and should be approached with a short iron.

11) The longest par five poses problems with out-of-bounds, an acute dogleg right and a wall across the fairway .

12) A longish par three (stroke index two) has four green bunkers.

13) Place the drive between the two fairway bunkers - but take one more club than you think you need.

14) A long hitter can get home in two with a good birdie chance.

15) A tough par four. The drive will kick towards the fairway bunker. A long second shot is needed to the guarded green.

16) With two fairway bunkers at 220 yards, hit it very straight!

17) The two green bunkers and water at the back, will cause trouble.

18) The green is large. Miss it and there's a difficult pitch.

Recommended Facilities

Isle of Man

17

ROWANY
Golf Club

Port Erin, Isle of Man.

Secretary: Martin Redmayne
01624-622726.
Clubhouse: 01624-834108.

ROWANY Golf Club has not had an illustrious history. But it has had Greg Norman on the course.

And motor racing ace Nigel Mansell is a member.

Indeed it was Nigel who was responsible for introducing Greg to the 18-hole course at Port Erin, on the island's south west coast, in September, 1988.

On his first round with Nigel Mansell, captain Paul Grounds and president Bryn Jones, Greg Norman made the par of 70.

In an afternoon foursome, when Tony Corrin stepped in for the president, Norman had a gross of 68. He was complimentary about the course and said the slowness had caught him out.

The club was founded in 1895 as the Port Erin Golf Club on the suggestion of a group of English 'toffs' visiting the new course on the Langness Peninsula at Castletown.

There were objections from some Port Erin residents, who saw a golf course as competition for visitors' money, much of which was spent on hiring boats for fishing trips.

But a nine-hole course was opened on rented farmland. It was extended to 18 holes in 1905.

By 1911 it was considered good enough to host an exhibition match by professionals and in 1912, when a new clubhouse was opened, Harry Vardon (the 1911 Open winner) Ted Ray (the 1912 winner) and George Duncan (who was to win in 1920) visited the course to play a match with Bill Leaver.

The club changed its name to Rowany in 1925, after the land on which it was originally established. A 1970 bid to restore the original name was unsuccessful.

After much uncertainty and negotiation the club leased the course from the Port Erin Commissioners in 1977, after individual lessees had held sway for many years.

As Alan Reid wrote at the end of his 1995 centenary history of the club: "...there have been times during its evolution that the club has sputtered and stalled; but always there has been some dedicated individual or group behind the scenes with the foresight and belief in the membership to continue to help its development."

FACT FILE

An undulating seaside course of 18 holes, 5840 yards. Par 70. SSS 69. Record 66.
Restrictions: Societies make contact initially by phone.
Fees: £10 to £15.
Dress code: Smart casual..
Shop opening: Summer 8.30 am to 11pm; winter 9am to 5pm.
Facilities:

TO THE CLUB
Rowany Drive, Port Erin.

Course Information

Hole	Yards	Stroke	Par
1	284	13	4
2	218	6	3
3	297	11	4
4	324	15	4
5	504	8	5
6	416	4	4
7	393	1	4
8	167	17	3
9	403	3	4
10	539	9	5
11	370	5	4
12	355	2	4
13	196	7	3
14	294	14	4
15	315	10	4
16	153	12	3
17	285	18	4
18	327	16	4
OUT	3006		35
IN	2834		35
TOTAL	5840		70

1) A short par four with a blind pitch shot to a well bunkered green.

2) A long par three from an elevated tee with out-of-bounds right.

3) An accurate second shot is needed to this elevated green, protected by a deep cross bunker.

4) A good drive and a delicate pitch and run to a green sloping away.

5) A blind pitch shot to a bowl green is the challenge on this par five.

6) A long tee shot into the wind is rewarded with a mid iron second.

7) Rising gently uphill, this requires a fairway wood or long iron to a narrow green. There's sand and gorse if you miss on the right.

8) The tee shot must carry all before it to reach the green.

9) A tee shot left will set up a long to mid iron second shot.

10) A straight drive is vital on this tight par five.

11) To overshoot the three-tiered green means trouble.

12) A great hole. Keep the drive right and take a mid iron to the elevated green with a narrow entrance.

13) A strong par three. Miss the green either side for a difficult pitch!

14) There's gorse to the right and left of the green on this par four. A tight tee shot to the landing area will open the approach.

15) The green slopes away and needs a well placed approach shot.

16) Another good par three with sand and gorse on both sides.

17) A good drive placed left will set up a pitch and birdie chance.

18) A good drive left of centre sets up the mid to short iron shot, depending on the wind direction, to this scenic closing hole.

Recommended Facilities

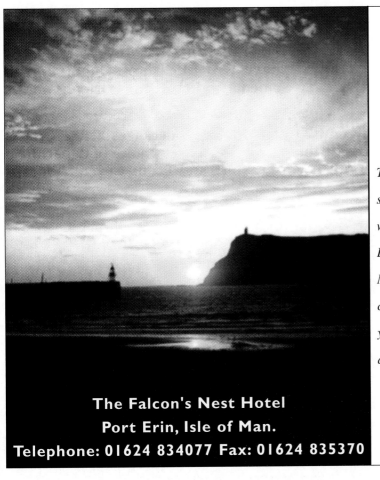

Isle of Man

Teeing off in the Isle of Man?

Fly there in just 30 mins with

Comed Aviation Ltd.

BLACKPOOL

Tel: 01253 349072 Fax: 01253 349073

ISLE OF MAN

Blackpool

DOMESTIC FARES

Route	Single	Return	Apex
Blackpool to Isle of Man	£49	£90	£80
Isle of Man to Blackpool	£49	£90	£80

DOMESTIC FARE RULES

1) One way or return valid for 6 months.
2) Apex return to be purchased 14 days in advance. No refunds. No changes.
3) Hand baggage not exceeding 10kgs. Comed reserve the right to restrict this allowance for operational reasons.
4) Failure to cancel reservations will incur an admin. charge of £20.00 per ticket

Day	Dep	Arr	Flt.No.5W
FROM BLACKPOOL TO RONALDSWAY ISLE OF MAN			
	0800	0830	201
Mon-Fri	1230	1300	203
	1730	1800	205
FROM RONALDSWAY ISLE OF MAN TO BLACKPOOL			
	0900	0930	202
Mon-Fri	1330	1400	204
	1830	1900	206

Central Reservations:

0161 489 2864

or

01253 349072

Check in time 15 minutes prior to departure

Blackpool handling / enquiries: Servisair
Ronaldsway handling / enquiries: Manx Airlines

MYLCHREESTS CAR RENTAL

GROUP	WEEKEND PER DAY		WEEKLY	
	CAR	**£**	**CAR**	**£**
X	ROVER 100 3 Door	17.25	ROVER 100 3 Door	99.00
A	ROVER 100 5 Door	18.75	ROVER 100 5 Door	111.00
B	ROVER 200 5 Door	20.00	ROVER 200 5 Door	125.00
C	ROVER 400 5 Door	21.25	ROVER 400 5 Door	145.00
E	MONTEGO ESTATE	23.75	MONTEGO ESTATE	185.00

- Weekend rentals any time Friday to any time Monday minimum 3 day within office hours
- Child/Baby seats available
- Rover Automatic and Minibus available. Tel for qoute.
- All rates include full insurance (NO EXCESS) and V.A.T. as at 01.08.95
- Cars available from our Sea Terminal or Airport offices

All drivers must be over 23 and under 75 and have held a full drivers licence for over one year. Please advise on any endorsements.

All booking enquiries to:-
Ronaldsway Airport   Ballasalla   Isle of Man IM9 2AS

☎ 01624 823533

21

22

The Isle of Man
A Golfer's
Paradise

If you've only ever associated golf with Scotland, the USA or golf breaks in Portugal or Spain, then you've been missing out. Golfing in the Isle of Man can be a truly memorable experience. Although just 33 miles long by 13 wide, the Island has eight golf courses.

And challenge it will be, for the Island's courses will tax even the 'Greg Normans' of this world and there is one additional and very major distraction when golfing in the Isle of Man...the breathtaking views. Whichever course you play, you'll be surrounded by sensational scenery - stunning coastal views, cliffs plunging into the sea, rolling countryside and heather moorlands - it's enough to make even the grimmest score seem bearable.

Thanks to our favourable climate, golfing is virtually a year-round activity. What's more, that special warm Manx welcome extends equally to the club houses where the visiting golfer will seldom be a stranger for long.

From championship golf courses to our one nine hole golf course, golfing in the Isle of Man is a very special experience...Just imagine a golfing break in the Isle of Man, from the UK only an hour away by air or a leisurely ferry crossing lasting a little under four hours...No passport control, no jet lag, just the vexing question of which one of our eight magnificent courses to try today.

If you've never 'played a round' in the Isle of Man...why wait any longer?

Telephone 0345 686868 or fax (01624) 686800 for your free 'Golfing on the Isle of Man' leaflet today.

Alternatively write to: Isle of Man Department of Tourism and Leisure, Sea Terminal, Douglas, Isle of Man, IM1 2RG.

YOU'D BE SURPRISED

...what you can pack into an island just 33 miles long!

A prime golfing getaway, the Isle of Man is a gentle world apart from the rest of the British Isles.

The island is home to eight challenging golf courses, all within a short drive of each other - which means that golfers are never more than a few minutes away from a round!

But when you are not perfecting your swing, or your partner has loyally watched one round too many, what else can you do on the 33-mile-long holiday island?

The Isle of Man is a paradise for vintage transport enthusiasts; home to five Victorian transport systems that operate as efficiently today as they did 100 years ago.

Today the Manx Electric Railway, the oldest of its kind, operates between the capital Douglas, and Ramsey.

Horse-drawn trams ply the length of Douglas Promenade and steam trains whistle their way between Douglas and Port Erin.

10,000 years of heritage

Visitors with the slightest sense of history will be captivated by the dramatic and fascinating Story of Mann - an imaginative heritage trail which begins at the award-winning Manx Museum in Douglas and takes you on a journey of discovery to sites all over the island.

Nine major heritage attractions collectively unravel 10,000 years of often turbulent Manx history, tracing the paths of nomadic hunters, Viking kings and medieval knights.

A tour along the island's craggy coast-line will reveal medieval stone castles and open air museums as well as the worlds largest working water wheel, and the island's 1,000-year-old parliament.

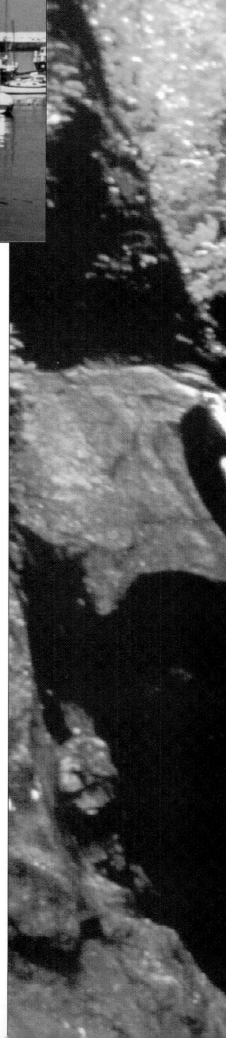

Simply great for walking

Just 13 miles long, by 13 miles wide, the Isle of Man is a place of outstanding natural beauty. The differing terrains are ideal for walkers, keen to enjoy the island's rugged coastline, dramatic scenery, wooded glens and unique wildlife.

For dedicated walkers there are three long distance routes, of 14, 28 and 90 miles.

For those who prefer a more leisurely pace, there is an excellent choice of shorter walks, taking you down the island's leafy lanes, natural glens and rushing waterfalls.

Gorgeous Gardens

The unspoiled charm of Ballalheannagh Gardens is bound to enchant visitors to the island.

Open to the public, the gardens are set in 20 acres spread over deep valleys and streams, dotted with waterfalls and stone bridges. Its varied aspects give Ballalheannagh a series of gardens, each different in character and interest.

Fabulous Fishing

Set in the middle of the Irish Sea, steeped in maritime traditions, the island makes an ideal anchor for keen fishermen, offering reservoir fishing as well as salmon and sea trout.

Creatures great and small

The Isle of Man is a breeding ground to all creatures great and small and continues to excite animal lovers with its unique range of rare species.

Among the more unusual is the Manx cat - which has no tail and the four-horned Loaghtan sheep, the only surviving truly Manx breed of farm animal.

One of the most important Manx wildlife sanctuaries of all is the Calf of Man, a tiny island just off Mann's southern coast.

Boat trips to the calf often take you past Atlantic grey seals, while summer visitors can sail out to deeper waters to see the basking sharks.

The taste of Man

Feast your eyes on the island's unique range of dishes, including its world famous kippers, Manx lamb, 'White Whiskey,' real ales and 'Queenies' - small, sweet scallops.

The Isle of Man is also justly proud of its Druiddale cheese - named after one of the typically scenic areas on the island - and, not to be missed, is its traditional Manx ice cream.

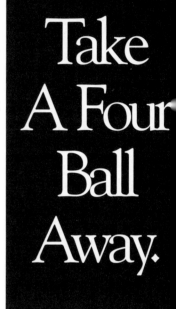

Local Facilities

For a perfect round, start at the nineteenth!

The Golf Course at Mount Murray is stunning. A fair but formidable challenge to the more experienced golfer it also has a forgiving nature for those of lesser ability.

Its 6709 yards (6406 yards off the forward tees and 5808 yards for the ladies) are of championship standard and make for a truly memorable round of this most ancient of games.

Under the guidance of resident professional Andrew Dyson, Mount Murray offers you the best of all worlds.

▶ **90 superbly appointed en-suite rooms including de-luxe four poster feature rooms.**

▶ **Two restaurants, and two bars.**

▶ **Unrivalled leisure facilities:-**18-hole championship length golf course • Floodlit, covered driving range • Indoor swimming pool with steam room and sauna suite • Superbly equipped fitness and aerobics centre • All-weather tennis courts • Crown-green bowling • Snooker room • Hair and Beauty studios • Multi-purpose sports hall...(and exhibition centre)

To find out more about the Mount Murray Experience contact: Jeremy Leeds, Mount Murray Hotel & Country Club, Santon, Isle of Man IM4 2HT. Telephone: 01624 661111 Fax: 01624 611116.

Merseyside

A GUIDE TO CLUB FACILITIES

Club Hire	Trolley Hire	Buggy Hire	PG Practice Ground	PN Practice Nets
DR Driving Range	Catering	Tea & Coffee	Bar	Games Room
Squash & Tennis	Bowling Green	Swimming Pool	Fishing	Changing Room
Lockers	Showers			

Copyright © Freedom Design

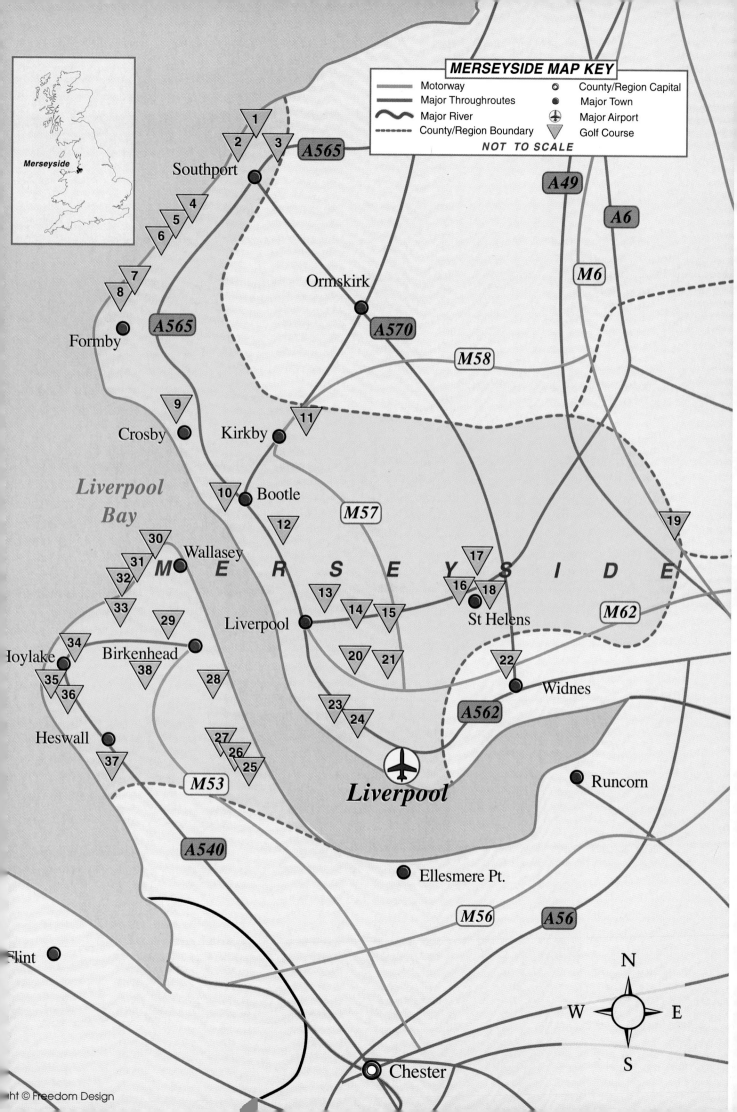

MERSEYSIDE MAP KEY

Motorway		County/Region Capital	
Major Throughroutes		Major Town	
Major River		Major Airport	
County/Region Boundary		Golf Course	

NOT TO SCALE

Merseyside

A565

A49

A6

M6

Southport

A565

Ormskirk

A570

M58

Formby

Crosby

Kirkby

Liverpool Bay

Bootle

M57

M E R S E Y S I D E

Wallasey

St Helens

M62

Liverpool

Birkenhead

Hoylake

Heswall

Widnes

A562

M53

Liverpool

Runcorn

A540

Ellesmere Pt.

M56

A56

Flint

Chester

N

W E

S

ht © Freedom Design

ALLERTON
Golf Course/Club

Allerton Road, Liverpool L18 3JT.

Owners: Liverpool City Council
Professional: Barry Large
0151-4287490.

ALLERTON is a municipal facility of two golf courses situated in the leafy suburbs of South Liverpool.

It was originally the private estate of the Fletcher family, who built a nine-hole golf course for their own use. The 18-hole course was constructed in the 1920s after the land, originally Home Farm, was bequeathed to the City of Liverpool.

The mansion house, which was the Fletcher family home, was partly destroyed by fire in 1947 and is now derelict. However, the obelisk that stood in the Fletchers' garden still remains near the putting green.

It was reputed to have been placed by the Fletchers as a landmark for family members sailing up the River Mersey, which can be seen from the golf course.

The Fletchers' stables and coach house now house the professional's shop, locker rooms, members' bar and function room.

The 18-hole course is pleasant to play and offers birdie chances. It is a very popular course and booking is essential. The nine-hole course is basically a par three course aimed at learners of all ages. There are no bunkers or serious hazards.

The greens are usually fast and have some very unusual shapes.

FACT FILE

Parkland courses - 18 holes over 5494 yards. Par 67. SSS 66; 9 holes over 1841 yards. Par 34.

Restrictions: Book for the 18-hole course seven days in advance.

Fees: 9 holes - £3.80. 18 holes £6.40.

Dress code: None.

Shop opening: 7.45am to dusk.

Facilities:

TO THE CLUB
Allerton Road is off Queen's Drive.

Course Information			
Hole	Yards	Stroke	Par
1	439	1	4
2	417	9	4
3	461	3	4
4	174	13	3
5	340	5	4
6	279	17	4
7	330	11	4
8	114	15	3
9	233	7	3
10	284	16	4
11	353	4	4
12	181	8	3
13	299	18	4
14	350	2	4
15	338	14	4
16	340	12	4
17	332	6	4
18	230	10	3
OUT	2787		33
IN	2707		34
TOTAL	5494		67

1) A longish par four played slightly uphill to a large green surrounded by bunkers.

2) Not as long as the first hole. The drive must be between two mature trees and then downhill to a large green.

3) The longest on the course, with woodland and copses each side.

4) One shot to the green but it is up a steep gradient.

5) A straightforward drive but the hole is blind due to the slope.

6) A slight dogleg with a narrow entrance to the sloping fairway and the green is elevated.

7) A wide but slanted fairway and a row of bunkers short of the green.

8) A very short par three played across a ravine with many bunkers round the green. The ball can roll back into the ravine.

9) Across the ravine again to a large green.

10) An easy drive but the green is ringed by deep bunkers.

11) It is heavily wooded to the left with several fairway bunkers.

12) A par three with out-of-bounds left and right.

13) A short par four that's relatively easy.

14) This slight dogleg calls for an accurate drive due to the restricted entrance to the fairway, through trees.

15) A deceptive hole due to the plateau green.

16) Beware the lonesome pine that restricts the drive on this slight dogleg to a large green.

17) Another slight dogleg with an undulating fairway that is tricky.

18) On this par three the main problem is that the ball tends to roll over the back of the green.

Recommended Facilities

Merseyside

5

ARROWE PARK
Golf Centre

Arrowe Park Road, Birkenhead,
Wirral, Merseyside L49 5LW.

Bookings: 0151-6771527.
Professional: Colin Didsbury
0151-6771527.

THE Arrowe Park course opened in 1932 on the site of a country park.

Although it is a municipal golf course, it is quite long and has a good pedigree, having been used as a qualifying course for the Open when it was held at Royal Liverpool in 1947. Famous names like Henry Cotton, Dai Rees and Sam Snead played their qualifying rounds here.

As a municipal layout, the course has had to be simplified but the original championship tees still exist and are used in competitions.

When the course was built, the clubhouse was a large house that is now a children's home and it has benefitted from charity events at Arrowe Park.

In June 1996, the Merseyside Municipal Championship was held over the course and the Arrowe Park team won the scratch section.

One of the club's leading players, David Ball, also won the Wirral Open and set the Arrowe Park course record of 66.

This is a very popular course and weekend play needs to be booked a week in advance. The Arrowe Park Golf Club plays over the course and has facilities in the clubhouse.

FACT FILE

A parkland course of 18 holes, 6387 yards. Par 71. SSS 70. Record 66.
Restrictions: Unrestricted play. Societies book with the pro.
Fees: £6 (pensioners & juniors £3).
Dress code: Smart casual.
Shop opening: Daylight hours.
Facilities:

TO THE CLUB

From junction 3 of the M53 to the A551.

6

Course Information

Hole	Yards	Stroke	Par
1	300	13	4
2	300	11	4
3	394	3	4
4	138	17	3
5	458	1	4
6	396	7	4
7	391	9	4
8	168	15	3
9	505	5	5
10	493	8	5
11	213	16	3
12	487	6	5
13	202	12	3
14	460	2	4
15	192	18	3
16	445	4	4
17	335	14	4
18	510	10	5
OUT	3050		35
IN	3337		36
TOTAL	6387		71

1) A tight tee shot with out-of-bounds both sides.

2) A sharp dogleg left with out-of-bounds left. The green is generous.

3) A long straight par four, usually into the wind.

4) A heavily bunkered short hole requiring an accurate mid iron shot.

5) A long, straight par four with a long second shot.

6) With out-of-bounds left and trees to the right, this straight par four needs accuracy.

7) A medium length dogleg right. The second shot is played to a bowl-shaped green.

8) An elevated short hole with the green tilted towards you.

9) This long par five is the first hole with no immediate out-of-bounds to consider.

10) A slightly uphill par five but reachable in two.

11) A longish par three with a copse to the left and possible bail-out right.

12) Hit the drive down the right and the green is on.

13) A long, tight par three to a narrow green with trouble just short left and right.

14) This calls for a very tight drive between mature oaks.

15) A par three angled across the line of the hole.

16) An excellent par four. The fairway is undulating, there's an out-of-bounds right and trees left.

17) An uphill tee shot to a well bunkered green.

18) A deep depression will gather the ball if you try for the green in two.

Recommended Facilities

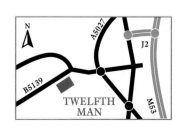
Merseyside

BIDSTON
Golf Club

Bidston Link Road, Wallasey,
Wirral, Merseyside L44 2HR.

Secretary: J. J. Gleeson
0151-6383412.
Professional: Alex Rowland
0151-6306650.

ALTHOUGH founded in 1909, many changes have been forced on the Bidston course in recent years.

The club is one of several in the north west of England to have been adversely affected by the building of motorways.

In the late 1970s the M53 project took 20 acres, including the second, third, fourth and part of the fifth.

In building four new holes and completely changing the round, some of the character went out of the course.

However, the financial compensation and a grant from the Sports Council enabled the club to build a new clubhouse in 1982.

Fire had seriously damaged the previous clubhouse in 1972 and it took 12 months of voluntary effort to restore the building.

The Bidston 18-hole course is a short distance inland from the Wallasey and Leasowe courses on the coast.

The club's origins came from a 1908 decision by the Borough of Wallasey to allocate a piece of land for use as a municipal golf course.

Known now as The Warren, this course came into play in 1909 and soon had three golfing societies playing over the links.

Congestion was a problem on the tight, nine-hole course and in 1913 the three societies merged as the Bidston Golf Club and moved to a new site, creating nine holes on what is now the back nine.

In the 1920s the club extended to 18 in two phases

For many years the only access to the course was via Bidston railway station and its direct rail access from Liverpool made the course popular with stage stars appearing in Liverpool.

The 16th hole is named Shady Nook, after the song made popular by Donald Peers.

Bidston was also popular with media people. For about 50 years, the Liverpool Press Club held the annual meeting at the golf club.

FACT FILE

A links and parkland course of 18 holes, 6140 yards. Par 70. SSS 70. Record 68.

Restrictions: Visitors welcome weekdays except 9.30 to 11.30am Tuesday to Thursday. No visitors at weekends. Societies make contact in advance.

Fees: £22.

Dress code: Smart casual.

Shop opening: 8.30am to 6pm.

Facilities:

TO THE CLUB

From junction 1 of the M53 onto Bidston Link Road and half a mile west of the A551.

Hole	Yards	Stroke	Par
1	268	17	4
2	144	15	3
3	367	7	4
4	410	3	4
5	509	9	5
6	300	13	4
7	462	5	4
8	427	1	4
9	176	11	3
10	439	2	4
11	398	6	4
12	179	16	3
13	409	4	4
14	302	18	4
15	514	8	5
16	164	12	3
17	326	10	4
18	346	14	4
OUT	3063		35
IN	3077		35
TOTAL	6140		70

Course Information

1) Not a friendly first hole, with out-of-bounds left and right, a ditch and a pond before reaching the well protected green.

2) A par three over the river with club selection important.

3) With out-of-bounds each side of the fairway, hit a precise second!

4) The green is hidden to the right - and the danger is from the out-of-bounds on the right.

5) A dogleg left with a generous fairway and a large sloping green protected by bunkers each side.

6) The elevated green with a cavernous front bunker is hard to hold.

7) A par four with a broad, straight fairway.

8) Stroke index one and difficult to make par. The tee shot is daunting with out-of-bounds left and a pond to the right.

9) A par three needing an accurate shot to find the green.

10) From a raised tee the drive must clear the trees to the fairway.

11) Into the wind. The green is best approached from the right.

12) Hit a bold straight shot to the elevated green.

13) Once over the tree and ditch-lined road, the fairway is wide and straight, leaving a not-too-difficult second shot.

14) A pulled tee shot finds the river. Watch, also, for the cross bunker.

15) The River Fender is down the left and the sunken green is hidden from the second shot. But no bunkers!

16) A topped shot is disastrous on this par three.

17) A broad fairway to a raised green that is hard to hold.

18) A simple finishing hole if the large cross bunkers are avoided.

Recommended Facilities

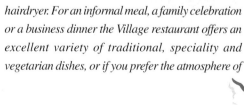

BLUNDELLS HILL
Golf Club

Blundells Lane, Rainhill,
Merseyside L35 6NA.

Owners: **Phil & Steve McKie**
01744-24892.
Professional: **Ray Peters**
0151-4300100.

THIS new, privately-developed 18 hole course is ideally set on sloping parkland between Prescott and St. Helens, with superb views of Merseyside and North Wales.

The club opened in two phases, beginning with 12 holes in June, 1994, with the clubhouse and final six holes a year later.

The handsome modern clubhouse is built at the top of Blundells Hill, sheltered by woods on the north and east, and looks out over the fan-shaped course on the north side of the M62 at junction seven.

It has quickly become a popular golfing venue, approachable and informal while observing a 'smart and casual' dress code.

The course has wide fairways, large bunkers and big, undulating greens. Water plays an important part with several ponds and ditches coming into play on five holes, starting with the fourth.

The water-ways are connected to a landscaped lake which serves as a moat to the landing zone on the 10th.

The directors of the company aim to make Blundells Hill a champion-ship golf course and it is constantly being developed.

Tiger Tees have been built on several holes, increasing the yardage in some cases and bringing fairway bunkers into play.

The club has established its own 'Open' for men during July and there are similar tourneys for seniors and ladies.

The club recognises that golf societies have a major role in making a club successful. There are several options for societies to visit on Tuesdays and Wednesdays and even on Saturdays and Sundays on a limited basis.

Blundells Hill has a major function room and caters for all types of social events.

FACT FILE

A parkland course of 18 holes, 6256 yards. Par 71. SSS 70.

Restrictions: Societies telephone the owner.

Fees: Weekdays £20 per round or £25 per day. Weekends £30 per round or £40 per day.

Dress code: Smart and casual.

Shop opening: 7.45am till 8pm summer.

Facilities:

TO THE CLUB

Junction 7 on the M62/57.
Take the A5080 towards Widnes, the club is 2 miles on the right.

Course Information

Hole	Yards	Stroke	Par
1	350	11	4
2	492	9	5
3	177	16	3
4	446	1	4
5	373	7	4
6	302	13	4
7	139	18	3
8	449	2	4
9	525	4	5
10	521	3	5
11	319	14	4
12	149	15	3
13	348	17	4
14	406	5	4
15	186	12	3
16	389	8	4
17	194	10	3
18	491	6	5
OUT	3253		36
IN	3003		35
TOTAL	6256		71

1) A downhill dogleg with out-of-bounds on the right. Play the tee shot with a long iron for position.

2) A slight dogleg to the right with two well-placed bunkers on the right.

3) A good par three, well bunkered to the left, trees on the right and water at the front of the green.

4) A nightmare! Trees left, trees right - and water in front.

5) An underrated hole. Watch the lateral water hazard on the right.

6) Uphill to a plateau green well guarded by bunkers left and right.

7) Miss the Mackenzie green and take four. Out-of-bounds behind.

8) A great long and straight par four with a downhill tee shot.

9) A long uphill par five with a slight dogleg left to a plateau green and large, deep bunkers left and right.

10) A long downhill par five with out-of-bounds left for the tee shot.

11) Not as simple as it looks. It's out-of-bounds left and there's a ditch some 40 yards short of the bunkers.

12) A good par three to a plateau. Bunkers, water and out-of-bounds wait for the misdirected shot.

13) A shortish dogleg. The bunkers can be carried.

14) A testing hole. A dogleg left with trees and bunkers.

15) Another good par three with a big, undulating green.

16) A good drive is needed on this dogleg with four fairway bunkers.

17) A long, flat par three with a big green.

18) A testing par five. A dogleg right with well positioned fairway bunkers and an elevated two-tier green, well protected.

Recommended Facilities

Merseyside

BOOTLE
Golf Course/Club

Dunnings Bridge Road,
Litherland, Liverpool L30 2PP.

Secretary (club): John Morgan
Clubhouse: 0151-9286196.
Professional: Alan Bradshaw
0151-9281371.

BOOTLE'S seaside links opened in 1934 as a municipal course but it is now leased to a private company and operates on a pay-and-play basis.

Bootle Golf Club plays over the course and has had a clubhouse on the site since the beginning.

The course was designed by Fred

Stephens, whose daughter Bunty, was one of England's finest players in the 1940s and 1950s; a Curtis Cup team member, captain, selector. She became president of the Ladies' Golf Union.

The Bootle course was built on the site of an old ammunition factory as a project to relieve local unemployment during the Depression.

There was a severe drought that year and the clubhouse opening was delayed by a fire that couldn't be extinguished due to lack of water.

In its early days the club amalgamated with two others - the Victory Golf Club and the Litherland Golf Club. In 1959 the club took the decision to take over the clubhouse on lease from the municipality, which was then Bootle Corporation.

The course has several memorable holes with lush greens and challenging approaches.

FACT FILE

A parkland/links course of 18 holes, 6242 yards. Par 70. SSS 70. Record 64.

Restrictions: Visitors welcome any time. Societies contact the pro in advance. Ladies' Tuesday morning.

Fees: £4.80 to £6.40.

Dress code: Smart and casual.

Shop opening: 7.15am to 8pm.

Facilities:

TO THE CLUB

From the motorways follow the Seaforth-Bootle docks signs.

Course Information

Hole	Yards	Stroke	Par
1	217	13	3
2	342	17	4
3	382	3	4
4	347	11	4
5	191	9	3
6	354	15	4
7	431	1	4
8	386	5	4
9	537	7	5
10	363	14	4
11	142	18	3
12	375	2	4
13	343	10	4
14	184	16	3
15	461	4	5
16	413	6	4
17	378	8	4
18	396	12	4
OUT	3187		35
IN	3055		35
TOTAL	6242		70

1) A long iron is needed on this tough par three into the wind.

2) An accurate drive down the left opens up the green.

3) A testing hole with out-of-bounds left and a ditch to carry.

4) A good drive will leave a short iron shot into the green.

5) A carry of 170 yards over a lake on this very picturesque hole.

6) A birdie chance is for the taking on this modest par four hole.

7) Stroke index one. A dogleg left to a small, elevated green.

8) A pond at the left calls for care off the tee. Watch out for the bunker 70 yards short of the green.

9) A monstrous par five of 537 yards calls for two excellent shots.

10) Downhill from the tee and an uphill approach to the green.

11) A par three through trees to an undulating green.

12) A dogleg right with trees to the right and a ditch crossing at average driving distance.

13) Out-of-bounds left and a pond right. So be straight!

14) A long iron shot on this par three hole with a lake to carry.

15) A dogleg left par five with a ditch crossing the fairway at about 200 yards and out-of-bounds left after the elbow.

16) A straightforward but long par four, tree-lined along the left.

17) An accurate drive is needed on this most picturesque hole on the course. Three deep bunkers guard the green.

18) It's out-of-bounds right off the tee on this slight dogleg right. No fewer than four pot bunkers guard the green.

Recommended Facilities

THE

Hillcrest

H O T E L

The Hillcrest Hotel has 49 comfortable bedrooms all with bathrooms (some have a whirlpool bath), satellite television, direct dial telephone, trouser press, hair dryer and hospitality tray.

The tropically-themed Palm Restaurant, overlooked by the cocktail bar is a lively venue at lunchtime and throughout the evening. Whilst Nelson's Bar, a traditional oak beamed pub, serves a wide range of drinks in a nautical setting, with regular entertainment.

Discount packages are available for parties of 12 or more (subject to availability).

CRONTON LANE, WIDNES, CHESHIRE, **WA8 9AR** TELEPHONE **0151 424 1616** FACSIMILE **0151 495 1348**

Merseyside

BOWRING PARK
Golf Course/Club

Roby Road, Huyton,
Merseyside L36 4HD.

Enquiries / Bookings
0151-2256335.
Professional: Dave Weston
0151-4891901.

THE Bowring course was built after the gift of the 80-acre Roby Hall Estate to Liverpool City Council in 1907.

Alderman W. B. Bowring offered the estate as a recreation area to celebrate the 50 years he and his father had served on the council.

The estate was renamed Bowring Park and developed in two principal areas - a park and a nine-hole golf course that opened in 1911. It was later extended to 18 holes.

Believed at the time to be the first municipal golf course in England, it was developed and improved by the city council and is still owned and managed by them.

After sixty years as a popular venue with golfers from far and near, the M62 motorway project cut through the middle of the course in 1973.

Nine holes failed to retain the interest of many golfers, merely through the lack of challenge, and in the next 20 years several attempts

were made to bring what was to be the back nine into play.

Due to drainage problems the project was not completed until the Liverpool City Leisure Services took over the management in 1993.

The department invested heavily into Bowring with an extensive drainage system, tree planting and upgrading of the tees and greens.

The course was returned to an 18-hole layout and the continuing development programme is attracting golfers back to Bowring Park.

There is no advance booking; golfers simply turn up and pay at the shop.

There is a pleasant warm up to the round as the first hole is clear and not too long. After a short second hole the third is designed to stretch the golfer a little.

After playing the fifth - the only par five on the course - golfers cross the bridge to play holes five to 11 on 'the back area.' These holes are a little more demanding, over undulating ground with several water hazards.

Players return to the clubhouse side to play the more straightforward holes 12 to 18.

The Bowring Park Golf Club plays over the course and has bar facilities for members.

Former Prime Minister Harold Wilson (later Lord Wilson) who was for many years the MP for Huyton, was president of the club.

FACT FILE

A parkland course of 18 holes, 6147 yards. Par 70.

Restrictions: None.

Fees: £2.30 to £4.50

Booking Office opening: 8am till dusk.

Facilities:

TO THE CLUB ▷

From junction 5 of the M62 on to Roby Road, Huyton.

Course Information			
Hole	Yards	Stroke	Par
1	378	8	4
2	170	15	3
3	437	3	4
4	333	12	4
5	478	10	5
6	383	7	4
7	402	4	4
8	324	16	4
9	402	2	4
10	245	6	3
11	440	1	4
12	291	14	4
13	150	18	3
14	362	11	4
15	324	13	4
16	340	5	4
17	329	17	4
18	359	9	4
OUT	3307		36
IN	2840		34
TOTAL	6147		70

1) A fairly easy start. The green is protected by mounds and bunkers.
2) A short par three, well protected by bunkers.
3) A difficult long par four with out-of-bounds down the left.
4) A difficult driving hole with a narrow entrance to the green.
5) A restricted driving hole due to a pond. The green is open.
6) Drive over the water hazard to a raised green with bunkers.
7) A difficult driving hole with an undulating fairway, out-of-bounds on the left and a lateral water hazard to the right.
8) A slight dogleg with heavy wooded areas to the left of the green.
9) A straightforward hole to a well-protected green, but a pond on the right makes the second shot difficult.
10) A short hole with bunkers short of the green.
11) A difficult dogleg, heavily wooded to the right, with the green guarded by mounds and bunkers.
12) An easy par four with no major hazards.
13) An easy hole that should renew confidence!
14) This hole requires a perfect drive. The fairway slopes and the green is at the lowest point.
15) An easy driving hole. The green is protected by mounds. Don't overshoot.
16) The green is easily driveable on this hole.
17) Drive into the dip and up to the green.
18) Awkward bunkers protect the green at the right. Otherwise it's relatively easy.

Recommended Facilities

Merseyside

BRACKENWOOD
Golf Course/Club

Brackenwood Lane, Bebington,
Wirral, Merseyside L63 2LY.

Bookings: 0151-6083093.
Professional: Ken Lamb
0151-6083093.

BRACKENWOOD is a municipal golf course owned by the Metropolitan Borough of Wirral. It is the venue of the annual Wirral Open tournament which attracts around 200 golfers each June, in aid of the St. John's Hospice.

The course was extended to 18 holes in 1980 after the old Bebington Corporation bought some adjacent farmland.

The clubhouse was converted from a hayloft and was extended in the early 1990s with the conversion of the farm stables.

The original house on the site is occupied by Brackenwood Golf Club, whose members play over the course.

Golf began on the site in 1934, when a nine-hole course was built on the site of a private estate.

The course is rather flat but is mature and gains its character from the many fine old trees.

The biggest challenge is hole 16, rated stroke index two on the card. It is the hardest driving hole with tight out-of-bounds to the left and dense trees to the right. The tricky green often takes three putts.

FACT FILE

A parkland course of 18 holes, 6285 yards. Par 70. SSS 70. Record 64.

Restrictions: Unrestricted play weekdays but booking is necessary for weekends. Societies make prior arrangements.

Fees: £6.

Dress code: Smart casual.

Shop opening: Dawn till dusk.

Facilities:

TO THE CLUB
Leave the M53 at junction 4.

Course Information			
Hole	Yards	Stroke	Par
1	336	11	4
2	137	16	3
3	424	4	4
4	473	1	4
5	325	17	4
6	197	7	3
7	516	14	5
8	362	9	4
9	350	10	4
10	202	6	3
11	343	15	4
12	561	8	5
13	190	12	3
14	409	5	4
15	331	13	4
16	433	2	4
17	293	18	4
18	403	3	4
OUT	3120		35
IN	3165		35
TOTAL	6285		70

1) A narrowing tree-lined fairway should be tackled with an iron off the tee but a well hit wood gains just a short pitch to the green.

2) A short hole with a well protected green.

3) Take steps to avoid the fairway bunkers on this lengthy hole.

4) Again, a long drive is needed to avoid the fairway bunkers.

5) A medium iron to the left side should leave an eight iron second.

6) A par three with a heavily guarded, very tricky green.

7) Accuracy is the key on this tree-lined fairway but the green can be reached in two. The green is large but tricky.

8) Another tree-lined fairway needing an accurate drive.

9) Playing safe on this dogleg should leave a seven iron second.

10) Wicked slopes make this hole a three-putter.

11) The bunkers can be driven but the green slopes heavily.

12) Two good woods are needed on this seldom reached par five.

13) An uphill par three that deceives. Take one club more!

14) The second shot must be at the pin as the green is long and narrow.

15) A well hit drive between the trees can get you there - but beware of the exceptionally sloping green.

16) The hardest driving hole with out-of-bounds left and dense trees right. The green is another three-putter.

17) A driveable par four hole if you avoid the trees.

18) Trees left and right make this another hard driving hole and the green is yet another tricky example.

Recommended Facilities

Merseyside

17

BROMBOROUGH
Golf Club

Raby Hall Road, Bromborough,
Wirral, Merseyside L63 0NW.

Secretary: Trevor Barrowclough
0151-3342155.
Professional: Geoff Berry
0151-3344499.

PROBABLY one of the first north west farmers to indulge his enthusiasm for golf was Mr. J. Hassall, who owned the land on which this attractive course stands.

After firing golf balls down the wide open spaces of his pastures, Mr. Hassall formed a club in 1903 and opened his nine-hole course the following year.

In so doing, he removed one of the most frequent disputes in the early world of golf; the one between landlord and tenant!

His son, Ernest Hassall, became a golfer of repute and reached the semi finals of the Irish Open in 1919. The Bromborough Golf Club extended the course to 18 holes in 1923.

During World War Two, the course was requisitioned for use as an American Army camp and was not re-opened until 1948.

Twenty years later, another setback struck the club. The M53 motorway sliced four holes off the course and it was the generosity of Lord Leverhulme, who is president of the club, that saved the day.

He purchased enough land to the south of the course to return it to 18 holes. In 1970 a new clubhouse was built.

A planting programme in 1977 enhanced the revised course and today the conifers - up to 30 feet tall - are an attractive feature.

Bromborough's par five 11th hole is reckoned to be the finest in the Wirral with its narrow, tree-lined fairway and water hazards.

The course record of 67 was set by Gordon Edwards, the 1995 English Seniors champion.

FACT FILE

A parkland course of 18 holes, 6650 yards. Par 72. SSS 73. Record 67.

Restrictions: Societies make arrangements by phone.
No visitors before 2.30pm on Saturday or all day Sunday.
Ladies' Tuesday morning.

Fees: £26 to £30.

Dress code: Usual golf attire.

Shop opening: 8am to 7.30pm summer; 8.15am to 5.30pm winter.

Facilities:

TO THE CLUB

Half a mile west of the railway station, in Raby Hall Road.

Course Information

Hole	Yards	Stroke	Par
1	312	13	4
2	427	5	4
3	535	7	5
4	151	17	3
5	435	1	4
6	176	15	3
7	540	9	5
8	409	11	4
9	383	3	4
10	160	16	3
11	486	4	5
12	354	12	4
13	335	14	4
14	457	8	4
15	448	2	4
16	157	18	3
17	486	10	5
18	419	6	4
OUT	3348		36
IN	3302		36
TOTAL	6650		72

1) A shortish par four with out-of-bounds all the way on the right.

2) An accurate tee shot is needed to avoid three fairway bunkers.

3) A long par five, slightly doglegged right with trees both sides.

4) A shortish par three over water to a green ringed by bunkers.

5) A long par four. The tee shot is over water. The hole doglegs to the right and the entrance to the green is narrow. Stroke index one.

6) Three deep bunkers dictate an accurate tee shot.

7) A long dogleg left par five where accuracy is all important.

8) A good tee shot is required on this par four hole to set up the second shot to a large green.

9) A great par four. The tee shot over water has to be accurate to see the green, which is over a valley.

10) A short hole over a valley to a Mackenzie green.

11) A shortish par five. Again, the tee shot is all important, with trees left and water right.

12) Four bunkers wait to catch the wayward tee shot.

13) A short dogleg par four needing an accurate drive to avoid three fairway cross bunkers.

14) Two long shots will reach this long, narrow green.

15) Drive to the left to open up the green on this long par four.

16) A medium length par three. Again, the green is ringed by bunkers.

17) A good tee shot over a valley gives the chance of reaching the green in two on this par five.

18) A great finishing hole needing a very accurate drive and second shot to a well protected green.

Recommended Facilities

CALDY
Golf Club

Links Hey Road, Caldy,
Wirral, Merseyside L48 1NB.

Secretary: T. D. M. Bacon
0151-6255660 (Fax 6257394).
Professional: Kevin Jones
0151-6251818.

ALTHOUGH it is believed golf was first played at Caldy as early as the 1890s, it would have been on a casual basis on local farmland.

The formation of a golf club was not considered until 1906, when the Caldy Manor Estates Company engaged John Morris, the professional at nearby Hoylake (Royal Liverpool), to survey the land along the east bank of the River Dee.

Work on laying out a nine-hole course began under Morris's direction early in 1907, and the Caldy Golf Club was formed in June. A clubhouse was built about the same time.

The development of the village and the golf club received a boost with the opening of Caldy railway station on the former Hoylake to Hooton line.

The club became a limited company and acquired the course in 1923. Six years later, enough land was purchased on the east side of the then railway to extend to an 18-hole course of championship length. The new course opened in 1931. Changes to the layout were made when more land was bought in the 1940s.

After nearly 70 years of development and progress, the club had outgrown the clubhouse and its various extensions and a new clubhouse was built in 1974.

The old house, on the northern boundary, was converted to a private residence and the course was revised to place the first tee and the 18th green in front of the new clubhouse.

The old railway line was closed and the land returned to use as a bridal way.

A coastal protection scheme, completed in 1993, solved the problem of erosion that affected several holes by the early 1980s.

The course is divided into the links section (holes three to 10) on the seaward side of the Wirral Way bridle path and the parkland section of 10 holes.

The course is a severe test of golf, as indicated by its standard scratch score of 73. There are four par five holes of well over 500 yards.

Caldy was used as a qualifying course for the European Open in 1981.

In 1996, four Caldy club members were in the Cheshire county team, with Phil Bailey being captain.

FACT FILE

A links and parkland championship course of 18 holes, 6675 yards. Par 72. SSS 73. Record 68.

Restrictions: Visitors on weekdays only. Societies make advance arrangements. Visitors book in advance.

Fees: £33 to £38.

Dress code: Usual golf attire.

Shop opening: Dawn till dusk.

Facilities:

TO THE CLUB

On the west side of the Wirral peninsula, just south of Caldy village.

Course Information

Hole	Yards	Stroke	Par
1	405	9	4
2	156	13	3
3	389	5	4
4	342	15	4
5	538	7	5
6	377	1	4
7	557	11	5
8	157	17	3
9	411	3	4
10	188	12	3
11	528	6	5
12	437	2	4
13	355	18	4
14	393	10	4
15	346	14	4
16	416	4	4
17	149	16	3
18	531	8	5
OUT	3332		36
IN	3343		36
TOTAL	6675		72

1) A wide open tee shot. Long handicap players beware the gorse on the second shot. It plays half a club longer than it looks.

2) This par three can play 50 yards longer into the wind.

3) A dogleg right. Be accurate with distance on the second shot or it will vanish over the cliff!

4) Drive to the right centre - and don't be too strong with the second.

5) With the tee on the cliff edge, a hooked shot must be avoided.

6) A drive down the left gives a better opening to the green. The longer handicap player should play this hole as a three-shotter.

7) The second shot must hug the out-of-bounds to open the green.

8) The tee is on high ground. A straightforward one-shot hole.

9) A dogleg right. Avoid the trees on the right. A pond is not visible from the fairway and awaits the over-strong pulled second shot.

10) Ideally the tee shot is played slightly left of the green with a fade.

11) A double dogleg needing an accurate drive. Caldy members play their second shot for the middle of the clubhouse, to open the green.

12) The gardens on the right are the bane of the player who slices.

13) A straightforward two-shot hole. The safe side is left.

14) A diagonal ridge on the fairway forces a choice. Long hitters go left to get a good angle for the second shot.

15) A dogleg right. Don't be tempted to cut the corner!

16) The tee shot has to hug the right of the fairway to get the best line for the second shot on this par four.

17) The best hole, needing imagination and a feel for distance.

18) A tough challenge, needing planning, decisions and heart! Start by aiming for the largest house on the hillside.

CHILDWALL
Golf Club

Naylor's Road, Gateacre,
Liverpool L27 2YB.

Manager: K. Jennions
0151-4870654 (Fax 4870882).
Professional: Nigel Parr
0151-4879871.

CHILDWALL Golf Club has had three different courses since it was founded in 1913.

The present course of 18 holes dates from 1939 and was laid out by James Braid.

It is located not at Childwall but at Gateacre, a little to the east and on the south side of the M62 between junctions 5 and 6.

Like the course, the clubhouse is of some architectural note, being in the style of the Royal Birkdale clubhouse by the same architect, Alderman Shennan. It was refurbished in 1996.

The present course came about as the result of an attempt to get the club to pay a greatly increased rent for the previous course, at Childwall Hall.

Four club members, Messrs. Treneman, Sloss, Green and Foreman, bought 200 acres in a remote spot at Gateacre and passed them on to the club at the same price.

It was the second move forced on the club by disputes over leases. In 1922 they left their original site opposite Woolton Hall, in Woolton, Liverpool, where they had been founded as the Woolton Hall Golf Club in 1913.

During World War Two the club was kept going by Joe Preston, Sam Foreman, Tommy Roberts, Ingram Legge, Charles Doyle and a handful of stalwarts who organised dances and whist drives at a time when membership was low and transportation was difficult.

The course is now a fine parkland layout that has benefited over recent years from previous tree planting programmes and changes to the hazards, making it an intriguing and challenging course to play.

The Childwall team were the winners of the 1996 handicap fours over 36 holes, held by the Lancashire Union of Golf Clubs and Childwall is the scene of an annual warm-up between the Lancashire squad and the Lancashire PGA.

The club gives charitable support to the R.N.L.I. from a summer tournament.

FACT FILE

A parkland course of 18 holes, 6425 yards. Par 72. SSS 71. Record 67.

Restrictions: Visitors welcome only on weekdays. Ladies' day Tuesday. Societies contact the Secretary.

Fees: £23.50 to £32, with member £9.50 and £14.50.

Dress code: Smart casual.

Shop opening: 8.30am to 6.30 pm.

Facilities:

TO THE CLUB

From junction 6 of the M62, take the Huyton turn-off and then left at the second set of lights, into Wheatfield Road.

Course Information

Hole	Yards	Stroke	Par
1	400	9	4
2	498	5	5
3	177	15	3
4	389	1	4
5	314	14	4
6	173	17	3
7	352	12	4
8	485	8	5
9	424	3	4
10	512	6	5
11	320	13	4
12	387	2	4
13	156	16	3
14	492	11	5
15	408	7	4
16	150	18	3
17	407	4	4
18	426	10	4
OUT	3212		36
IN	3258		36
TOTAL	6470		72

1) A slightly downhill par four with bunkers on both sides.
2) Out-of-bounds along the right and then downhill to a two-tier green the size of a postage stamp!
3) A great par three with a peculiar-shaped green.
4) The fairway slopes to the right, making the ditch a tempting place. A very small green makes this the toughest hole.
5) Hitting the fairway is hard but long hitters can drive this par four.
6) A well guarded par three. The green is generous but hard to read.
7) A dogleg to the left. Keep it down the left to get the best approach.
8) It's downhill but the length makes this a difficult par five.
9) A great par four. There's sand on the left and trouble on the right. The second shot is difficult to a sloping, well guarded green.
10) Fairway bunkers galore on this downhill dogleg. A good par five.
11) It's a short par four but the fairway is small with out-of-bounds right and bunkers both short and all around the green.
12) A dogleg round the out-of-bounds on the right. The fairway slopes to the right and the green is hard to hit.
13) An uphill par three. The length is deceiving.
14) Bunkers guard the fairway and the green on this par five.
15) A great tree-lined par four up the hill. The green is long.
16) A pretty par three but the well defended green is hard to hit.
17) There's a ditch right and short of the front-sloping green.
18) A fantastic finishing hole! A ridge in the middle of the fairway and a valley just short of the green can cause problems.

Recommended Facilities

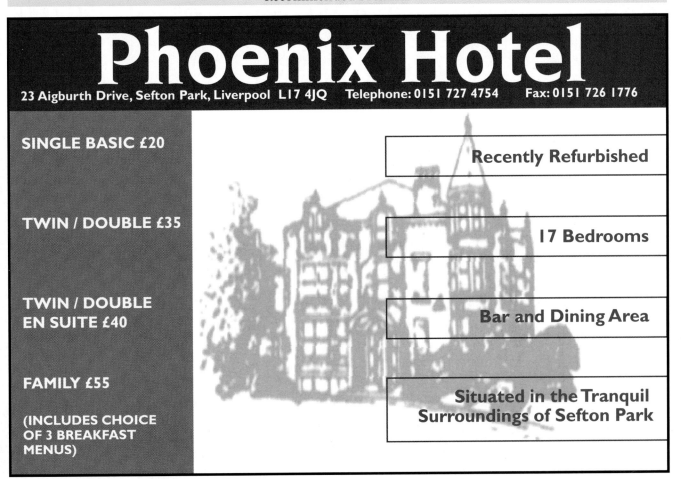

Merseyside

23

EASTHAM LODGE
Golf Club

117 Ferry Road, Eastham,
Wirral, Merseyside L62 0AP.
Secretary: C. S. Camden
0151-3273003.
Professional: Bob Boobyer
0151-3273008.

THE origins of the Eastham Lodge club can be traced back to 1922 when the Port Sunlight Golfing Association was formed at Lever Brothers Ltd.

Members hoped the company would agree to convert an unused section of the Edgeworth Estate into a golf course and this came about in 1930.

A nine-hole course was designed by Sandy Herd, the 1902 Open Championship winner and the Port Sunlight Golf Club was formed in 1932.

But the members' enthusiasm was not matched by ability and W. H. Davies, the Wallasey professional, English International and member of the Ryder Cup team, was engaged to give a series of lectures and demonstrations.

In 1934, Lever Brothers built a large wooden clubhouse, opened by Lord Leverhulme, to replace two converted railway coaches.

After World War II the company agreed to extend the layout and Guy Farrar, Secretary of Royal Liverpool, helped in redesigning the course. Six new greens and three fairways were built.

The course was lost, however, when a motorway scheme came through the land. The company offered a site at Eastham. In 1974 the Port Sunlight club was dissolved and Eastham Lodge Golf Club was launched with financial help from the North West Sports Council, Bass North West Ltd., and several members of the club.

The third Viscount Leverhulme opened the new clubhouse in 1976 and the club prospered. In 1980 a £42,000 extension to the clubhouse was opened by Ian Bradshaw, the club's most successful golfer, and a further six holes were opened a year later.

Ian Bradshaw joined the club at the age of 10 and went on to win the Cheshire Stroke Play Championship several times, was runner-up in the 1979 Brabazon Trophy and the 1982 English Amateur Championship. He represented England in 1979. The Ian Bradshaw lounge was named in his honour.

The course is a pleasant parkland layout of 15 holes, with three holes played a second time. It is a flat course but most of the holes are subtle doglegs and the many mature trees make for a test of accuracy.

Plans are in progress to make it a full 18-hole course by 1998.

President of Eastham Lodge is Sir Bobby Charlton CBE.

FACT FILE

A parkland course of 15 holes, 5953 yards. Par 69. SSS 69. Record 67.

Restrictions: Societies may play Tuesday or Friday by prior arrangement. Visitors phone in advance but can not play at weekends.

Fees: £22.

Dress code: Smart casual.

Shop opening: Dawn till dusk.

Facilities:

TO THE CLUB

From junction 5 of the M53 follow signs to Eastham Country Park.

Course Information

Hole	Yards	Stroke	Par
1	159	17	3
2	321	15	4
3	358	7	4
4	206	11	3
5	461	1	4
6	205	9	3
7	337	3	4
8	331	13	4
9	515	5	5
10	418	2	4
11	363	10	4
12	189	12	3
13	331	14	4
14	515	6	5
15	418	4	4
16	155	16	3
17	384	8	4
18	287	18	4
OUT	2893		34
IN	3060		35
TOTAL	5953		69

1) A short hole to start. There are two bunkers in front of the green but don't be long, either!

2) An easy driving hole. Stay slightly left. The green is offset right.

3) A picturesque dogleg left. Drive over the oak tree at left.

4) The best short hole on the course. Bunkers surround the green.

5) A good drive is needed to tackle this long par four hole - a dogleg to the right. There are some lovely trees at the apex of the hole.

6) Another good short hole. Don't hit the overhead cables.

7) A pretty hole through trees to a slightly elevated green.

8) Be adventurous - take the short-cut on the dogleg right!

9) A good par five hole, known locally as a slog up the A41.

10) A testing par four. Drive between trees for a good approach.

11) The drive must be down the right of the fairway on this slight dogleg left to a Mackenzie green.

12) A lovely short hole with out-of-bounds left.

13) Same as the eighth.

14) Same as the ninth

15) Same as the 10th.

16) A short and tricky hole. The green is on top of a mound.

17) A good drive is required on this moderate par four. The second shot is to a narrow green.

18) This short par four can be driven but beware the cross bunkers just short of the hole.

Recommended Facilities

Merseyside

25

FORMBY
Golf Club

Golf Road, Formby,
Merseyside L37 1LQ.
Secretary: R. I. F. Dixon
01704-872164 (Fax 833028).
Professional: Clive Harrison
01704-870390.
Clubhouse: 01704-872164.

BECAUSE of its sheltered aspect, a golfer could forget that Formby was a links course. The sea is visible only twice and the stately pine trees and high dunes filter out much of the noise from wind and foreshore.

But hitting the ball down these championship standard links gives that immediate feedback from firm, springy turf, fast seaside greens and natural sandy bunkers.

Many of Formby's holes weave their way well below the surrounding dunes, creating a feeling of privacy that is rare on a links course.

And another factor is that the course does not stretch 'out and back' but has no fewer than 11 changes of direction.

Like several links, this course has had the problem of coastal erosion and three new holes have been built over the years.

Founded in 1884, Formby lost its first clubhouse in a fire and the present elegant building with its distinctive clock tower was completed in 1901.

All the major amateur championships have been held here with the exception of the Walker Cup.

In 1934, Diana Fishwick (Critchley) defeated the American, Glenna Collett, in a memorable final of the British Ladies Amateur Championship.

The Amateur Championship has been staged at Formby three times, including the 1984 event when Jose-Maria Olazabal beat Colin Montgomerie and went on to complete a unique hat-trick by winning the British Boys' and British Youths' titles.

Formby has never hosted an Open Championship due to lack of the necessary facilities but the course is used in the final qualifying rounds when the Open is held at Royal Birkdale (and in 1996 for the

Royal Lytham event). The championship length was re-measured in 1996 as 7040 yards.

In 1997 Formby hosts the European Ladies' Amateur Championship and, in 1998, the English Amateur Stroke Play Championship (the Brabazon Trophy).

The course record at the start of 1996 was 65, set by Neil Coles in a Pro-Am tournament in 1965. The amateur record of 66 was set in 1991 by Ian Pyman and M. J. C. Hudson.

The club has Dormy House accommodation for men.

Formby Golf Club has no lady members and no management link with the ladies' club.

FACT FILE

A links course of 18 holes, 6496 yards (visitors). Par 72. SSS 72. Record 65.

Restrictions: Visitors must contact in advance. No visitors before 9.30am. Restricted on Wednesdays, weekends and Bank Holidays. Handicap certificates required.

Fees: £50 per day or round.

Dress code: Usual golf attire. Jacket and tie required upstairs.

Shop opening: 8.15am to 6pm.

Facilities:

TO THE CLUB

One mile west of the A565, near Freshfields railway station.

Course Information

Hole	Yards	Stroke	Par
1	394	11	4
2	372	9	4
3	499	3	5
4	310	15	4
5	153	17	3
6	385	7	4
7	368	13	4
8	480	1	5
9	444	5	4
10	178	16	3
11	376	12	4
12	385	4	4
13	370	10	4
14	408	6	4
15	393	2	4
16	115	18	3
17	486	8	5
18	380	14	4
OUT	3405		37
IN	3091		35
TOTAL	6496		72

1) A deceptively easy-looking drive requires a very accurate shot. The railway runs along the right, behind the trees.

2) Another deceptive drive needing local knowledge to find the green.

3) Cross-bunkers force the drive to the right and then more cross-bunkers inhibit the second shot.

4) A classic short par four with bunkers at strategic points.

5) Don't be left of the green on the first of the par three holes.

6) A good drive is needed to allow a long blind shot to the green.

7) Believe the marker post! Fir trees on the right block out a dangerous sloping green.

8) A long dogleg par five through pines and other varieties. Keep the drive to the right to find the two-level green.

9) A long par four straight into the prevailing wind. It's a tricky green.

10) Beware of the large bunkers left and right of the green.

11) Clear the sandhills with the drive to find the plateau green.

12) Another classic par four needing a good medium iron to the green.

13) The green is situated in a bowl. Beware the bunkers.

14) A dogleg right. Watch the bunkers each side at about 200 yards.

15) A good drive to the left of the tree reveals a green guarded by two large sandhills.

16) This short par three is well bunkered at the front and left.

17) Don't try to cut the corner on this dogleg left!

18) A heavily bunkered hole to a green 50 yards long. Check where the flag is before you start your round.

Recommended Facilities

BLUNDELLSANDS HOTEL

THE SERPENTINE, BLUNDELLSANDS, CROSBY, MERSEYSIDE L23 6YB
TELEPHONE: 0151-924 6515 FACSIMILE: 0151-931 5364

"Ideally situated for Formby Golf Course, the majestic Victorian red brick building that is the Blundellsands Hotel is a haven for golfers and their families alike.

Just a few minutes walk from the beach, the hotel delightfully couples the elegance of a bygone era with every comfort of the modern day. All its 41 en-suite bedrooms are tastefully furnished, and offer satellite TV, trouser press, hair dryer, and tea and coffee making facilities.

Car parking at the hotel is free, secure and plentiful, and for those not driving, the local railway station is less than 100 yards away, providing a frequent and easy link to Formby within minutes.

The hotel has a delightful restaurant, offering both an a la carte and Table d'hôte Menu, and has a pianist playing most evenings. Add to this the cosy welcoming atmosphere of the Copper Bar and you have all the ingredients for a relaxing evening after a hard day on the fairway!

We look forward to welcoming you soon."

STAGECOACH
HOTELS PLC

Merseyside

27

FORMBY LADIES
Golf Club

Golf Road, Formby,
Merseyside L37 1YL.

Secretary: Mrs Val Bailey
01704-873493.
Professional: Clive Harrison
01704-870390.

FORMBY is one of the few surviving all-ladies golf clubs in the world. The club was formed in 1896 with a nine-hole course on ground leased from Formby Golf Club, where the ladies previously played.

Since the 1920s the Formby Ladies Golf Club has been fully self-governing and the time has long passed since the club was referred to as 'the ladies branch.'

Today at Golf Road the two clubs exist side by side but independently, although Clive Harrison acts as professional for both and the pro shop facilities are shared.

The ladies' links are surrounded on three sides by 'the long course' and the characteristics are the same. Golf writers have long admitted that the only difference between the two 18-hole courses is one of scale - not skill.

The idyllic atmosphere created by the sand dunes, the pine woods, the heather and wild flowers is common to both. The wild life includes kestrels, swallows, pheasant and red squirrels.

Although only 5374 yards, the par and scratch score of 71 indicates the difficulty. The westerly wind is troublesome and the course is noted for its small, hard-to-hit greens.

The story of the Formby Ladies Golf Club was told in a centenary history written by freelance golf writer and broadcaster Patricia Davies.

Luckily for the research, many records and letters dating back to 1896 were discovered in some old lockers a few years ago after being thought lost in a fire which badly damaged the clubhouse in 1953.

The ladies played over 'the long course' from the beginning and the first reference to a plus-handicap golfer at Formby was Miss Mary Bushby, who returned a score in 1885 of 72 plus 5 = 77.

The Formby Ladies Golf Club was launched in 1896 with its own course and clubhouse - and a proud claim to having accommodation superior to that of the nearby West Lancashire Ladies Golf Club, at Blundellsands.

Formby's best player Beryl Newton (nee Brown) was the Lancashire ladies champion eight times between 1921 and 1937. From her home in the Isle of Man she sent her club medals for the centenary exhibition.

After World War Two, Frances 'Bunty' Stephens was Lancashire champion from 1948 to 1955 and again in 1959 and 1960. She twice won the British title and had several Curtis Cup honours.

FACT FILE

A links course of 18 holes, 5374 yards. Par 71. SSS 71.

Restrictions: Societies and visitors write to the Secretary. Handicap certificates required.

Fees: £28 to £33.

Dress code: Collar and tie in clubhouse after 4pm.

Shop opening: As for Formby Golf Club.

Facilities:

TO THE CLUB

One mile west of the A565 Southport to Liverpool road, near Freshfield station.

Course Information

Hole	Yards	Stroke	Par
1	261	10	4
2	417	4	5
3	129	16	3
4	287	8	4
5	122	17	3
6	412	2	4
7	251	14	4
8	428	6	5
9	322	12	4
10	422	1	5
11	307	9	4
12	158	15	3
13	385	5	4
14	301	13	4
15	374	3	4
16	128	18	3
17	324	7	4
18	346	11	4
OUT	2629		36
IN	2745		35
TOTAL	5374		71

1) A short par four needing great accuracy.

2) A par five with the prevailing wind blowing into the heather.

3) A short hole with plenty of bunkers. The wind dictates the choice of club.

4) Play to the left on this picturesque par four, then to the right side of the green to avoid a large bunker.

5) A classic par three with the green set into the side of a hill.

6) A dogleg par four from an elevated tee needs two good shots.

7) The green is well guarded on this driveable par four.

8) The longest hole can be a slog in the wind.

9) Orchids grow in the approach to the fairway on this tough par four.

10) An elevated tee gives a rare view of the sea. It is easy to run through the green with the approach.

11) 'The tree hole' that claims a sliced tee shot.

12) A par three that the great Edith Wilson called a gem.

13) A long par four that can be a bit of a slog.

14) A short par four with trees on the left and heather on the right.

15) A hidden green makes the second shot hard to judge. A hollow and a large bunker are the problems.

16) A very short par three, usually played with a cross wind.

17) Position off the tee is all important on this par four.

18) A straightforward par four with cross-bunkers to carry for the second shot.

Merseyside

GRAND NATIONAL
Golf Club

Aintree Golf Centre,
Aintree Racecourse,
Ormskirk Road, Liverpool L9 5AS.
Secretary: George Cowley
0151-5235157.
Professional: Liam Kelly
0151-5237323.

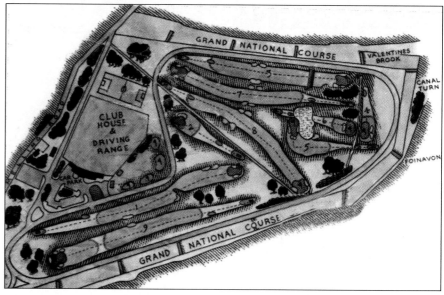

THIS nine-hole course lies in the heart of the Grand National racecourse, bordered by those famous fences such as Becher's Brook, Canal Turn and Valentine's.

Golfers even have the chance to play across the original Becher's Brook, a small stream which bisects the course. The management takes pride in the condition of the tees and greens - winter versions never have to be used - achieved through their long tradition of turf husbandry on one of the world's most famous race-courses.

It is a pay-and-play course with keen prices and the added factor of being one of the longest nine-hole courses in the country. Eighteen holes check out at more than 6600 yards. Among the selection of standard golf course hazards, including a deep lake and numerous bunkers, the course has one that is thought to be unique.

Stretched imaginatively across the third fairway is a replica steeple-chase fence fronted by a wide ditch designed to catch the second shot. This is a 'fun' substitute for a cross-bunker. Aintree is probably unique among golf courses in having both the opening and closing holes played over 500 yards.

Both holes are stern driving tests , particularly the last hole, which stretches for 550 yards in front of the famous racecourse stands and, when played into the prevailing wind, is a formidable challenge to any golfer.

Adjacent to the golf course is a 30-bay driving range. Liam Kelly, the well-known teaching professional, is on hand to advise beginners and improvers.

FACT FILE

A parkland/links course of 9 holes, 6624 yards. Par 72. SSS 72. Record 72.

Restrictions: Societies make contact in advance. Visitors can also book in advance. Competitions Sunday am.
Fees: £5 to £10 (pay-and-play).
Dress code: Usual golf attire.
Shop opening: 9.30am to 8pm.
Facilities:

TO THE CLUB ⟩

From the M57 and M58 follow the sign for Liverpool, then for Aintree Racecourse.

Course Information

Hole	Yards	Stroke	Par
1	555	5	5
2	204	13	3
3	451	1	4
4	148	17	3
5	262	9	4
6	207	15	3
7	451	3	4
8	484	7	5
9	550	11	5
10	555	6	5
11	204	14	3
12	451	2	4
13	148	18	3
14	262	10	4
15	207	16	3
16	451	4	4
17	484	8	5
18	550	12	5
OUT	3312		36
IN	3312		36
TOTAL	6624		72

1) A 555 yard opening par five, quite generous but be sure to hit the fairway!

2) Probably the most challenging tee shot on the course, a par three is an excellent result.

3) A well placed bunker on the right and a very unusual water hazard makes this a challenging par four.

4) A medium length par three, bunkers left and Becher's Brook running diagonally. Don't relax!

5) A short dogleg right par four round a lake. The angle of approach is the secret to success.

6) Off the back tee, 207 yards to a very narrow raised green, water hazard left and bunker short.

7) A small landing area off the tee, an angled ditch and a well guarded green make this a great hole.

8) Par five off the back, par four from the normal tee. Whichever way, this uphill dogleg right is tough!

9) It's not over yet! Another 550 yard par five usually into the wind with out-of-bounds left.

Recommended Facilities

GRANGE PARK
Golf Club

Prescot Road, St. Helens,
Merseyside WA10 3AD.

Secretary: David Wood
01744-26318.
Professional: Paul Roberts
01744-28785.
Clubhouse: 01744-22980.

EVERY Midsummer's Day the ground rent for the club's 18-hole course is handed by the captain to the chairman of Pilkington's, the international glass manufacturers.

The ground rent for this prime piece of parkland at the highest point in St. Helens is a single red rose!

This lunch ceremony has been held since 1969, when Pilkington's sold the land to the golf club for £40,000 on a 999-year lease.

Not wishing to increase the cost to the club, Lord Pilkington said there would be a nominal rent.

The captain recalled from his student days that nominal rents were either a peppercorn or a rose at Midsummer. He suggested a rose be the annual rent. Lord Pilkington, a proud Lancastrian, accepted and stipulated it should be a red rose.

The captain at the time was Bert Fairclough, who recalled the 'red rose clause' in his 1991 centenary history of Grange Park. It was just one of many absorbing stories.

The club was founded in 1891 as the St. Helens Golf Club and a nine-hole course was laid out by the professional at Hoylake (Royal Liverpool), John Morris, who was the nephew of golfing legend Old Tom Morris, of St. Andrews.

The course, which opened in June, 1892, was on the opposite side of Prescot Road to today's course.

In 1911 the club became the Grange Park Golf Club Ltd., to finance an 18-hole course, which was opened in 1913 with an exhibition match between Harry Vardon, the five-time Open champion, and Ted Ray, the 1912 champion. The winner was Ted Ray.

The 1913 course was on the north side of Prescot Road and six more changes of a major nature were forced on the club in the next 56 years.

Probably the greatest golfer in the club's history was J. W. 'Jackie' Jones, who took up the game at 13 because of poor health and died on the first tee at Grange Park 58 years later.

He twice won the Lancashire Amateur Championship (in 1948 and 1954) and in 1948 he also won the Liverpool and District title and was a semi finalist in the English Amateur Championship.

Jones set course amateur records at Fleetwood, Royal Lytham and West Lancashire as well as his home course.

Perhaps his greatest achievement was in the British Open at Royal Lytham in 1952, when he was fourth on the leader board after two rounds (with 143) and was drawn to play the last two rounds with Bobby Locke, who won the title. Jones won the silver medal presented to the leading amateur.

Grange Park hit the headlines in 1975 when, for the first time on a British golf course, the head greenkeeper led his staff out on strike a week before the Captain's Prize.

Retired head greenkeeper Walter Sumner, who had spent 50 years with the club, returned to supervise members in a rescue operation.

FACT FILE

A parkland course of 18 holes, 6422 yards. Par 72. SSS 71. Record 65.

Restrictions: Societies phone the Secretary/Manager. Casual visitors contact the pro.

Fees: £23 to £35.

Dress code: Smart casual.

Shop opening: 8.30am till dusk.

Facilities:

TO THE CLUB

On the A58, one and a half miles south of St. Helens town centre.

Course Information

Hole	Yards	Stroke	Par
1	344	12	4
2	353	14	4
3	361	4	4
4	206	10	3
5	483	16	5
6	478	6	5
7	347	8	4
8	151	18	3
9	443	2	4
10	323	17	4
11	456	1	4
12	449	3	4
13	487	9	5
14	185	11	3
15	492	5	5
16	157	15	3
17	346	7	4
18	361	13	4
OUT	3166		36
IN	3256		36
TOTAL	6422		72

1) An easy opening par four to a front sloping green.
2) The long slope down to the green and out-of-bounds behind it, calls for a firm chip or a careful pitch and run.
3) Beware the fairway sloping towards the bunkers.
4) Under-clubbing is a common fault on this long par three.
5) An easy long hole. Some pin positions call for a precise approach.
6) It takes two big shots to clear the ditch.
7) A tee shot to the left of the fairway opens up a good approach to the narrow, elevated green.
8) It's best to err on the right hand side on this par three.
9) Two good shots will reach the rear-sloping green, in front of the clubhouse. It's out-of-bounds behind the green, of course.
10) Keeping clear of the out-of-bounds, a ball on the right of the fairway opens up the bunkered green.
11) A handicap golfer will be happy with five on this stroke one hole.
12) A ditch on the right of the sloping fairway attracts fades and slices.
13) On this picturesque par five hole, two lusty shots will open up the green for an accurate pitch.
14) The greenside bunkers await a wayward tee shot.
15) With out-of-bounds all along the left, this hole plays its full length to a narrow Mackenzie green.
16) Best advice - hit the green!
17) While the big hitter may chance a shot to the green, two modest shots round the dogleg should set up a par.
18) Use the wide fairway to avoid the out-of-bounds on the left.

Recommended Facilities

Merseyside

33

HAYDOCK PARK
Golf Club

Newton Lane, Newton-le-Willows
WA12 0HX.

Secretary: J. V. Smith
01925-228525.
Professional: Peter Kenwright
01925-226944.
Clubhouse: 01925-224389.

THERE were fewer than 10 golf clubs in England when the Haydock Park club was formed on January 5, 1877. The Wigan Observer reported that the club's first prize meeting was held on May 2.

The course was a nine-hole layout at Haydock Park, half a mile from the club's present location at Golborne Park.

The move, in 1922, was a considerable step up for the club. Instead of a humble sports pavilion on rough pastureland, they moved into an 18th century mansion on 90 acres of ideal parkland turf in a leasing agreement with the Legh Estate.

The lease has been renewed periodically and golf is guaranteed on the site until the year 2020.

Fascinating glimpses of golf club life between the two world wars were given in the club's centenary booklet. They came from the diaries of former secretary Jim Unsworth.

He recalled a competition in 1925 which was a disaster due to the long rough. "Eighty balls and one small caddy were lost."

Don Bradman, the famous Australian batsman, visited the course in 1934 and played in a foursome and another Australian of note, Rugby League player Bill Shankland, became the club pro in the 1930s.

Many clubs suffered the loss of territory during World War Two but the Haydock Park club actually had an American Forces base on the last six holes.

The course was not returned to 18 holes until 1951, and the 'occupation' is remembered in an annual competition for the Burtonwood Golf Association Trophy, which was donated by the Americans.

In the 1980s the club produced three lady players of note. Amanda Bromilow (nee Brown) became the Lancashire Girls and Lancashire Ladies champion and her sister, Jacqui Brown, has become a professional, along with Tina Yarwood.

FACT FILE

A parkland course of 18 holes, 6043 yards. Par 70. SSS 69. Record 65.

Restrictions: No visitors Tuesdays and weekends unless introduced by a member. Societies make arrangements with the Secretary.

Fees: £25.

Dress code: Usual golf attire,

Shop opening: 8.30am to 6.30pm.

Facilities:

TO THE CLUB

From junction 23 of the M6 to the A580 and then one mile east.

Course Information

Hole	Yards	Stroke	Par
1	408	3	4
2	182	9	3
3	490	13	5
4	119	16	3
5	523	12	5
6	362	6	4
7	310	14	4
8	191	7	3
9	438	2	4
10	363	8	4
11	375	4	4
12	151	17	3
13	449	1	4
14	283	18	4
15	495	11	5
16	328	15	4
17	380	5	4
18	196	10	3
OUT	3023		35
IN	3020		35
TOTAL	6043		70

1) A good par four, usually played with a long iron second shot.

2) A par three with a small green and bunkers left and right.

3) After a good drive, beware the out-of-bounds right of the green.

4) A ring of bunkers and a sloping green call for a precise shot on this short par three hole.

5) A nice par five with a fairway bank that partly obscures the green.

6) Tee off from an elevated tee to a fairway that slopes right towards the out-of-bounds.

7) The two-tier green can make the short iron second shot difficult.

8) Another two-tier green makes this a testing par three.

9) Stroke index one, usually played into the prevailing wind.

10) This straightforward par four has a narrow, well guarded green.

11) A good driving hole. It's a dogleg right with out-of-bounds all the way down the right.

12) An easy par three but beware any crosswind from the left.

13) A good hole needing a drive left of centre for the best line to the green, but troublesome in the wind.

14) A tee shot placed in the right spot could make a birdie.

15) A dogleg par five with out-of-bounds right of the green.

16) Avoid the bunkers off the tee and it's a straightforward hole.

17) A good tee shot is required on this dogleg left.

18) A good par three to finish by the clubhouse.

Recommended Facilities

Merseyside

HESKETH
Golf Club

Cockle Dicks Lane,
off Cambridge Road,
Southport, Merseyside PR9 9QQ.

Secretary: Peter B. Seal
01704-536897.
Professional: John Donoghue
01704-530050.

HESKETH is the oldest of the six golf clubs in Southport and has a place in the golfing history of the region.

It was from Hesketh that the Lancashire County Golf Union was formed in 1910 and the first county championship was held there, with the home player, G. F. Smith, being the winner.

In 1924 the club again led the way when the captain, J. Rayner Batty, was the instigator and first president of the English Golf Union.

Hesketh's name stayed at the forefront as the venue of top events, including the Dunlop Southport Tournament, won on more than one occasion by Henry Cotton.

The club's fame was boosted by the achievements of the Bentley brothers in the 1930s. Both became English Amateur champions, Harry in 1936 and Arnold in 1939. Harry also won the amateur titles of Germany, France and Italy and was in the Walker Cup team in 1934, 1936 and 1938.

The present course dates from the turn of the century but it was partly built over the original 12 holes laid out in 1885, when the club was formed under the title Southport Golf Club, four years before Birkdale.

In 1891 the members voted to quit the course in the sand dunes north of Southport because of unruly behaviour from residents of a neighbouring 'shanty town.'

The club moved to a leased site on the Scarisbrick Estate, where their professional, George Strath, laid out a new course.

The 'shanty town' having been removed, the club returned in 1902 to their original location, where the new heir to the Hesketh family estates had built a new course and clubhouse. A merger took place and the name was changed to Hesketh Golf Club.

The course is regarded as a true test of golf and poses problems to amateurs and professionals alike.

Recognition of the course continues with its use as a qualifying course for the Open when held at Royal Birkdale, the venue of the 1995 County Championship and recent events such as the British Senior Amateur Championship and the British Girls' Amateur Championship.

FACT FILE

A links course of 18 holes, 6407 yards. Par 71. SSS 72. Record 64.

Restrictions: Societies by prior arrangement. Visitors may play weekdays except 12.30 to 2pm (members only) and Tuesday am (ladies).

Fees: £25 to £40.

Dress code: Smart casual.

Shop opening: Dawn till dusk.

Facilities:

TO THE CLUB

One mile north of Southport on the A565 off Cambridge Rd.

Hole	Yards	Stroke	Par
1	383	7	4
2	151	15	3
3	319	11	4
4	178	17	3
5	363	9	4
6	451	1	4
7	430	5	4
8	348	13	4
9	436	3	4
10	329	18	4
11	185	14	3
12	425	4	4
13	471	10	5
14	393	2	4
15	375	6	4
16	187	16	3
17	505	8	5
18	478	12	5
OUT	3059		34
IN	3348		37
TOTAL	6407		71

Course Information

1) Not a difficult par four but an uneven lie is likely for the second.

2) Only the best aerial shot will hit the green, perched on a sand dune.

3) Trees left, bunkers right. This short par four calls for accuracy.

4) The green is surrounded by bunkers. A good shot is vital.

5) A ditch down the left and a blind second into the prevailing wind make this a good test.

6) About 450 yards of undulating fairway with out-of-bounds all along the left. Stroke index one is deserved.

7) The longest hole. Watch for the ditch 100 yards from the green.

8) A very tight tee shot, best played down the left. The green is small.

9) A ditch runs all the way on the left so a long, straight ball is needed to find the green in two.

10) No problems here. A definite birdie chance.

11) Get close to this Mackenzie green - or be in the three-putt zone.

12) A ridge of hummocks at good drive length make this one difficult.

13) A ditch runs down the left and cuts across the fairway at drive length and with a pond on the right it makes for a difficult tee shot.

14) A tight drive with out-of-bounds down the right and then played to a blind green.

15) The church steeple is a good line for the blind tee shot.

16) A well bunkered hole, played into the prevailing wind.

17) No bunkers but plenty of trees. A sharp dogleg left to a blind green. Only a hero or an idiot will try to be there in two!

18) This green can be reached in two but the entrance is very narrow.

Recommended Facilities

HESWALL
Golf Club

Cottage Lane, Gayton, Heswall,
Wirral, Merseyside L60 8PB.

Secretary: R. J. Butler
0151-3421237 (Fax same).
Professional: Alan Thompson
0151-3427431.

THIS course, with a splendid location on the Dee Estuary, was founded in 1901. Set in gently rolling parkland, it has that ideal combination of isolation, superb views and interesting wildlife.

The marshes adjacent to the course are a bird sanctuary with international status.

In common with other Wirral clubs, Heswall enjoys views of the Welsh hills that are quite inspiring on those days when the atmosphere is crystal clear.

The course is split by the Wirral Way bridal path and with the holes changing direction several times, the wind factor is all part of the challenge.

The club hosted the Cheshire County Championships in 1996.

Club professional Alan Thompson is the EGU's North West Regional Coach and the Cheshire county youth coach. In the last 10 years or so, four of the club's young players have been in the county youth team and Christopher Sands holds the Heswall course record of 62.

Among several players who play at representative level, Fiona Brown has played for England at all levels and was a reserve in the 1996 Curtis Cup. She has won both the English and Welsh Ladies Stroke Play championships in recent years.

Another Heswall member, Andrea Dunn, has won the Welsh Ladies Matchplay championship.

FACT FILE

A parkland course of 18 holes, 6554 yards. Par 72. SSS 72. Record 62.

Restrictions: Handicap certificates required. Unrestricted except for Bank Holidays. Societies Wednesday and Friday by prior arrangement.
Fees: £30 to £35.
Dress code: Usual golf attire.
Shop opening: Dawn till dusk.
Facilities:

TO THE CLUB

One mile south of Heswall, off the A540.

Course Information

Hole	Yards	Stroke	Par
1	421	5	4
2	393	11	4
3	337	9	4
4	209	13	3
5	494	7	5
6	396	15	4
7	434	1	4
8	160	17	3
9	509	3	5
10	450	4	4
11	148	14	3
12	490	6	5
13	350	10	4
14	431	2	4
15	327	12	4
16	151	16	3
17	520	8	5
18	334	18	4
OUT	3353		36
IN	3201		36
TOTAL	6554		72

1) A demanding long opening hole with out-of-bounds left off the tee.

2) A blind tee shot onto the left-to-right sloping fairway. The greenside bunkers are large.

3) The third but shortest par four so far. Avoid that fairway bunker from the tee. Anything short of the green gets wet!

4) A superb par three. Try to hit the green but watch the slope.

5) On a still day this is a reachable par five but a stream is waiting for a poor second shot.

6) Your approach through the tree lined fairway really needs a fade to the left.

7) A long par four dogleg left with trees to avoid on the second shot.

8) On this par three all the danger is on the left.

9) This par five gets narrower as you approach the green. Bunkers make a very narrow approach shot to the flag.

10) A challenging par four. It's out-of-bounds left and water to the right off the tee. The green is well guarded.

11) A tricky par three. The narrow green needs accuracy off the tee.

12) A dogleg par five past a pond with a sloping, elevated green. Be careful not to overclub.

13) A good tee shot flies the fairway bunker to open the dogleg left.

14) Trees on the fairway and a ditch waiting for a flat tee shot.

15) Anything left is in trouble and the second needs to be inch perfect.

16) An uphill par three to a green surrounded by bunkers.

17) A long par five with water and a narrow fairway.

18) A dogleg right and a guarded green make this a tricky finish.

Recommended Facilities

HILLSIDE
Golf Club

Hastings Road, Southport,
Merseyside PR8 2LU.

Secretary: John G. Graham
01704-567169.
Professional: Brian Seddon
01704-568360.
Clubhouse:
01704-569902 (Fax 563192).

IN the stretch of sandhills to the south of Southport, where three championship links courses rub shoulders, Hillside occupies the middle ground. The 'neighbours' are Royal Birkdale (to the north) and Southport and Ainsdale.

The Hillside club was formed in 1911 and moved in 1923 to its present location with a new 18-hole layout designed by Fred Hawtree.

Members proudly claim that since the back nine holes were redesigned in the 1960s, their course is just as good as Birkdale. Perhaps it is only the lack of space for marquees and grandstands that has kept Hillside away from the honour of staging an Open Championship.

However, many other championship events have been staged at Hillside since 1967, and in 1991 it was the final qualifying venue when the Open was held at Royal Birkdale.

Major events held at Hillside include: the British Amateur Championship (1979), the British Ladies Championship (1977), the European Tours PGA Championship (1882), the European Amateur Championship (1991, for the first time in England), the English Amateur Stroke Play Championship for the Brabazon Trophy (1995), the Army Championship (1995), and the Mid-Amateur Championship (1996). In the PGA event of 1982, Tony Jacklin clinched his last major trophy in a dramatic play-off against Bernhard Langer.

The layout of the course is almost scrupulously correct in its design balance, the two nines having a very similar length and each having two par threes, five par fours and two par fives.

From the back markers it measures 6850 yards and from the yellow tees (which visitors would play) it is a more moderate 6204 yards.

Playing this excellent course builds to a climax in the high dunes of the back nine, where the towering tees of the 11th and 17th give a commanding and possibly daunting view of the fairways.

When the magazine Golf World produced a list of the top courses in the British Isles in 1990, Hillside was placed at 19.

FACT FILE

A links course of 18 holes,
6850 yards (championship). Par 72.
SSS 74. Record 66.

Restrictions: By arrangement with the Secretary, visitors have access Monday to Friday from 9.04 to 11.52am and from 2 to 4pm; with limited access Sunday from 2 to 4pm.

Fees: £35 to £45.

Dress code: Usual golf attire.

Shop opening: Dawn till dusk.

Facilities:

TO THE CLUB

From the A565 Liverpool to Southport road, turn into Hastings Road on the seaward side, near Hillside railway station.

Course Information

Hole	Yards	Stroke	Par
1	399	7	4
2	525	13	5
3	402	3	4
4	195	9	3
5	504	15	5
6	413	1	4
7	176	17	3
8	405	11	4
9	425	5	4
10	147	18	3
11	508	8	5
12	368	12	4
13	398	2	4
14	400	14	4
15	398	4	4
16	199	16	3
17	548	10	5
18	440	6	4
OUT	3444		36
IN	3406		36
TOTAL	6850		72

1) A tough start of almost 400 yards.
2) A straightforward par five with a fast, tricky green.
3) Even with a good drive you face a testing second shot on this first-class dogleg hole.
4) This is a good short hole, normally into a breeze. Play one club more than you think.
5) If in doubt on this par five, play short of the cross-bunker for your second.
6) Stroke one on the card; beware those greenside bunkers.
7) Don't be short on this par three.
8) Drive down the left and second shot left!
9) A difficult par four. For the second shot aim long and left.
10) Well, it looks easy!
11) A fabulous view down to the fairway. Concentrate to stay safe.
12) A new plantation has made this tighter than index 12 suggests.
13) Another hard par four. The second shot is longer than you think.
14) Don't go in the bunker from the tee and take one more club to the green.
15) Take an iron off the tee on this par four.
16) Make sure you hit the right tier on this tricky green.
17) Watch the two fairway bunkers. Don't leave yourself a short pitch.
18) Play an iron from the tee and keep out of those greenside bunkers!

Recommended Facilities

Merseyside

41

HOYLAKE
Municipal Golf Course

Carr Lane, Hoylake,
Wirral, Merseyside L47 4BQ.

Bookings: 0151-6322956.
Clubhouse: 0151-6324883.
Professional: Simon Hooton.

THE ladies of the Royal Liverpool Golf Club started to play on a nine-hole course on this site in 1929.

In 1932 the old Hoylake Urban Council bought enough land to double the course and the man selected to design it was the great James Braid.

The Hoylake Municipal Golf Course was formally opened in April, 1933, with an exhibition match in which James Braid and George Duncan played two other professionals, W. H. Davies and W. H. Kenyon.

Braid is second from the left on the front row in the picture below.

Henry Cotton came to see the course and played a round with the first professional, Danny Thwaite.

The new course cost £20,000 and a further £3,000 went on building a clubhouse.

From the early days of municipal ownership, private golf clubs were formed to play over the course and they include: Grosvenor Grange Ladies, Hoylake Golf Club, West

Hoyle Golf Club and the Irby Golf Club. Both Hoylake and West Hoyle also have ladies' golf clubs.

Like all seaside courses, the weather is an important factor. In the prevailing wind, Hoylake's front nine can be a stern test for a municipal course.

Course Information

Hole	Yards	Stroke	Par
1	342	10	4
2	418	4	4
3	175	18	3
4	334	17	4
5	447	3	4
6	371	5	4
7	167	11	3
8	429	1	4
9	390	8	4
10	178	16	3
11	399	7	4
12	477	13	5
13	324	12	4
14	360	9	4
15	479	14	5
16	203	15	3
17	463	2	4
18	357	6	4
OUT	3073		34
IN	3240		36
TOTAL	6313		70

1) The fairway is wide but the second shot is tricky with seven bunkers surrounding the green.

2) A tough hole unless downwind. There is no run on this fairway.

3) A par three often affected by the wind. And those huge bunkers.

4) The easiest par four and driveable in one with the wind behind.

5) A tough par four with no run off the tee shot and the second shot restricted by out-of-bounds on both sides.

6) Taking account of the out-of-bounds, there is still a problem with a road across the fairway, stopping a low running drive.

7) A great par three with bunkers, ditches and then a pond to avoid.

8) A ditch across the fairway at 235 yards is the decider here.

9) Played off a plateau tee but there is no run on the drive.

10) A fine par three. Seven bunkers guard the very fast green sloping front to back, with trees at the back.

11) The first step is to miss the fairway bunker at 215 yards.

12) A great par five with fairway bunkers and trees to consider.

13) Aim left from the tee and hope there's no wind!

14) A short par four. It's out-of-bounds left and a very tricky second shot is needed to the sloping green.

15) Hit the ball straight and it runs for ever. Gorse at the right of the green is the main concern.

16) Keep straight. There are bunkers all over the place.

17) If it's windy play this as a five.

18) A great finishing hole. Avoid that fairway ditch and be ready to hit an accurate approach shot.

Recommended Facilities

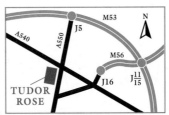

HUYTON & PRESCOT
Golf Club

Hurst Park, Huyton Lane, Huyton, Merseyside L36 1UA.

Secretary: M. H. Devenish
0151-4893948; Fax: 0151-4890797.
Professional: Malcolm Harrison
0151-4892022.
Clubhouse: 0151-4891138.

THERE were water features on the Hurst Park Estate long before golf came to be played there early in the 20th century.

Indeed, designers of modern golf courses could learn a thing or two from the landscape architects of the 18th century.

Although, perhaps fountains and statues behind the ninth green would be overdoing it somewhat!

There are no such follies at Huyton and Prescot but the tee for the fifth hole is built on an island that was actually part of the water garden created in the 1870s.

There is a chance of causing a splash on half a dozen other holes, mainly in the ditch that meanders through the course.

The estate had its own well, which is still intact under the secretary's office.

Golf was first played in the grounds in 1905 at about the time the Atherton family bought the estate and its Georgian manor house. It was not until 1948 that the golf club bought the estate from the Athertons and formed a limited company to run the club.

The manor house clubhouse met a crisis in 1961 when timber rot was discovered and the old minstrel gallery had to be removed.

A crisis of greater dimensions was the news in 1965 that a motorway was to be built across the course, taking two of the holes.

With support from the BICC Group, Prescot Council and the Lancashire County Council, the club purchased new land and built a new course, which was opened in 1972.

It's a parkland course noted for several testing and picturesque par three holes.

Recent additions have been new showers and a safety fence bordering the lane next to the club.

Huyton and Prescot is host to the annual Roy Castle Cause for Hope competition in aid of the fund established by the late entertainer towards a cancer research hospital in Liverpool.

FACT FILE

A parkland course of 18 holes, 5839 yards. Par 68. SSS 68.

Restrictions: Societies by arrangement with the Secretary. Ladies day Tuesday. No visitors weekends unless with a member.

Fees: £22 to £50. With member - £6 and £12.

Dress code: Smart casual - no jeans or collarless shirts.

Shop opening: 8.30am to 6pm.

Facilities:

TO THE CLUB

The course is off Huyton Lane (B5199). From the M57 exit at junction 2.

Hole	Yards	Stroke	Par
1	449	1	4
2	364	7	4
3	352	15	4
4	405	3	4
5	153	9	3
6	368	5	4
7	178	11	3
8	348	13	4
9	322	17	4
10	356	14	4
11	160	18	3
12	407	2	4
13	496	8	5
14	177	12	3
15	356	6	4
16	401	4	4
17	338	10	4
18	209	16	3
OUT	2939		34
IN	2900		34
TOTAL	5839		68

Course Information

1) A long drive needed and an accurate second shot. A very difficult start to your round.

2) A good drive down the right side of the fairway needed, avoiding the water on the left with your second shot.

3) Long iron or fairway wood for position, with a delicate short iron second to a difficult green.

4) A good drive needed to avoid the bunker left with trouble on the right.

5) The only advice on this hole is hit the green.

6) Dogleg left, avoiding the trees left with your drive, leaves a straightforward second.

7) A difficult par three if you don't hit the green with your tee shot.

8) Take notice of the marker with your tee shot and avoid the water with your second shot.

9) Avoid the cross bunkers and big tree right, a good birdie chance.

10) The second shot is the key to this hole. A difficult green to hold.

11) This is the easiest par three on the course, but no time to relax.

12) Two good long shots required, a par on this hole is a good result.

13) Can be reached in two, but watch out for out-of-bounds left and right.

14) A good tee shot needed avoiding the water right.

15) A straightforward drive, judge the distance right for your second and you will leave a birdie opportunity.

16) Sharp dogleg left with a good tee shot needed. With the second shot you can use the slope on the left of the green.

17) You can take some of the corner off with your tee shot, watch out for the two-tier green.

18) Watch the car park left - hope you had a good day!

Recommended Facilities

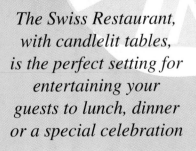

LIVERPOOL
Municipal Golf Course

Ingoe Lane, Kirkby,
Liverpool L32 4SS.

Enquiries: 0151-5465435.
Professional: David Weston
0151-5465435.

LIVERPOOL Municipal, or Kirkby Golf Course as it is better known, was built to championship length of 6700 yards before World War Two.

But it was lost to agriculture during the war and not reinstated as a true golf course until the 1960s.

After such a long break it was a gradual process to build a regular clientele and as golf gained popularity, so did this municipal course.

Now it is in fine condition after a major improvement programme by the Liverpool Leisure Services Directorate, who took over control in 1993.

Drainage was the first problem to be solved, followed by planting schemes to define the fairways more clearly and give the course a more pleasing appearance.

The pre-war pitch and putt course was not reinstated but the Kirkby course has its own practice field on the south side of the River Alt, where learners and improvers can iron out those glitches in their game.

The first fairway is alongside the River Alt and although generous enough to allow a margin for error, some golfer still go fishing.

Golfers cross the river by bridge to the second hole and enjoy the wide open spaces of the biggest course near Kirkby.

Regular patrons are quick to praise the recent improvements, which have made the course an excellent test for golfers.

The course has its own professional, Dave Weston, and the facilities expected of a golf club. There is an on-site shop and cafe/bar open to visitors.

FACT FILE

A parkland course of 18 holes, 6706 yards. Par 72. SSS 72. Record 68.

Restrictions: Societies contact the professional in advance. Visitors must phone to book.

Fees: £3.25 to £6.40.

Dress code: Smart casual.

Shop opening: 8am to 9.30pm weekdays, 7am to 9.30pm weekends.

Facilities:

TO THE CLUB

M62 to M57 junction 6, and follow the Fazackerley signpost. The course is 200 yards on the right.

Course Information

Hole	Yards	Stroke	Par
1	357	12	4
2	484	6	5
3	331	14	4
4	442	1	4
5	487	8	5
6	187	13	3
7	311	18	4
8	359	10	4
9	433	4	4
10	187	16	3
11	371	9	4
12	315	17	4
13	495	15	5
14	459	3	4
15	467	2	4
16	380	7	4
17	224	11	3
18	417	5	4
OUT	3391		37
IN	3315		35
TOTAL	6706		72

1) A straight drive to an open green. The River Alt is on the left.

2) Cross the bridge to play this hole. A straight drive to a green surrounded by trees.

3) An easy drive downhill on this slight dogleg to a small green.

4) Another slight dogleg but the fairway is nice and wide. The green is protected by mounds.

5) An open aspect finishing on a small Mackenzie green.

6) The River Alt presents a water hazard to the right on this easy par three protected by mounds and bunkers.

7) A pleasant par four to the backdrop of a wooded green.

8) A par four with a wide fairway parallel to the railway track, playing downhill to a small, bunkered green.

9) Back across the river to play this par four, a slight dogleg.

10) A par three down a wide, tree-lined fairway to a large green.

11) A large open green lies at the end of this undulating fairway.

12) A dogleg with a wide fairway and another inviting, open green.

13) Another wide dogleg but this time the green is small and wooded at the back.

14) This long par four has a water hazard, a wide fairway and a large green protected by mounds.

15) Another generous fairway, quite undulating.

16) An elevated green is the target from the tree-lined fairway.

17) A long par three with a raised green.

18) A downhill dogleg with a tree-lined fairway.

Recommended Facilities

Merseyside

LEASOWE
Golf Club

Leasowe Road, Moreton,
Wirral, Merseyside L46 3RD.

Secretary: Don Whiteside
0151-6775852 (Fax 6041424).
Professional: Neil Sweeney
0151-6785460.

WHAT a fascinating story the members of Leasowe can tell about the origins of the club.

Their founder was England's greatest amateur golfer and their first humble course had changing facilities in a lighthouse!

Why John Ball wanted to form his own club will never be known. Leasowe Golf Club's centenary book, in 1991, asked the question and wondered if it was due to the prohibition of Sunday golf at his home club, Royal Liverpool?

Or perhaps he was upset at not being invited to be captain of that famous Hoylake club after winning both the Amateur Championship and the Open, in 1890?

Surely he wasn't trying to make a monument to his brilliant championship double, which has never been repeated?

In all probability none of these were the reasons, the book concluded.

Ball and his fellow founders, all with farming expertise, laid out their nine holes, Ball was duly elected captain, and Leasowe Golf Club was registered with the R and A in May, 1891.

An arrangement was made with Mrs. Williams, the lady keeper of the lighthouse, to provide a room for changing until a small pavilion was built.

After two years, however, the club quit the lighthouse links in favour of a site on the Wallasey side of Leasowe Castle. A nine-hole course was laid out by Ball and Jack Morris, the professional at Royal Liverpool.

Ball was captain for the first four years. After winning his fifth Amateur title in 1899, he was made a life member. In 1904 the course was extended to 18.

On the playing side, the Leasowe links share many of the valued characteristics of the coastal courses of the Wirral and its immediate neighbour to the east is Wallasey Golf Club.

In recent decades few golf clubs have had such a succession of traumas as those which befell

Leasowe. Happily, they now seem to be over.

In 1963 the clubhouse burned down. In the 1960s and 1970s the issue of sand removal and tipping brought detrimental publicity. The problem of coastal erosion and loss of holes seemed insurmountable until recent years. Burglars stole the Captain's Medallion, a beautiful piece of jewellery given in 1891 by John Ball but it was luckily recovered by a third party. And as recently as 1990 a severe storm flooded part of the course.

On the positive side, the club completed ownership of all the course in 1984 and opened a new clubhouse in 1988.

Leasowe is a men-only golf club and that in itself is something of note in the 1990s.

FACT FILE

A links course of 18 holes, 6263 yards. Par 71. SSS 70. Record 63.

Restrictions: Societies and visitors book in advance.

Fees: £20 to £25.

Dress code: Usual golf attire.

Shop opening: 8am to 6.30pm in summer; to 4.30pm in winter.

Facilities:

TO THE CLUB

From the end of the M53 head into Wallasey and follow Leasowe Road to the Castle Hotel.

Course Information

Hole	Yards	Stroke	Par
1	252	17	4
2	302	11	4
3	138	16	3
4	456	1	4
5	335	9	4
6	563	5	5
7	387	7	4
8	277	15	4
9	439	3	4
10	451	2	4
11	297	14	4
12	159	18	3
13	316	12	4
14	441	6	4
15	411	4	4
16	367	10	4
17	482	8	5
18	190	13	3
OUT	3149		36
IN	3114		35
TOTAL	6263		71

1) A short par four reachable with a good drive.

2) Slightly longer, with a blind tee shot and a ditch short of the green.

3) Par three with a narrow, bunkered green.

4) A straightforward drive but the second shot is blind and there are tricky mounds round the green.

5) The fairway is narrow and there are big slopes in the green.

6) A narrow driving hole due to out-of-bounds down the left but it opens out for the second shot.

7) A dogleg left with bunkers on the corner and then short of the green. The out-of-bounds is at the left and back of the green.

8) A short par four reachable with a good tee shot.

9) Drive over the market garden (out-of-bounds) and then take a long iron to the green.

10) Watch for the bunkers 220 yards from the tee.

11) The ditch down the left and in front of the green is a problem.

12) The two-tier green is protected by bunkers right and bushes left.

13) A tight driving hole through bushes with out-of-bounds right, a ditch on the left and bunkers round the green.

14) The ditch is behind the green on this long par four.

15) A dogleg right with a water hazard at 280 yards on the left.

16) The ditch appears down the left, there are bunkers at good driving range and out-of-bounds behind the green.

17) A par five to a tight green with hollows at the sides.

18) A tough par three with bunkers surrounding the green.

Recommended Facilities

LEE PARK
Golf Club

Childwall Valley Road, Gateacre,
Liverpool L27 3YA.

**Secretary: Mrs. D. Barr
0151-4873882.
Clubhouse: 0151-4879861.**

THIS pleasant parkland course was founded in 1950 and was designed by Frank Pennink. It has many lovely tree-lined fairways and tip-top greens and an ongoing programme of improvements enhances the course each year.

Although more than 6,000 yards in length, the course is flat and ideal for the older, high-handicap golfer.

Nevertheless, it poses problems for the more accomplished player, as proved by the course record of 68.

The clubhouse facilities have recently been greatly improved, but Lee Park has not had a resident professional for several years.

Societies are welcomed but must be 12 or more in number.

FACT FILE

A parkland course of 18 holes, 6125 yards. Par 71. SSS 69. Record 68.

Restrictions: Visitors welcome. Societies (12 or more) make prior arrangements for Monday, Thursday or Friday only.

Fees: £21 to £26.

Dress code: Usual golf attire.

Facilities:

TO THE CLUB

The course is on the B5171, from the A562. From the M62 leave at junction 6.

Course Information

Hole	Yards	Stroke	Par
1	389	9	4
2	139	17	3
3	535	7	5
4	398	3	4
5	204	13	3
6	545	1	5
7	354	11	4
8	170	15	3
9	361	5	4
10	123	18	3
11	375	6	4
12	333	12	4
13	139	16	3
14	479	8	5
15	443	2	4
16	499	4	5
17	310	10	4
18	329	14	4
OUT	3095		35
IN	3030		36
TOTAL	6125		71

1) A slight dogleg par four. Watch out for the pond on the left, short of the green.

2) This par three poses no problems with the right club.

3) A long par five, played from a new elevated tee.

4) Take account of the ditch about 100 yards short of the green.

5) Not an easy par three with out-of-bounds left and trees right.

6) A long par five even for the big-hitters. Stroke index one.

7) A short par four. Drive left of the big tree to stay safe.

8) A well bunkered par three of moderate length.

9) A great hole. Drive past the big tree to this sharp dogleg left.

10) A deceptively simple, well bunkered short hole.

11) This dogleg to the left needs a good drive.

12) A good straight drive and the going is easy.

13) Another of those deceptively simple short holes.

14) A nice straight hole calling for a good drive.

15) This par four is very long from the back tee. Stroke index two.

16) A good par five. It's out-of-bounds left and right.

17) This dogleg left needs an accurate second shot.

18) A nice short par four to finish.

Recommended Facilities

MERSEY VALLEY
Golf Club

Bold Heath, Widnes WA8 3XL.

Professional: John Woolley
0151-4246060.
Management: 0151-4246060.

DESIGNED and constructed by St. Mellion Leisure Ltd., the development arm of St. Mellion International, this 18-hole, par 72 course was opened in 1995.

It covers some 125 acres adjacent to the A57 Liverpool to Warrington road and is two miles from junction 7 of the M62.

The course is level, although the greens and fairways have gentle undulations. A comfortable round of golf can be completed in just over three hours.

The course is run on a pay-and-play basis where both members and visitors pay green fees. The aim is to provide golf that is affordable to both regular and casual users.

Water comes into play on several holes and thousands of trees have been planted to give the course a parkland setting.

All the greens have been laid down to the best bent/fescue mixtures to provide top quality putting surfaces.

An outstanding feature of the Mersey Valley course is the superb drainage and, coupled with the natural free-draining soil, this ensures all-year play.

Fairways were sown well in advance with quality fescues, with the rough and semi-rough sown in the same seed mixtures.

The practice area can also be used year-round, thanks to a raised teeing area with tee mats. Both the ninth and 18th greens are located in front of the club-house.

FACT FILE

A parkland course of 18 holes, 6300 yards. Par 72. SSS 70. Record 70.

Restrictions: Members pay and play. Visitors and societies phone in advance.

Fees: £15 to £20.

Dress code: Usual golf attire.

Shop opening: Dawn till dusk.

Facilities:

TO THE CLUB

From junction 7 of the M62, one and a half miles on the A57 towards Warrington. The club is on the left.

Course Information

Hole	Yards	Stroke	Par
1	343	15	4
2	128	18	3
3	501	5	5
4	326	8	4
5	279	16	4
6	494	7	5
7	182	13	3
8	433	3	4
9	511	2	5
10	223	4	3
11	400	10	4
12	320	11	4
13	489	6	5
14	421	9	4
15	132	12	3
16	350	14	4
17	317	17	4
18	451	1	4
OUT	3197		37
IN	3103		35
TOTAL	6300		72

1) A comfortable opening hole with a wide fairway and a large green.

2) A short par three requiring a drive over water.

3) A tough par five of 501 yards with out-of-bounds on the left.

4) A dogleg par four with a super layout.

5) A short par four that's driveable by experienced golfers.

6) The second par five hole has ponds to the left and right of the fairway and a downhill approach to the green.

7) This is a tricky par three to an elevated green.

8) A lovely par four hole with ponds guarding the green.

9) It's long and has a wide fairway. A real driving hole.

10) Arguably one of the toughest par threes in the north west.

11) A straightforward par four of moderate length with a bunker guarding the entrance to the green.

12) A dogleg par four to an elevated green.

13) This par five presents a birdie chance to the average golfer.

14) A slightly uphill drive and second shot to an elevated green.

15) A spectacular par three. The green is behind a lake.

16) A dogleg par four hole with a very wide fairway.

17) With the wind behind, this short par four is driveable

18) A superb finishing hole - a par four that's rated stroke index one.

Recommended Facilities

Merseyside

53

PRENTON
Golf Club

Golf Links Road, Prenton,
Birkenhead, Merseyside L42 8LW.

Secretary: W. F. W. Disley
0151-6081053.

Professional: Robin Thompson
0151-6081636 (Fax 6091580).

THOSE palmy days when a golf club could be started for £25 are part of any account of Prenton's history.

Agricultural land was rented for £10 a year and £10 was earmarked to lay out the course. The clubhouse was a rented shack.

That was in 1905, after a February meeting had agreed to start a golf club. The course was in play in the spring, with jam jars set into the ground to serve as the holes. They were often full of water, however, and a young member earned the princely sum of one shilling for suggesting that tins with holes punched in the bottom would be a good substitute.

The response was so great that the club was on the move within three months to a larger site of more than 50 acres, including land that is today's Walker Park.

Water supply was a problem on the new course and the club resorted to collecting rainwater from the roof of the shack, which had been bought for £35. A clubhouse was opened in 1908 and forms a part of the present clubhouse.

The club's first greensman, Seph Francome, was a leading athlete and in 1912 he was given 14 days leave in order to represent Great Britain in the Olympic Games in Stockholm.

It was recognised around this time that the course needed improving but no sooner had the work started that World War One broke out and part of the course was lost to cattle grazing.

The 1920s was a productive period, starting with the engagement of Colt, Mackenzie and Company to redesign the course. The design was actually done by Dr. Alister Mackenzie and the new course was opened in May, 1923, with an exhibition match between A. G. Havers and Abe Mitchell.

A new 40-year lease lasted from 1922 until the eventual purchase of the course.

In the 1920s, Prenton had two professionals of international repute, W. H. Davies, who later joined Wallasey Golf Club, and E. W. Jarman, who later joined West Lancashire. Jarman was succeeded by his brother, Bobbie, who had a 50-year association with the club and was elected to honorary membership.

Damage to the clubhouse from German bombing in World War Two was finally made good by 1953 and the club's consultant course architects, Hawtrey and Son, were asked to plan a new 18th hole.

It was almost 20 years before 'the untidy pit' in front of the clubhouse, was replaced.

FACT FILE

A parkland course of 18 holes, 6411 yards. Par 71. SSS 71. Record 65.

Restrictions: Societies by prior appointment. Ladies' days Tuesday and Thursday.

Fees: £25 to £30.

Dress code: Usual golf attire; smart casual in the clubhouse.

Shop opening: 8.30am to dusk.

Facilities:

TO THE CLUB

Off the A552, two miles west of Birkenhead. From the M53 use exit 3.

Course Information

Hole	Yards	Stroke	Par
1	256	17	4
2	396	3	4
3	161	13	3
4	368	9	4
5	396	5	4
6	548	1	5
7	141	15	3
8	284	11	4
9	506	7	5
10	418	6	4
11	511	10	5
12	393	12	4
13	436	4	4
14	443	2	4
15	215	14	3
16	186	18	3
17	392	8	4
18	361	16	4
OUT	3056		36
IN	3355		35
TOTAL	6411		71

1) A relatively easy par four for the average player. Beware the ridge on the green.

2) A two-shotter if the ball is not pulled into the out-of-bounds.

3) A short uphill hole needing a firm and straight hit.

4) The tee shot must land on the fairway on this downhill dogleg.

5) A five would be fine on this par four full of trouble.

6) The longest hole, often played into the wind, needs three good shots to have any chance of par.

7) Choice of club decides the outcome on the shortest hole.

8) The wise move is a medium iron from the tee and a short approach or chip - but be straight!

9) A long uphill haul. Just keep them straight!

10) Another hole needing a straight hit. The green slopes to the left.

11) A good par five with out-of-bounds on both sides and fairway bunkers at the top of the hill.

12) A par four with a blind tee shot. The green bunkers spell trouble.

13) A difficult par four best tackled along the left - but take a good look at the fairway bunkers first.

14) Another tough one. A drive down the centre of the fairway is vital.

15) A long par three with a long green, sloping from the back.

16) A nice par three played to a well bunkered sloping green.

17) A testing two-shot hole. Take steps to avoid the cross bunkers at about 300 yards.

18) A challenging finish. There's out-of-bounds at the left but the main problem here is the steeply sloping green.

Recommended Facilities

The Bowler Hat Hotel offers 32 well appointed en-suite bedrooms with satellite TV, trouser press, tea/coffee making facilities and hair dryer.

The style of the hotel is that of a 19th Century Georgian Country House. The red brick facade is surrounded by over 100 car parking spaces and traditional landscaped gardens, and in the distance the welsh mountains form a panoramic backdrop to this charming hotel.

The award winning restaurant which is well patronised by residents and local discerning diners and has won 2 AA Rosettes (1995 &1996) reflecting the high standards of food and service.

Set in the heart of the Wirral with 16 golf courses within 20 minutes drive, the Bowler Hat hotel is the ideal base for your golfing holiday. We offer special rates for golf parties and society's.

2
Talbot Road
Oxton
Birkenhead
Merseyside
L43 2HH

Merseyside

55

ROYAL BIRKDALE
Golf Club

Waterloo Road, Birkdale,
Southport, Merseyside PR8 2LX.

Secretary: N. T. Crewe
01704-567920 (Fax 562327).
Professional: Richard Bradbeer
01704-568857.
Clubhouse: 01704-569913.

ONE of the north of England's premier clubs, Royal Birkdale was founded in 1889 and since 1954 it has been on the rota of Open Championship courses.

With its ideal location in the high sandhills to the south of Southport, the championship course is nearly 7000 yards but from the yellow tees it is a more comfortable 6292 yards, with a par of 71.

Birkdale's links are much favoured by overseas players because the fairways are mostly level and offer fair lies, unlike many British links courses where a good shot can be kicked away by odd humps and hollows.

At Birkdale the punishment tends to fit the crime!

The course was originally a nine-hole layout planned by George Lowe but the modern course is largely the result of the 1930s remodelling by Hawtree and Taylor.

The club's 'royal' designation was granted in 1951.

Royal Birkdale's name stands high on the list of Open Championship courses, having hosted no fewer than seven since the club was selected by the R and A in 1954. The next Open at Birkdale will be in 1998. The Australian maestro, Peter Thomson, won the 1954 championship with a four-round total of 283. It was part of his remarkable run of seven successive years in which he won four Opens and was runner-up in three.

In 1961 Arnold Palmer won at Birkdale with 284 and four years later Peter Thomson notched his fifth Open title with 285.

The Americans' penchant for the course showed in the results of the next three Open Championships staged there.

Lee Trevino's win in 1971 was in spite of taking a seven at the 71st after driving into the sand dunes on the left. He finished with 278 and beat Taiwan's Mr Lu by one stroke.

In 1976 Johnny Miller had a remarkable final round of 66 to take the title with a margin of six shots.

Tom Watson lowered the four-round tally to only 275 in winning in 1983.

The Australian, Ian Baker-Finch, took the last Birkdale Open title in 1991 with a score of 272.

But perhaps the most exciting day at Royal Birkdale came in 1969 when the destination of the Ryder Cup hung on the outcome of the final hole.

The teams were tied on 15 points when America's Jack Nicklaus and Britain's Tony Jacklin, level at the 18th, both reached the green in two. Each player missed his first putt. Nicklaus was four feet from the hole and Jacklin about half that distance. Nicklaus then sank his putt and in a wonderful gesture of sportsmanship he conceded Jacklin's putt.

The course record of 63 was set by Jodie Mudd in the 1991 Open.

After that event, the club took the major step of digging up, redesigning and rebuilding all the greens.

FACT FILE

A championship links course of 18 holes, 6292 yards. Par 71. SSS 71. Record 63.
(Category one, 6703 yards)

Restrictions: Visitors and societies make contact in advance. Handicap certificates required. Restricted tee-off at weekends.

Fees: £55 to £75.

Dress code: Usual golf attire.

Shop opening: 8am to 7pm.

Facilities:

TO THE CLUB

On the A565, one and a half miles south of Southport.

Merseyside

Course Information			
Hole	Yards	Stroke	Par
1	430	11	4
2	397	3	4
3	373	7	4
4	179	15	3
5	316	13	4
6	472	1	5
7	140	17	3
8	392	9	4
9	395	5	4
10	355	14	4
11	347	8	4
12	159	18	3
13	422	4	4
14	157	16	3
15	499	2	5
16	328	12	4
17	479	6	5
18	452	10	4
OUT	3094		35
IN	3198		36
TOTAL	6292		71

1) Opening with a long par four dogleg that has out-of-bounds on the right. The green entrance is narrow, needing a precise shot.

2) Danger behind the green dictates a carefully hit second shot.

3) Best advice is to take one more club than you think it needs.

4) The wind from the left can be the critical factor on this par three.

5) A pond awaits those who fancy their chances by cutting the corner.

6) A long dogleg with a bunker at the elbow on the right. Ditches and rough make it tough and the plateau green is well defended.

7) The high tee is sheltered, so the wind can surprise the golfer.

8) The best line on this dogleg right is down the right side from the tee but beware the bunkers. Playing safe at the left can leave a blind second shot, which has to be well struck.

9) With the fairway only partly visible from the tee, it's best to play the drive to the right on this moderate par four.

10) This dogleg left is a short par four but there's big trouble in scrub if you play too far left.

11) It's safer on the right - but taking a risk down the left can give a much better approach to the green.

12) Don't overhit the green on this par three.

13) The ditch down the left is a problem on this par four hole.

14) A par three where the sloping green decides the outcome.

15) A long par five with bunkers placed to catch the tee shot.

16) Driving down the left gives the best chance at the green.

17) A par five where an accurate drive is vital.

18) A long par four where the second shot may need one more club than seems obvious.

Just Perfect for Golf

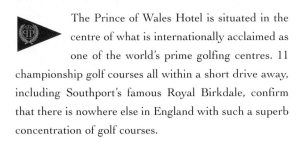

The Prince of Wales Hotel is situated in the centre of what is internationally acclaimed as one of the world's prime golfing centres. 11 championship golf courses all within a short drive away, including Southport's famous Royal Birkdale, confirm that there is nowhere else in England with such a superb concentration of golf courses.

Southport's Leading Hotel

The Prince of Wales has been the premier hotel in Southport for over a century, situated on Lord Street in the middle of shopping and entertainment areas. All 104 en suite bedrooms reflect the Victorian heritage and have satellite colour television, radio, direct dial telephone, hair drier, trouser press and welcome refreshments tray.

How to find us

You'll find us easily, as the hotel is conveniently located on Lord Street, with easy access for the M6, M62, M61 and M58.

PRINCE OF WALES
· H O T E L ·

SOUTHPORT
★ ★ ★ ★

Lord Street, Southport, Lancashire PR8 1JS Tel: 01704 536688 Fax: 01704 543488

A member of the Paramount Hotel Group

TO BOOK RING NOW ON 01704 536688

ROYAL LIVERPOOL
Golf Club

Meols Drive, Hoylake, Wirral,
Merseyside L47 4AL.

Sec: Grp. Capt. C. T. Moore CBE
0151-6323101.
Professional: John Heggarty
0151-6325868.

THE story of golf in northern England began at the Royal Liverpool club at Hoylake.

And what an illustrious story! The great names and the great events stretch back to the club's formation in 1869.

Although the Open championship is no longer held here, many other major events come to the famous Hoylake links as can be judged from the recent calendar.

In June 1995, the club hosted the 100th Amateur Championship, an honour for a club that instigated the tournament in 1885.

In May 1996, the Army Championship was held here, followed a month later by the EGU Northern Counties Championship and July's 75th anniversary match of the first international between Great Britain and Ireland and the United States.

That famous match at Hoylake gave the American golf administrator George H. Walker the idea of donating the trophy for a regular series, which began in 1922 as the Walker Cup. Royal Liverpool hosted the event in 1983.

The entire American Walker Cup team had previously been at Royal Liverpool, competing in the Amateur Championship in 1975, when up and coming British players such as Nick Faldo, Sandy Lyle, Nick Price and Mark James were chasing the honours. The title was won that year by the American, Marvin Giles.

In 1977, Sandy Lyle won the Brabazon Trophy at Royal Liverpool.

Going back to the beginning of the Hoylake story, golf began on a piece of rough ground known as the Warren, at the north end of the present links.

The nine-hole course was extended to 18 in 1871, when the club was granted its 'Royal' honour.

It was the home club of two legendary amateur players, John Ball and Harold Hilton. A record eight Amateur Championships were won by Ball between 1888 and 1912. In 1890 he won both the Amateur and the Open. Hilton won the Amateur title four times and the Open twice.

Jack Graham was another fine player of the same generation at Hoylake and holds a place with Ball and Hilton as the club's own 'great triumvirate.'

The Amateur Championship has been held at Royal Liverpool a record 17 times. It was here in 1930 that Bobby Jones won the second leg of his famous Grand Slam.

The Open Championship was held here on 10 occasions, although not since 1967, due to Hoylake's lack of space for marquees and stands.

This remains one of the great seaside championship courses - a stern test of nerve and accuracy.

The picture above is the rarely-used view of the clubhouse from the car park side.

FACT FILE

A seaside links course of 18 holes, 6835 yards. Par 72. SSS 74. Record 67.

Restrictions: Societies write to the Secretary. Visitors phone first. Handicap certificates required. No visitors before 9.30am or between 1 and 2pm. Ladies' day Thursday. Weekends limited.

Fees: £45 to £60 per round, with member £12 and £15.

Dress code: Usual golf attire.

Shop opening: 8am till dusk.

Facilities:

TO THE CLUB

The course is south west of Hoylake on Meols Drive (A540).

Course Information

Hole	Yards	Stroke	Par
1	429	5	4
2	374	15	4
3	505	7	5
4	184	13	3
5	424	1	4
6	383	9	4
7	198	17	3
8	479	3	5
9	392	11	4
10	412	12	4
11	200	14	3
12	393	4	4
13	159	18	3
14	521	8	5
15	459	2	4
16	533	10	5
17	393	6	4
18	397	16	4
OUT	3368		36
IN	3467		36
TOTAL	6835		72

1) A very tough opening hole. The tee shot must land close to the corner of the dogleg.

2) A slight dogleg right with a hard-to-hold sloping green.

3) A dogleg left needing a drive between two sets of bunkers and then a decision to play short or long.

4) A testing par three to a pedestal green ringed by deep bunkers.

5) Drive right of centre and then try to figure out the distance! It is not stroke index one for nothing!

6) A very tough hole needing a brave drive over the marker post.

7) A par three with variety - but not the controversial hole of old.

8) A famously difficult par five. Take care approaching the green, which falls away sharply each side.

9) Alongside the Dee estuary. Drive straight and hope for the best with the blind second shot!

10) A par four that often plays longer due to the prevailing wind. Grassy hollows guard the green.

11) Can you foil the bunker just short of the green on this par three?

12) Another dogleg left with an obvious route for big hitters.

13) The shortest hole. Be bold - and accurate.

14) Keep right to avoid the pot bunkers 100 yards from the green.

15) A long par four needing two very good long shots.

16) Direct the drive at the corner of the dogleg. The second shot is a long carry across the out-of-bounds, opening up the green.

17) Keep right, remember those three bunkers hidden from the tee.

18) An accurate tee shot between two sets of bunkers leaves a medium to long iron shot to a deep green.

Recommended Facilities

Merseyside

SHERDLEY PARK
Municipal Golf Course

Elton Head Road, St. Helens,
Merseyside WA9 4DE.

Professional: Peter Parkinson
01744-813149.
Clubhouse: 01744-815518.

OPENED in 1974, Sherdley Park is established as one of the top municipal golf courses in the north west, attracting players from a radius of about 25 miles.

Due to the popularity of the course it is necessary to book a tee six days before playing.

Professional Peter Parkinson designed the extension to 18 holes in 1974 but his claim to fame is connected with another course.

Playing at the West Lancashire Golf Club at Blundellsands in 1972, when he was the assistant pro, he had an incredible hole in one at the seventh by driving across the corner of the dogleg.

It is listed in the Guinness Book of Records as the longest hole in one in Britain, at 394 yards but the re-measured figure in the West Lancashire club's booklet states 387.

The Sherdley Park course is an undulating parkland layout that offers a good challenge to golfers of all handicaps.

Modifications had to be made in 1994 when the St. Helens link road from the M62 was built. Peter Parkinson did the design work for the changes.

Sherdley Park has an annual charity event for the St. Helens and Knowsley Hospice.

FACT FILE

A parkland course of 18 holes, 5974 yards. Par 71. SSS 69. Record 68.

Restrictions: None.

Fees: £6.20 to £7.40.

Dress code: Smart casual.

Shop opening: 6.30am till dusk.

Facilities:

TO THE CLUB

From exit 7 of the M62 onto the A570 for two miles, turning right at the second roundabout for 400 yards. Turn left into the park.

Course Information			
Hole	Yards	Stroke	Par
1	307	17	4
2	498	13	5
3	343	7	4
4	367	3	4
5	188	15	3
6	441	1	4
7	503	11	5
8	394	9	4
9	383	5	4
10	383	2	4
11	267	16	4
12	139	12	3
13	397	4	4
14	307	8	4
15	174	10	3
16	252	18	4
17	268	14	4
18	363	6	4
OUT	3424		37
IN	2550		34
TOTAL	5974		71

1) A gentle opening hole with a disaster area left of the fairway.

2) Again, trouble for players hitting to the left. The prevailing wind usually assists.

3) In the wind this hole plays longer than the yardage suggests.

4) A similar hole to number three.

5) There's a nice downslope to the green on this par three.

6) A long up-and-down fairway makes this a difficult par four.

7) A difficult hole. It's a dogleg left over a roadway.

8) The tee shot must be straight to stand a chance of par.

9) A good test of tee to green with an out-of-bounds fence on the left.

10) The dogleg left fairway falls to the right, making a difficult hole.

11) This par four is short and simple.

12) This is the most popular hole on the course. Two large trees in front of the green spoil many good shots.

13) Against the prevailing wind, two very good shots are needed to reach the green.

14) A steep up-and-down fairway makes it difficult to judge distance.

15) Disaster areas on both sides! Make the tee shot good.

16) It's a short par four but it plays much longer than its yardage.

17) With water to the right of the green, the second shot to the green is a good challenge.

18) Beware the ditch at long drive length.

Recommended Facilities

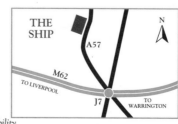

Merseyside

SOUTHPORT & AINSDALE
Golf Club

Bradshaw Lane, Ainsdale,
Southport, Merseyside PR8 3LG.

Secretary: A. G. Flood
01704-578000 (Fax 570896).
Professional: Mike Houghton
01704-577316.

ONE of the chain of fine seaside links courses in the Southport area, the club is on the opposite side of the railway to Royal Birkdale.

This important championship course stretches to 6612 yards from the back tees and 6217 from the yellow tees. Set among the sand dunes, it is a wonderful test for golfers with accuracy being of prime importance.

Several holes were laid out by James Braid when the club had to relocate part of the course in the 1920s.

A new clubhouse was then built at the Ainsdale end and in 1933 the club was recognised as one of the great courses when it was chosen to host the Ryder Cup. It resulted in a famous victory for Great Britain and Ireland. The Ryder Cup returned in 1937.

The clubhouse has an impressive room dedicated to Ryder Cup history, while other rooms affirm the club's sense of tradition in the form of great pictures, past and present.

Southport and Ainsdale Golf Club was established in 1906 as a nine-hole course on common land at Birkdale with only a wooden shed as a clubhouse.

Murmerings among the membership soon caused a move to a larger site to the south, where an 18-hole course was laid out and a large clubhouse was built, facing Liverpool Road, where it remained until the enforced move of 1922.

In the early 1990s the Ainsdale clubhouse was extended and refurbished, adding to the club's well known reputation for hospitality.

Hole	Yards	Stroke	Par
Course Information			
1	180	13	3
2	495	3	5
3	375	11	4
4	296	15	4
5	396	1	4
6	362	9	4
7	458	5	4
8	147	17	3
9	438	7	4
10	150	18	3
11	427	4	4
12	383	10	4
13	138	16	3
14	370	6	4
15	341	12	4
16	486	2	5
17	430	8	4
18	345	14	4
OUT	3147		35
IN	3070		35
TOTAL	6217		70

1) A well protected par three needing a straight hit with a long iron.

2) Avoid the sand for a chance of par on this straight hole.

3) From a raised to a bowl green. Just avoid the traps at the right.

4) A birdie chance. An iron off the tee is recommended.

5) A tough par four with a bottle-neck fairway to a raised and well bunkered green.

6) A dogleg right with a blind tee shot, maybe with an iron.

7) A dogleg left with a long, blind second shot.

8) The reverse Mackenzie green leaves no margin for error.

9) The tee shot is all important here. Keep it to the left.

10) A deceptive par three, perhaps with the same club as the eighth.

11) A long par four to a small green. The fairway can't be missed.

12) Play left from the tee on this par four.

13) A tricky short par three hole. The narrow green is well protected by bunkers.

14) A good driving hole between the hills. Beware the sloping green.

15) A picturesque short par four through pine trees.

16) The signature hole. It's a par five with a second shot carry over large hills called Gumbleys.

17) A tough par four alongside the railway. The tee is elevated and there are bunkers down the left.

18) This short par four has a blind tee shot and doglegs to the left. The second is slightly uphill and difficult to judge.

Recommended Facilities

Merseyside

SOUTHPORT
Municipal Golf Links

Park Road West, Southport,
Merseyside PR9 0JS.

Manager/Pro: Bill Fletcher
01704-535286.
Clubhouse: 01704-530435.

WITH so many fine clubs in the vicinity, it could be thought that a municipal course was not necessary. But this 18-hole promenade layout owned by Sefton Council is probably the busiest in Southport.

Being rather flat, it is ideal for beginners and veterans although the back nine can be tough, having several long par fours.

It is also handily positioned for tourists, at the north end of the Marine Lake quite near the town centre. They would be well advised, however, to book a tee well in advance. There is a club and trolley hire facility.

As well as being a popular pay-and-play facility, no fewer than five golf clubs play over the course.

They are the Park Golf Club (founded in 1924) the Alt club, the Southport and Southport Ladies' clubs and the Sefton Junior Golf Club.

The course was originally a nine-holer on land reclaimed from the sea but it was extended just before World War Two. The government then requisitioned the last nine to grow crops but the council reinstated the course after the war.

FACT FILE

A links/parkland course of 18 holes, 6139 yards. Par 70. SSS 70. Record 66.

Restrictions: Up to six days notice may be necessary. Societies make prior arrangements with the pro shop but can not play on Saturday.

Fees: £3 to £8 per round.

Dress code: Smart casual.

Shop opening: 8am to 7.30pm; 5.30pm in winter.

Facilities:

TO THE CLUB

Off Marine Drive at the north end of Southport promenade.

Course Information

Hole	Yards	Stroke	Par
1	376	11	4
2	395	5	4
3	539	1	5
4	476	7	5
5	330	13	4
6	190	15	3
7	425	3	4
8	132	17	3
9	373	9	4
10	289	14	4
11	292	10	4
12	460	2	4
13	129	18	3
14	412	8	4
15	451	4	4
16	165	16	3
17	420	6	4
18	285	12	4
OUT	3236		36
IN	2903		34
TOTAL	6139		70

1) A moderate par four to start. There's water to the right and the green is well bunkered.
2) A hard driving hole with a long iron into the green.
3) With trees to the left and right, be happy with a par!
4) It's well bunkered but you could look for a four!
5) There's water to the right and bunkers are the problem.
6) This long par three has a blind tee shot.
7) Stroke index one on the card, this long par four has water to the right and bunkers round the green.
8) Another par three with a blind shot. A good challenge in the wind.
9) There's water to the right of the fairway and the small green is well defended by bunkers.
10) A short par four with out-of-bounds on the left - so hit iron!
11) Trees surround the green with bunkers front left and right.
12) A long par four and a difficult hole in the wind.
13) Out-of-bounds left is the only risk on this short par three.
14) A par four with no bunkers! Watch the out-of-bounds at the left.
15) Another long par four, this time with water in front of the green.
16) Two well placed bunkers make the green hard to hit.
17) This very small green is also hard to hit and it is well guarded to the the left and right.
18) Play an iron off the tee on this short par four and keep clear of the trees at the right of the green.

Recommended Facilities

SOUTHPORT
Old Links
Golf Club

Moss Lane, Southport,
Merseyside PR9 7GS.

**Secretary: Brian Kenyon
01704-28207.**

ALTHOUGH the club was formed in 1926, golf has been played on the club's Churchtown site for much longer.

It was previously the home of Southport Golf Club, where the great Harry Vardon won the Leeds Cup in 1922.

J. H. Taylor, Alex Herd and Jack White also played there.

The assets of this club were acquired when the Old Links was formed as a limited company.

But it is known that the game started there in 1909, when the local YMCA took over the site as a golf course.

The Old Links layout differs from the other Southport courses in being a little inland from the resorts 'golf belt' and is on very lush parkland.

In recent years the course has been lengthened and re-arranged and the greens relaid. It is considered to be a good test for a consistent player of any handicap.

The club's fixtures diary recalls a fact that may astonish modern golfers. In the 1920s the size of the 'home green' was 180ft by 60ft!

FACT FILE

A parkland course of 9 holes, 6244 yards. Par 72. SSS 71. Record 69.

Restrictions: No visitors Sunday and Wednesday before 3pm. Societies make contact in advance.

Fees: £18.50 to £25.50 (day).

Dress code: Smart casual.

Facilities:

TO THE CLUB

Three miles north east of Southport, at Churchtown off the A5267.

Course Information

Hole	Yards	Stroke	Par
1	494	8	5
2	286	18	4
3	168	14	3
4	430	2	4
5	386	6	4
6	331	10	4
7	141	16	3
8	380	4	4
9	487	12	5
10	499	7	5
11	278	17	4
12	200	9	3
13	374	5	4
14	437	1	4
15	331	11	4
16	147	15	3
17	388	3	4
18	487	13	5
OUT	3103		36
IN	3141		36
TOTAL	6244		72

1) A difficult drive with out-of-bounds left and trees right. Three deep bunkers threaten the second shot but the chip to the green is easy.

2) With trees each side an accurate drive is needed. The second shot to the green is hard because of two large trees and a huge bunker.

3) The elevated green is well bunkered but it isn't a difficult par three.

4) Out-of-bounds to the left, trees to the right, and four deep bunkers at driving distance! And then there's water behind the green.

5) All the way down the left is out-of-bounds but there's a not-too-difficult chip to the sloping green.

6) Yet another out-of-bounds on the left with water at driving distance. The green is relatively easy.

7) One very accurate shot is needed here because there are trees all round the green and four troublesome bunkers.

8) With trees on both sides an accurate second shot is necessary. Beware the sloping fairway.

9) This is a longish par five but long hitters can reach the green with two accurate shots.

Recommended Facilities

Merseyside

69

WALLASEY
Golf Club

Bayswater Road, Wallasey,
Wirral, Merseyside L45 8LA.

Secretary: Mrs L. M. Dolman
0151-6911024.
Professional: Mike Adams
0151-6383888.

WALLASEY is a links course of pedigree, with a gallery of famous names woven through its history.

It is one of the chain of superb courses in the sandhills along the Wirral, West Lancashire and Fylde coasts.

Founded in 1891, the club opened with a course laid out by Old Tom Morris, of St. Andrews, but little of the great man's handiwork has survived the relentless advance of the sand. Only four Morris greens remain and several replacement holes have also been lost.

From Wallasey's original 240 acres, 100 were reclaimed by drifting sand. Today's course is as much the work of other great names of golf course construction - James Braid, Sandy Herd, Harold Hilton and Fred Hawtree.

The club's existence for many years depended on short-term leases until 1986, when a new lease of 100 years secured the foreseeable future.

The problem of drifting sand dunes also appears to have been solved by a coast road and the planting of marram grass.

Wallasey has a claim to fame as the home of Dr. Frank Stableford, a former club captain, who invented the scoring system that carries his name. He introduced his system in 1931 although he had invented it many years earlier while a member at the Glamorganshire Golf Club. The first Stableford competition was held at Wallasey in 1932 and is remembered in an annual tournament for the Stableford Trophy.

Playing the Wallasey course is a severe test not to be entered into by the faint-hearted. Accurate driving is essential if the golfer is to have any chance with the irons.

There is little that is straightforward. Several greens are elevated and are very fast. Large greens are unknown here and with so much sand heaped around, there is need of relatively few man-made bunkers. The standard scratch score of 73 tells it all.

Course Information

Hole	Yards	Stroke	Par
1	382	11	4
2	463	5	4
3	381	7	4
4	504	1	5
5	173	15	3
6	343	13	4
7	520	3	5
8	393	9	4
9	154	17	3
10	311	16	4
11	371	8	4
12	147	18	3
13	498	2	5
14	493	12	5
15	369	6	4
16	200	14	3
17	464	4	4
18	441	10	4
OUT	3313		36
IN	3294		36
TOTAL	6607		72

1) A straightforward par four. The second shot is to an elevated green.

2) Toughest on the course in the prevailing wind! A dogleg right with a long iron second shot.

3) A narrow landing area and an elevated green.

4) A long par five, with the best view on the course from the high tee.

5) This par three from an elevated tee is all carry.

6) A short par four with a ditch and out-of-bounds down the right.

7) Another long par five. There are bushes and out-of-bounds right and a good second shot is needed to avoid the bunkers.

8) A great hole. It's a dogleg right where positioning is vital.

9) This par three looks simple - but don't miss the green!

10) A sharp dogleg right. An iron off the tee for position and a short iron to an extremely elevated green. Don't leave it short.

11) Another wonderful hole. Your second shot must get to the back of the green because of the severe slope.

12) Deep bunkers and rough protect the green on this par three.

13) A straightforward par five needing a good drive.

14) Similar to 13 but in the opposite direction. The length is deceptive. Take more club that you first thought.

15) A dogleg left to a very elevated, hard to hold green.

16) A tough par three. It requires a fade to hold the green.

17) A long par four with a blind second shot. Keep to the right.

18) A great finishing hole. There's no flat area of the fairway, leaving a tough second shot to a large green.

Recommended Facilities

Merseyside

WARREN PARK
Golf Course

The Grange, Grove Road, Wallasey,
Wirral, Merseyside.

Professional: Steve Conrad
0151-6395730.
Clubhouse: 0151-6398323.

THIS municipal nine-hole golf course operated by the Metropolitan Borough of Wirral was formerly the estate of a Liverpool shipping magnate.

Golf began on the site in 1907, when the tycoon had a private seven-hole course laid out in the grounds.

During World War Two the house and grounds were requisitioned for the American Forces. The building housed an intelligence gathering unit and an anti-aircraft battery was placed in the grounds. An airstrip was laid on what is now the ninth fairway. The property was purchased by the local council after the war and returned to use as a golf course.

FACT FILE

A links course of 9 holes, 5890 yards. Par 72. SSS 69.

Restrictions: A municipal pay-and-play course with no restrictions.

Fees: £2.70.

Shop opening: Dawn till dusk.

Facilities:

TO THE CLUB

The entrance is 500 yards along Grove Road beyond the railway station.

Course Information

Hole	Yards	Stroke	Par
1	281	15	4
2	263	17	4
3	434	1	4
4	315	3	4
5	286	13	4
6	164	7	3
7	328	11	4
8	370	5	4
9	504	9	5
10	281	16	4
11	263	18	4
12	434	2	4
13	315	4	4
14	286	14	4
15	164	8	3
16	328	12	4
17	370	6	4
18	504	10	5
OUT	2945		36
IN	2945		36
TOTAL	5890		72

1) Quite an easy opening hole. Avoid trouble by using a sand iron.

2) A tight driving hole with trouble down the right and mounds down the left. Take a three wood or wedge into the wind.

3) The toughest on the course. It's a wide driving hole with rough and bunkers down the left.

4) A very tricky hole. You must hit the right side of the fairway for a good angle into the green.

5) Do you go for it or do you lay up? It's a real birdie chance.

6) The only par three on the course and quite tricky with bunkers short and both sides of the green.

7) From an elevated tee down the right to a protected green.

8) A downhill par four usually playing a driver from the tee to just past the bunkers, leaving a six to eight iron into a big, round green.

9) The only par five on the course playing a driver, a fairway wood and a wedge to a well bunkered green.

Merseyside

WEST DERBY
Golf Club

Yew Tree Lane, Liverpool L12 9HQ.

Secretary: A. P. Milne
0151-2541034 (Fax 2590505).
Professional: Nick Brace
0151-225478.
Clubhouse: 0151-2281540.

WEST Derby is a gentle, undula-ting parkland course situated close to the M62 and M57.

Founded in 1896, the course has matured well and all the fairways are tree-lined.

It is a busy club with good facilities and welcomes golfing societies by arrangement.

The course measures 6257 yards and has a par of 72. A brook running through the course comes into play on six holes. Recently, a new first green was laid.

The club celebrated its centenary in July, 1996, with a week of special events including charity days.

The Lancashire Seniors Champ-ionship was held at the club in 1996.

The club has marked the cen-tenary with an attractive plaque and decorative wall, pictured far right.

The attractively designed modern clubhouse enjoys fine views of the course.

FACT FILE

A parkland course of 18 holes, 6257 yards. Par 72. SSS 70. Record 66.

Restrictions: Societies contact the Secretary. Visitors phone the pro. Ladies' day Tuesday. No visitors at weekends.

Fees: £23 to £30.

Dress code: Smart casual. Jacket and tie after 7pm in clubhouse.

Shop opening: 9am till dusk.

Facilities:

TO THE CLUB

From the A57 (Prescot Road) onto Princess Drive and then Yew Tree Lane.

Course Information

Hole	Yards	Stroke	Par
1	301	13	4
2	320	16	4
3	344	11	4
4	380	1	4
5	284	14	4
6	546	10	5
7	131	17	3
8	479	7	5
9	161	9	3
10	553	4	5
11	437	2	4
12	190	15	3
13	421	3	4
14	131	18	3
15	485	8	5
16	397	5	4
17	321	12	4
18	376	6	4
OUT	2946		36
IN	3311		36
TOTAL	6257		72

1) A short dogleg right to an undulating green.

2) A straight par four but beware the brook in front of the green.

3) A slight dogleg left to a well bunkered green.

4) Keep on the fairway off the tee and take note of the brook.

5) Play across the Deysbrook again to the tight plateau green.

6) A long par five that doglegs around a pond on the left.

7) A short, well bunkered par three.

8) A long dogleg right to a small, tight green.

9) A well protected par three with out-of-bounds on the right.

10) One of the longest par fives on Merseyside with out-of-bounds on the right.

11) A difficult hole if a breeze is blowing. The green is tight.

12) A long par three with a narrow opening to the green.

13) Avoid the copse on the right on this par four hole.

14) A short hole with a generous green - but beware the pond.

15) Stay right off the tee to seek the best position on this long hole that doglegs to the left.

16) The fairway is narrow and the small green is well protected.

17) A straight drive off the tee will keep you clear of the out-of-bounds on the right.

18) The fairway off the tee is quite wide on this finishing par four.

Recommended Facilities

Merseyside

WEST LANCASHIRE
Golf Club

Hall Road West, Blundellsands,
Liverpool L23 8SZ.

Secretary: Douglas Bell
0151-9241076 (Fax 9314448).
Professional: David Lloyd
0151-9245662.
Clubhouse: 0151-9244115.

THE West Lancashire club was the pioneer of golf on the Lancashire coast. It was formed in 1873, just four years after the Hoylake club (Royal Liverpool).

Scottish businessmen, occupied in Liverpool's booming maritime economy, launched the game on each side of the Mersey.

West Lancashire's first 18 hole course was on the eastern side of the Liverpool to Southport railway, on land leased from the Blundell family. The first hole was played across what is now the Waterloo RUFC ground.

In 1894 the club acquired a parcel of land on the seaward side of the railway and solved the problem of too many short holes by relocating holes seven to 11.

The club's status in the early years was established when it was one of the 24 clubs that contributed to the cost of the Amateur Championship Trophy. The course was changed again in 1921, with nine holes being laid on the seaward side of the tracks and for nearly 40 years the Blundellsands course continued to be split by the railway, the two halves linked by an inadequate footbridge.

Since 1894 a ladies club had existed with a separate course on the west side of the tracks. In the late 1940s, sand encroachment led to the amalgamation of the two clubs.

The last step in the evolution of the course came in the 1950s when the club surrendered the land on the eastern side of the railway in return for 170 acres on the western side.

A fresh start was made with a new 18 hole course designed by C. K. Cotton, using some of the previous fairways. Cotton produced the ideal layout of two loops of nine with the ninth and 18th greens in front of a new clubhouse. It opened in June, 1961.

A welcome feature of the new layout was the installation of several elevated tees which gave golfers fine views of the Mersey, the Welsh mountains and, to the north, the Fylde Coast and Blackpool Tower. The new course produced a very stern challenge with a length of 6767 yards from the white tees and a par of 72. Even the yellow course, over 6238 yards, has a par of 70. The West Lancashire club has had many famous figures in its illustrious history, dating back to Harold Hilton, who became the club's first unpaid secretary in 1901, when he successfully defended his amateur championship at St. Andrews. Hilton made a record 33 appearances in that championship, winning four times. He won the Open Championship twice.

The record for the championship course is 68, set by Jim Payne on the final day of the Open qualifying rounds in 1991. He went on to win the amateur gold medal at Royal Birkdale and turned professional the next year.

The course at Blundellsands can also boast the longest hole-in-one in British golf, achieved in 1972 by assistant professional Peter Parkinson, when he took the very risky straight line on the 387-yard doglegged seventh. The feat is in the Guinness Book of Records.

An excellent outline history of the club, by Fred Lowe, published by the club in 1992, was the basis of this article.

FACT FILE

A championship links course of 18 holes, 6767 yards. Par 72. SSS 73. Record 68.

Restrictions: Societies contact the Secretary. Handicap certificates or proof of golf club membership required. Ladies' day Tuesday pm.

Fees: £28 to £50, £11 and £13 with member.

Dress code: Usual golf attire.

Shop opening: 8am to 6.30pm.

Facilities:

TO THE CLUB

Off the A565 Liverpool to Southport road at Crosby.

Course Information

Hole	Yards	Stroke	Par
1	433	7	4
2	490	2	5
3	158	15	3
4	412	11	4
5	478	5	5
6	156	18	3
7	370	13	4
8	448	3	4
9	403	9	4
10	355	14	4
11	557	1	5
12	178	16	3
13	363	12	4
14	440	4	4
15	391	10	4
16	531	6	5
17	175	17	3
18	429	8	4
OUT	3348		36
IN	3419		36
TOTAL	6767		72

1) A very difficult opening hole, purely because of its length.

2) A relatively easy par five for many golfers.

3) A nice picturesque hole - but treacherous when the wind blows.

4) A long and tough par four that makes a late turn to the right and has a small green that drops away at the right.

5) A par five with potentially troublesome mounds along the left.

6) A difficult par three because the green is long and narrow and is surrounded by four large bunkers.

7) Dubbed 'Folly,' this short dogleg par four has a hard-to-hit green.

8) A very long dogleg par four; only the length makes it tough.

9) A short and simple par four. Position off the tee is the key.

10) Another simple par four but, into the wind, quite long and tough.

11) The railway runs all along the right. At 557 yards into the prevailing wind, three excellent shots are needed to get par.

12) Very deep bunkers guard the green on this tough par three.

13) Position off the tee is the key to a par four. The three bunkers on the left edge of the fairway are the main hazards.

14) Probably the hardest on the course needing two excellent shots.

15) A nice, simple, picturesque par four.

16) Two very good long shots should see a birdie on this par five.

17) Possibly the hardest par three. Only an excellent shot will do!

18) One of the most demanding tee shots you will ever play. There is a 100 yard stretch of water on the right at driving range.

Recommended Facilities

The Hillcrest Hotel has 49 comfortable bedrooms, all with bathrooms (some have a whirlpool bath), satellite television, direct dial telephone, trouser press, hair dryer and hospitality tray.

The tropically-themed Palm Restaurant, overlooked by the cocktail bar is a lively venue at lunchtime and throughout the evening. Whilst Nelson's Bar, a traditional oak beamed pub, serves a wide range of drinks in a nautical setting, with regular entertainment.

Discount packages are available to parties of 12 or more (subject to availability).

CRONTON LANE, WIDNES, CHESHIRE, **WA8 9AR** TELEPHONE **0151 424 1616** FACSIMILE **0151 495 1348**

Merseyside

WIRRAL LADIES
Golf Club

93 Bidston Road, Birkenhead,
Wirral, Merseyside L43 6TS.

Secretary: David Kelly
0151-6521255 (Fax 6534323).
Professional: Angus Law
0151-6522468.
Clubhouse: 0151-6530566.

WIRRAL is a ladies' club that has always allowed men to be members. Furthermore, in the second year of the club's existence, 1895, there were three male trustees, two of whom were life members.

In many cases it was due to family connections, the men also being members at Royal Liverpool, only a few miles away.

Over the years it has sometimes caused a little confusion. For example, when a group of 24 male members booked a group holiday at Royal St. Davids, at Harlech, they each found posies of flowers in their rooms for the 'Wirral Ladies.'

And when two builders, members of the club, sent entry forms for a golf competition at the annual conference of the builders' federation, they received replies refusing their entries which read: "Dear Mrs. - We do not allow ladies to play in the golf competition."

The men gained equal status with the ladies at Wirral in 1952 and today the membership is evenly divided. There are also more than 30 junior members, the majority of which are boys.

The ladies retain their exclusive vote at annual meetings and the management is, in the main, in their hands. The men have their own committee.

The Wirral Ladies' Golf Club was founded in 1894 and the first course was of nine moderate holes covering about 1500 yards. By 1907, they were playing over 18 holes and in the next few years the course evolved to about 4500 yards, while today's course covers 4966 yards.

The club marked the 1994 centenary with an ambitious extension and improvement of the clubhouse facilities.

FACT FILE

A parkland course of 18 holes, 4966 yards. Par 70. SSS 70. Record 71.

Restrictions: Visitors must have handicap certificates. Societies make contact in advance.

Fees: £20 to £25.

Dress code: Usual golf attire.

Shop opening: 8am to 6pm.

Facilities:

TO THE CLUB

From the Mersey Tunnel, follow the Hoylake sign and turn left up the hill towards the observatory.

Course Information

Hole	Yards	Stroke	Par
1	367	13	5
2	113	17	3
3	345	3	4
4	291	11	4
5	345	5	4
6	346	1	4
7	316	9	4
8	115	15	3
9	252	7	4
10	257	12	4
11	274	6	4
12	162	16	3
13	418	2	5
14	345	10	4
15	346	4	4
16	238	14	4
17	144	18	3
18	292	8	4
OUT	2490		35
IN	2476		35
TOTAL	4966		70

1) The fairway is open but there's a water hazard to the left and a bunker about 130 yards from the pin.

2) A short par three with a heavily guarded green.

3) The fairway is narrow but a good tee shot brings a birdie chance.

4) A short dogleg par four with bunkers left and right and trees behind the green.

5) Play the tee shot to the right of the fairway to open up the green.

6) On this hole, play up the left of the fairway to open up the green.

7) A tricky little green with a narrow fairway approach.

8) A short par three with a small green.

9) A dogleg left par four. Play up the right to avoid the frontal bunker.

10) A short par four that needs a very accurate tee shot.

11) Try to fade right round the trees on this dogleg par four.

12) A big bunker can foil hopes on this par three.

13) The longest on the course. All the trouble is on the right.

14) A straightforward par four but the landing area is small for long hitters. It's out-of-bounds behind the green.

15) A par four dogleg to the left. Watch out for the mid-length bunker.

16) A much shorter dogleg, this time to the right.

17) A par three with a small green surrounded by trees.

18) There's a water hazard on the left and it's out-of-bounds back left with a wall at the right.

Recommended Facilities

Merseyside

WOOLTON
Golf Club

Doe Park, Speke Road,
Woolton, Liverpool L25 7TZ.

Secretary: S. H. King
0151-4862298 (Fax. 4861664).
Professional: Alan Gibson
0151-4861298.
Clubhouse: 0151-4480228.

A Georgian gentleman's home is the domain of Woolton Golf Club, at Doe Park, in the south of Liverpool.

The club moved in when it was founded in 1901 and research into the history of the building is being done for inclusion in the club's centenary book.

However, the clubhouse has been fundamentally altered since its days of grace and ease.

The compact course covers 80 acres of rolling parkland and is little changed from its early days. It is noted for its excellent, springy fairways. An automatic irrigation system with pop-up sprinklers was installed in 1996.

Each hole has its own characteristic and together with the mature tree-lined fairways, present the golfer with a challenging and enjoyable round.

The course is split by a road, with holes one to eight and 17 & 18 on the clubhouse side.

The building is in the process of a major refurbishment, costing more than £500,000 over several years. The locker rooms and showers have been rebuilt, the roof has been renewed, and the total refurbishment of the ground floor rooms began in 1996.

The programme is aimed at having the club and course in peak condition for the centenary.

Woolton Golf Club gives a welcome to golfing societies and has a 27-hole golf and catering package for groups of 20 or more. Corporate days are also encouraged.

FACT FILE

A parkland course of 18 holes, 5706 yards. Par 69, SSS 68.

Restrictions: Societies contact the Secretary/Manager; visitors contact the professional.

Fees: £20 to £30, with member £8 and £12.

Dress code: Smart casual.

Shop opening: 8am to 6pm, or dusk in winter.

Facilities:

TO THE CLUB

From the end of the M62, turn left at Childwall five-ways and the club is left off the A562 dual carriageway down School Lane.

Course Information

Hole	Yards	Stroke	Par
1	260	17	4
2	375	5	4
3	307	11	4
4	162	15	3
5	325	9	4
6	427	1	4
7	155	13	3
8	344	7	4
9	464	3	4
10	341	12	4
11	150	16	3
12	501	2	5
13	204	10	3
14	403	6	4
15	155	14	3
16	530	4	5
17	347	8	4
18	256	18	4
OUT	2819		34
IN	2887		35
TOTAL	5706		69

1) An easy par four if you can avoid the out-of-bounds on the right.

2) Out-of-bounds along the right and a brook just short of the green.

3) A short par four. Driveable for big hitters in summer.

4) A par three of modest length but it's tricky, with awkward bunkers.

5) A dogleg to the right, with out-of-bounds on the right and cross-bunkers about 35 yards from the green.

6) A long and difficult par four with a ridge, a big tree on the left and cross-bunkers 100 yards from the green. Stroke index one.

7) A troublesome array of bunkers greets short shots to the green.

8) A sharp dogleg to the right. Watch out for cars on the right.

9) Another long and difficult par four with out-of-bounds on the right.

10) Watch the bushes down the left on this straightforward hole.

11) Even more than hole seven, this is not a par three to leave short.

12) A tricky par five with trees on both sides.

13) A two-tier plateau green is the challenge on this par three.

14) A slight dogleg left with a depression at driving distance, and a big hollow at the right, 100 yards short of the two-tier green.

15) Aside from the sand, there's a huge depression right of the green.

16) The longest on the course. A fairway gully midway and bushes for the last 100 yards on the right.

17) A slight fade off the tee is needed on this difficult par four.

18) A short par four - but there are trees left and right and a ring of bunkers protecting the green.

Recommended Facilities

MAGNIFICENT MERSEYSIDE

Out & About in *Merseyside*

Liverpool is a vibrant and exciting city to visit. It is alive with entertainment and attractions whilst at the same time having a strong cultural identity.

Its rich heritage is underlined in being short-listed for the City of Architecture and Design 1999.

Listed Buildings abound in the area, many of them built to classical designs, such as the Walker Art Gallery, Liverpool Museum and Central Libraries, and St. George's Hall.

The Town Hall is the jewel of Liverpool's historic buildings with its Golden Minerva sitting proudly atop the golden dome.

Both the St. George's Hall and the Town Hall have been refurbished and have a programme of events, public openings, exhibitions, conferences and business and private functions.

The Liver Building and the two cathedrals are but three more from Liverpool's great spectrum of architecture.

The restored Albert Dock has three times been winner of the Best Large Attraction in the North West.

Liverpool can also boast of being one of the greenest cities in Britain with 2,400 acres of parkland and open spaces.

Croxteth Hall and Country Park Estate is set in 500 acres of woodland with a working farm animal collection, miniature railway and adventure playground.

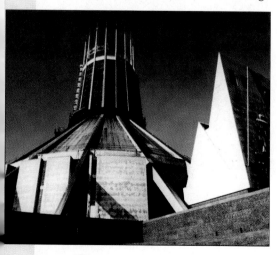

The city is steeped in popular culture; the birthplace of the Beatles, the home of two outstanding Premier Division football clubs, the location of the Grand National and the base of the Royal Liverpool Philharmonic Orchestra.

Across the River Mersey, the Wirral Peninsula offers contrasting rural tranquility, scattered with gems like Port Sunlight Village, beautiful Ness Gardens overlooking the Dee Estuary, West Kirby and Hilbre Island.

The former dockland in Birkenhead is being redeveloped, linking attractions by a tramway giving visitors a taste of days gone by.

Relics of Merseyside's great industrial past are to be seen all round the region, particularly in St. Helens, the heart of UK glass manufacturing, and Prescot, a former centre of clock and watch making.

E X

Golf Club Treasurers and Committee Members:

GET 'ON COURSE' IN YOUR MARKETING!

The wide world of golf is on the move. More golfers now want to travel to play other courses. And this can bring much-needed revenue to golf clubs.

Is your club geared to take advantage of this growing trend?

A full colour brochure or leaflet - professionally designed and produced with high quality photography and editorial copy - is the first step in securing or developing your golf revenue.

Not many clubs currently have the kind of literature that will inspire golfers to pick up the phone and make arrangements for a visit.

Meanwhile, the newer courses and country club complexes are going all out to promote their venues.

It's time to get 'ON COURSE.' It's time to call in expert help to promote your club. It's time to call On Course Publications Ltd., on **01253-781000.**

We also produce Business Cards, Letterheads, Corporate Stationery, and Sponsored Score Cards (in full colour), Hole Planners, Notice Boards and Year Books.

On Course Publications Ltd., Freedom House, 32-34 Wood Street, Lytham St. Annes, Lancashire FY8 1QR. A Freedom House Company. Registered in England No. 3125892.

Readers Response

Thank you for reading 'Where To Play Golf' in the British Isles - North West England Edition, the first book in The World Compendium of Golf Courses series. We hope that you have enjoyed the detailed features on this region's vast array of golf courses and we look forward to bringing the world of golf to your fingertips through future editions.

PRE-RELEASE DISCOUNTS FOR READERS

If you would like to be informed of release dates and places to buy other books in this series covering the regions of the world, simply register with our Reader Service Bureau, free of charge and we will not only keep you updated with our releases but also give discount vouchers to spend with your retailer. To register telephone:

In Europe (UK Office) +44 (0)1253 781000.
In U.S.A. (Florida) (813) 4459030.
Rest of the World (Head Office) +44 (0)1253 789789.

If however you have any general comments or questions, please feel free to fax or write to us at the following address;

On Course Publications Ltd.,

Freedom House
32-34 Wood Street,
Lytham St. Annes,
Lancashire,
England FY8 1QR
Telephone: +44 (0)1253 781000
Fax: +44 (0)1253 780101

Future Editions

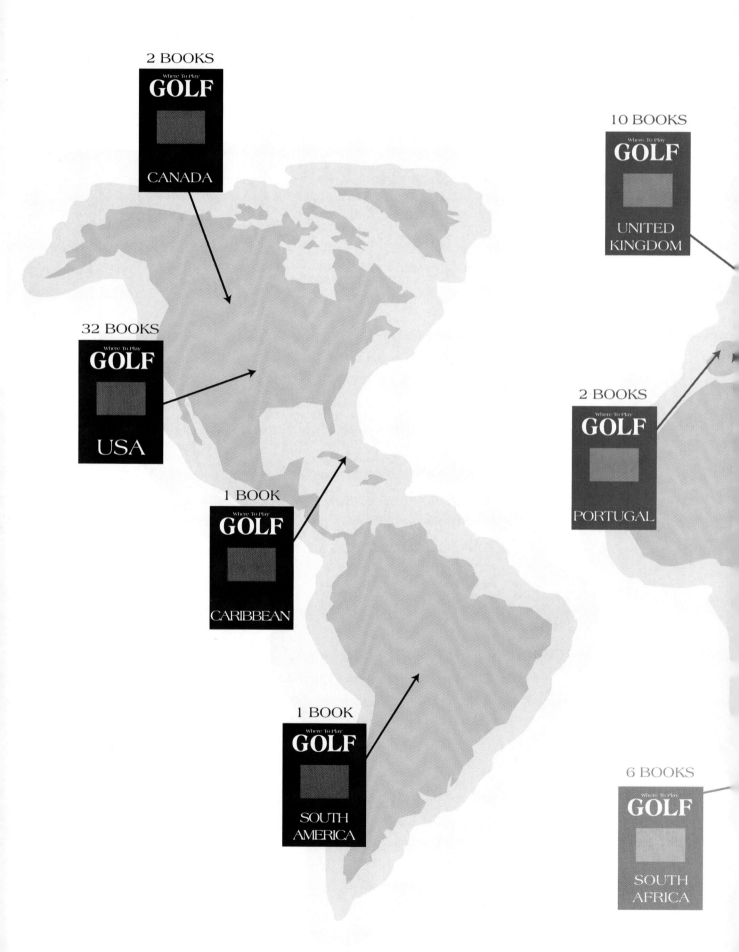

CALL: +44 (0) 1253 781000 FOR PUBLICATION SCHEDULE

THE WORLD COMPENDIUM
— OF GOLF COURSES™ —

5 BOOKS

Where To Play
GOLF

GERMANY

3 BOOKS

Where To Play
GOLF

ITALY

2 BOOKS

Where To Play
GOLF

FRANCE

3 BOOKS

Where To Play
GOLF

SPAIN

1 BOOK

Where To Play
GOLF

JAPAN

2 BOOKS

Where To Play
GOLF

AUSTRALIA

1 BOOK

Where To Play
GOLF

NEW
ZEALAND

PLAYERS

	DATE	SCORE	RD 1	RD 2	RD 3	RATE 1-10
A						
ACCRINGTON						
ALLERTON						
ALSTON MOOR						
APPLEBY						
ARROWE PARK						
ASHTON & LEA						
B						
BACUP						
BARROW						
BAXENDEN						
BEACON PARK						
BECKSIDE						
BENTHAM						
BIDSTON						
BLACKBURN						
BLACKPOOL NORTH SHORE						
BLACKPOOL STANLEY PARK						
BLUNDELLS HILL						
BOOTLE						
BOWRING						
BRACKENWOOD						
BRAMPTON						
BRAYTON PARK						
BROMBOROUGH						
BURNLEY						
C						
CALDY						
CARLISLE						
CARUS GREEN						
CASTERTON						
CASTLETOWN						
CHARNOCK RICHARD						
CHILDWALL						
CHORLEY						
CLITHEROE						
COCKERMOUTH						
COLNE						

	DATE	SCORE	RD 1	RD 2	RD 3	RATE 1-10
D						
DALSTON HALL						
DARWEN						
DEAN WOOD						
DOUGLAS						
DUNNERHOLME						
DUXBURY PARK						
E						
EASTHAM LODGE						
EDEN						
EUXTON PARK						
F						
FAIRHAVEN						
FISHWICK HALL						
FLEETWOOD						
FORMBY						
FORMBY LADIES						
FURNESS						
G						
GARSTANG						
GATHURST						
GRAND NATIONAL						
GRANGE FELL						
GRANGE-OVER-SANDS						
GRANGE PARK						
GHYLL						
GREEN DRIVE						
GREAT HARWOOD						
GREEN HAWORTH						
H						
HALTWHISTLE						
HAYDOCK PARK						
HERONS REACH						
HESKETH						
HESWALL						
HEYSHAM						
HILLSIDE						
HOUGHWOOD						
HOYLAKE						
HURLSTON HALL						
HUYTON & PRESCOT						

RECORD

	DATE	SCORE	RD 1	RD 2	RD 3	RATE 1-10
I						
INGOL						
K						
KENDAL						
KESWICK						
KING EDWARD BAY						
KIRKBY LONSDALE						
KNOTT END						
L						
LANCASTER						
LANSIL						
LIVERPOOL MUNICIPAL						
LEASOWE						
LEE PARK						
LEYLAND						
LOBDEN						
LONGRIDGE						
M						
MARSDEN PARK						
MARYPORT						
MERSEY VALLEY						
MOUNT MURRAY						
MORECAMBE						
MYTTON FOLD						
N						
NELSON						
O						
ORMSKIRK						
P						
PEEL						
PENRITH GOLF CENTRE						
PENRITH						
PENWORTHAM						
PLEASINGTON						
PORT ST. MARY						
POULTON-LE-FYLDE						
PRENTON						
PRESTON						

	DATE	SCORE	RD 1	RD 2	RD 3	RATE 1-10
R						
RAMSEY						
RISHTON						
ROSSENDALE						
ROWANY						
ROYAL BIRKDALE						
ROYAL LIVERPOOL						
ROYAL LYTHAM						
S						
SEASCALE						
SEDBERGH						
SHAW HILL						
SHERDLEY PARK						
SILECROFT						
SILLOTH						
SILVERDALE						
SOUTHPORT & AINSDALE						
SOUTHPORT MUNICIPAL						
SOUTHPORT OLD LINKS						
ST. ANNES OLD LINKS						
ST. BEES						
STONYHOLME						
STONYHURST PARK						
T						
TOWNELEY						
U						
ULVERSTON						
W						
WALLASEY						
WARREN						
WEST DERBY						
WEST LANCASHIRE						
WHALLEY						
WILPSHIRE						
WINDERMERE						
WIRRAL LADIES						
WOOLTON						
WORKINGTON						

On Course Publications

A TEAM EFFORT

Let us introduce the team at OCP
whose efforts bring this array of beautiful courses
and information to golfers worldwide.
There are many more people who have assisted
outside the company, far too numerous to
mention, whom we thank greatly.

The Support Team

CHAIRMAN: Mark Sampson

MANAGING DIRECTOR: Mike Orme

FINANCIAL MANAGER: Michaelle Kelly

RESOURCES MANAGER: Susan Houston

ADMINISTRATORS:
Rachel Somlo • Harriet Voss • Sara Tudor

The Editorial Team

EDITORIAL DIRECTOR: Barry Band

OPERATIONS DIRECTOR: David Wilson

RESEARCHERS:
Mark Sampson • Gerry Taylor • Mike Turner • Andy Ellis

PHOTOGRAPHERS:
Donald Campbell-Thomson • Warren Smith • David Wilson
Roger Boyes • David Clark • Mike Turner

Design Team

STUDIO MANAGER: Steven Gill

DESIGNERS:
John Stirzaker • Chris Tominey • Ange Carson
Gary Lees

PAGE COMPOSITION: Stephen Pearson

REPROGRAPHICS: Michael Jackson (BTS)

The Sales Team

SALES DIRECTOR: Chris Smith

Janet Horton • Ian Blyth • Robert Haggart
Vanessa Thompson • Christian Hingley • Kathryn Bainbridge
George Thewlis

YOUR CLUB PROFESSIONAL CAN PROVIDE YOU WITH THREE WAYS OF AVOIDING THE ROUGH

Ninety-five years ago, three prominent professional golfers of the day formed The Professional Golfers' Association of G.B. and Ireland. They decreed that the Association should become a hallmark of service, honesty, fair dealings and courtesy'.

Today the Association has 4000 qualified Members working throughout the world dedicated to the delivery of that early code of ethics. The strength of such an Association coupled with the personal attention its Members can bring ensure VALUE when you visit your PGA Professional.

Notes

Notes

Notes

Notes

Notes

Notes

Published by:
On Course Publications Ltd
32-34 Wood Street, St. Annes-on-Sea, Lancashire FY8 1QR
Telephone: +44 (0)1253 781000. Facsimile: +44 (0)1253 780101
Company Registered in England No. 3125892.

A FREEDOM HOUSE GROUP COMPANY